P9-DSY-511

To Carol and Bill
special thoughts
for special friends

LOVE LETTERS
TO AND FROM
A MONK

Seoyanne Nott

LOVE LETTERS TO AND FROM A MONK

My Aunt's Letters and His Responses

Compiled by Suzanne Saunders Taylor

Copyright © 2014 by Suzanne Saunders Taylor.

Library of Congress Control Number:		2014905436
ISBN:	Hardcover	978-1-4931-8636-5
	Softcover	978-1-4931-8637-2
	eBook	978-1-4931-8635-8

All rights reserved. No part of this book may be reproduced or transmitted in any form or by any means, electronic or mechanical, including photocopying, recording, or by any information storage and retrieval system, without permission in writing from the copyright owner.

This book was printed in the United States of America.

Rev. date: 06/19/2014

To order additional copies of this book, contact:
Xlibris LLC
1-888-795-4274
www.Xlibris.com
Orders@Xlibris.com
611164

CONTENTS

Introduction

She was 45 the first time she fell in love and married her husband, George. He was the same age and had never married before. Both were teachers: she elementary and he high school. When he died at the age of 70 she felt compelled to send a note to his Williams College roommate of his death. Thus began 20 years of a new relationship between this Episcopalian Monk and the recently retired college professor. Left behind and given to me for safe keeping were over 300 letters from the Rev. Bonnell Spencer, class of 1931 Williams, and my aunt Edna May Saunders Sole, with a BA from what is now Central Connecticut State University and an MFA from Boston University.

It is in the story told by the letters that we come to view two exceptionally educated professionals dealing not only with issues of religion, education and politics, but also with their deep feelings for each other. In many ways the letters weave a tale of romance. Did he lead her on and then retreat to the sanctity of his priesthood? Did she entreat and entice him? The story revealed in these letters tells of two philosophically differing viewpoints on religion: A Unitarian vs. an Episcopalian. The story also reveals each one's capacity for caring and nurturing, not only of others but of each other. Did one love more than the other? Therein lies the tale.

To understand the correspondence a brief report about Bonnell (Bonnie) and Edna May will set the stage for this play of words. Bonnell Spencer was Phi Beta Kappa at Williams and definitely very popular while there. He acted in several plays and also belonged to the Players Club in New York City, exhibiting a fondness for acting and the stage all his life. He was an accomplished author of numerous religious books and also a pastor and teacher of future seminarians. He graduated cum laude from Williams in 1931, and then went on to graduate from Oxford University with a master's degree in literature.

In 1933 he entered the General Theological Seminary in New York City and was ordained a deacon of the Order of the Holy Cross in 1936. In 1937 he was ordained a priest and life professed on January 6, 1940.

When he began to correspond and visit my Aunt he was in his 70s. In his 80s he traveled to Ghana where he set up a new school to train future priests. An ardent alum of Williams he often attended their reunions. Unable to provide much financial support for the college due to the vow of poverty he was required to take, he did write Williams once that he was able to persuade his prior to provide a modest donation to the college. Thus he was pleased that he would not be responsible for reducing the overall percent of his classes' contributing donors.

Edna May began teaching in a one room school house at the age of 17 where she had to tend the fire and teach all manner of students from ages 5 to 15. Ultimately she became a professor of education and taught many others to become teachers. At the same time she also taught the 6th grade in a demonstration school in New Britain, Connecticut. She had liberal and strong beliefs, supporting such organizations as NARAL (National Abortion Rights League), WCTU (Women's Christian Temperance Union), LWV (League of Women Voters), ACLU (American Civil Liberties Union), and NEA (National Education Association) as well as two state unions (Connecticut Education Association and the Connecticut State Employees Association). She became a Unitarian but worked vigorously for ecumenism by participating in numerous church collaborations such as the CRCC (Capitol Region of Council of Churches).

Her degree in fine arts inspired her to focus on the beauty about her, painting her front door purple upon her return from travel in Italy, where her favorite color was suggested as an ideal accent by architects there. She was always properly attired in hat and gloves. She traveled extensively and was exceptionally well read. She had a strong code of ethical beliefs and conduct. Once she wrote the IRS that she had enclosed more taxes than were actually due because she had been late in filing her taxes. On another occasion when alighting from her car in a parking lot she noticed that the neighboring car was scratched and left a note with her name and phone in case she had caused the damage. She did not learn to drive until age 70 after her husband had died and she needed to get about, so she was a careful driver. Her temerity led us all to conclude that should she ever be accosted on the park path she traveled on her frequent trips to the state capitol, the offender would be lectured until he desisted. At five foot one and a half inches she was a formidable, but very attractive woman who looked 20 years younger than she was. She found intellectual exchange exhilarating, but she had been accustomed to a married life of love.

The letters that follow depict the development of this new friendship as it began in 1974 and lasted until 1996. Early on my aunt kept copies of her letters to Bonnell Spencer as well as his responses. All the letters were handwritten. I suspect that one of the reasons she retained copies of her letters was that she first wrote a draft and then recopied the words over in perfect penmanship. She also wanted to keep what she had written so she would know what she had said. As time went by this became more important to her as she struggled with the onset of Alzheimer's, unknown to most of her friends and family until she was approaching 90.

Edna May and Bonnie

PART ONE

1974 - 1977

September 23, 1974
West Park, New York
Dear Edna,

It is a deep grief to me to learn of George's death. I cannot claim really to have been close to him—even when we roomed together we went our own ways. But I have always been very fond of him, and admired him greatly. I find myself feeling an emptiness when I realize I shall not see him again here. But I trust we shall get together on the other side.

Please accept my deepest sympathy. May God bless and uphold you in your time of sorrow.

Faithfully yours,
Bonnell Spencer NTC

March 27, 1975
Dear Edna,

Thank you for copy of the Memorial Service. It is a beautiful and deserved tribute. I wish I could have been with you for it. I am most grateful to have a copy which I shall treasure.

I hope I may have a chance to visit you sometime. It is a case of so near and yet so far, since I do not seem to be in your vicinity very often.

I have completely recovered from my operation—it went off beautifully with no complications whatever. You might pass that news on to Harvey when you are next in touch with him.

All best wishes for a blessed Eastertide.

Faithfully yours,
Bonnie

May 27, 1975
Santa Barbara, California
Dear Edna,

Thank you for your card. I am happy to report that I am fully recovered and never felt better in my life. I am out here in California for a meeting of the Order. I do hope sometime I can get into your neighborhood and see you again. All best wishes.

As ever,
Bonnie

July 27, 1975
Dear Bonnie,

We are happy about your report of excellent health; it is most heartening.

Whenever you find it convenient, if you wish, we would like to have you visit our house. Bring a friend if you like. George and I had planned to send you an invitation before the catastrophe hit us. I have learned to drive so that I could pick you up at an airport or station. Harvey and Anne would also like to see you.

I recently returned from Europe—England, Holland, Switzerland, and the art centers in northern Italy. George and I had planned to find England in the spring so I took him with me in my heart, but it was rather painful at times—he was the best traveling companion—heightening all the rich experiences in a way that was his alone. I found Padua an inspiration and hope to find some courses in architecture this winter.

Sincerely,
Edna May Sole

August 9, 1975
Whitly House, Texas
Dear Edna Mae,

Your letter had to be forwarded to me here in Texas where I am for this month seeing our new edition of the breviary throughout the press, and it has only just reached me. I do so wish I could accept you invitation to visit but next month I have only a very brief period at West Park to pack up things and then after a series of appointments, I end up in Santa Barbara, California, where I am to be stationed next winter. There will simply not be a moment to visit anyone.

I am happy to learn of your visit to Europe. I am sure it did you good to get away and to be in contact with so many interesting and beautiful things. George would have desired you to do just that, and he was with you in spirit as well as in your heart.

Please give my regards to Harvey and Anne. It is a real disappointment to me not to be able to see you all at this time, but my transfer to California came as a surprise and requires considerable adjusting, not unpleasant, but time consuming. I shall bear your invitation in mind, and if an opportunity comes later, shall try to see you.

As Ever,
Bonnie

August 25, 1975
Dear Bonnie,

We regret that we shall be unable to see and talk to you in the near future, but we understand and are happy for you that you have the opportunity in such a beautiful spot with a delightful climate. The invitation to visit will remain open if and when you wish to come.

It is good to know that you can help others with their problems; the world is in such a state of confusion. It worries me to see the decay of the family unit, which is essential to a healthy state, and the disregard for religion. Surely we all need some form of religion to guide our paths. I don't believe there is any one creed for everyone.

George's nephew had a baby boy born last February that reminds me of George, such a good loveable little fellow I stayed there a while to help when Betsy and Brian came home from the hospital. At one week he insisted on joining the family at the table for breakfast. I am trying to do my part in people projects like the Salvation Army and the League of Women Voters. May your future hold all that is good and beautiful.

Sincerely,
Edna May

[tucked in the letter was a Christmas Card and a note]

Dear Bonnie,

This fresco was my first love—it was the unmistakable purity of Fra Angelico shining through. Unfortunately, this copy cannot be compared to the original I saw in San Marco.

Note from Edna: 12/27/75

Imagine my chagrin when I reached home and realized that I had forgotten to include any holiday dress for the Christmas package. In our first snowstorm (a very beautiful one) I was trying to make the post office before closing time I arrived five minutes before. In atonement I am sending another book properly decorated. I am sorry for the confusion.

Sincerely,
Edna May

November 16, 1975
Mount Cavalry Retreat House
Santa Barbara, California
Dear Edna,

Your letter has lain unanswered for so long because I thought I should wait until I could write you from here so that you would have my new address. I got here Friday morning and am comfortably settled in my room. Unfortunately it is a long way from Connecticut but perhaps you will be traveling out this way sometime. If you are ever in these parts be sure to visit us. We have accommodations for you and you will find we have one of the most spectacular views anywhere. Please give my love to Harvey and Ann when you see them. I am sorry to have moved so far away just as I was getting in touch with you all again. But so it goes.

As ever,
Bonnie

[card December 1975]
Mount Cavalry Retreat House
Santa Barbara, California
Dear Edna,

Thank you for your letter and the lovely card. The picture is one of my favorites also. You will not believe that this card is a reproduction of an icon painted by one of the members of our Order. If you do visit us here you will be able to see his studio and collection of icons. I do hope you will come this winter or spring. At the moment I do not have many appointments. If you can make it and let me know sufficiently in advance I am sure I can find a time when I could be here. We do not have a definite charge for people who stay with us, but leave it to them to recompense as they see fit. I do not know how long I shall be stationed here, such assignments being usually left indefinite, but I expect it to be for quite a while. So do come and visit us. We shall make you feel completely at home.

I hope you are having a Blessed and Merry Christmas. I am glad you are able to be with your husband's nephew and his new family. My former classmate, Harvey (Hob), wrote me about the renovations you made on the house. I am sure that was very wise and I hope someday to see them. But meanwhile do come visit out here.

All the best.

As ever,
Bonnie

January 4, 1976
Mount Cavalry Retreat House
Santa Barbara, California
Dear Edna,

Thank you for sending me the lovely book on Ravenna so beautifully decorated. You certainly are most kind to have sent a second present. However I must inform you that so far the first has not arrived. Probably it got caught in the Christmas rush and is still somewhere en route. I mention this so you will know why I have never thanked you for it.

It is good to hear from someone who appreciated the snowstorm that everyone mentions, usually with moans and groans. I happen to love winter and snowstorms, and they are the one thing I miss out here—so I am envious.

I hope the New Year is bringing you much joy and that you will be visiting us this spring.

Love,
Bonnie

January 8, 1976
Mount Cavalry Retreat House
Santa Barbara, California
Dear Edna,

Your first book finally arrived. It too is beautiful and is especially appreciated since I spent a month in Perugia in the summer of 1933. So it brings back old and very happy times. Thank you again. You are much too kind.

As Ever,
Bonnie

January 20, 1976
Dear Bonnie,

The mail really came through: your most unusual Christmas card with its message, the letter, and the card. I am happy that the book on Perugia called forth such good memories. The beauty of Assisi still haunts me, especially that unforgettable Umbrian Valley, glorious by day and by night. Somehow I felt close to George there.

We are having a truly old fashioned winter with weekly snows so that we keep clean and sparkling. I like to walk in the snow among the stars for the crisp air and the stark trees seem to provide just the right background for the promises they hold forth.

I thoroughly enjoyed my two little boys, Brian and Andrew, at Christmas; they were quite fascinated by some xylopipes I have found at Schwartz in New York. "Children's faces looking up, holding wonder like a cup."

I believe I can visit Mount Cavalry sometime in April. Which part is best? Or is this an inconvenient month for you? Is another month better? Please be perfectly candid.

Sincerely,
Edna May

January 25, 1976
Mount Calvary Retreat House
Santa Barbara, California
Dear Edna,

Thank you for your letter. I answered at once to assure you April is fine for your visit. It will be best if you can come during the week, as we tend to get a bit crowded on weekends. Also April 11-17 is Holy Week, which will find things a bit austere. So you may want to avoid it. April 26-30 I am conducting a retreat here and I am not sure how crowded we shall be. Any other time in April will be fine, and even those dates are possible though you may find them less convenient. I do hope you will visit us for I am eager both to see you and to have you enjoy our remarkable views.

I am glad to learn that you enjoy winter—especially such as you are having this year. I enjoy them too—so I am very envious. We are still having summer—clear, bright days with the temperature in the 70's. It is rather a bore!

All the best.

As ever,
Bonnie

February 10, 1976
Dear Bonnie,

Thank you for being frank about April. I thought a Tuesday arrival and a Thursday departure might be prudent. Which is more convenient for you—April 6 till April 8 or April 20 till April 22? Either is all right for me. I do not wish to be a bother. I plan to fly United, which leaves Bradley Airport (Connecticut) at 7:45 in the morning and arrives at Santa Barbara at 1:48 in the afternoon. I presume I can get a cab at the airport. If for any reason this excursion should prove untimely, just let me know for I have had to learn down through the years to adjust to change even when it is sudden. If it is feasible, I should like to see you, your collection of icons, your views, and what a monastery is like.

Anne and Harvey came to supper on a Sunday to enjoy my two little boys with their mummy and daddy—all was most harmonious. Little Brian sat contentedly on Harvey's lap—like a monarch surveying his surroundings while Andrew, not to be ignored, played London Bridge around the two. When I was this child's age, I shared her sentiments for I was raised with two brothers. In later years, however, I realized my good fortune. I daresay, you are accustomed to a more sophisticated humor, but I have always cherished the natural spontaneity of little ones; although I prefer British humor to the American.

All the Best
Edna May

February 16, 1976
Mount Cavalry Retreat House
Santa Barbara, California
Dear Edna,

It is good news indeed that you can visit us in April. I suggest April 20-22 may be preferable, as that is Easter Week. The earlier dates would fall in Lent, which is a less pleasant time to visit in a monastery. But if it should turn out that the earlier date is more convenient for you do not hesitate to change. On whichever date, we shall meet you at the Santa Barbara airport at 1:48 p.m.

I gather you are still getting snow. We had a week of rain out here, which was badly needed. It is clouding up again now. Perhaps more is on the way. We can use it.

All best wishes.

As ever,
Bonnie

March 15, 1976
Dear Bonnie,

This morning I made all the reservations for my California jaunt. Unless some unforeseen disaster looms upon the horizon, I shall arrive in United at the airport in Santa Barbara at 1:48 p.m. at Tuesday, April 20. It is most kind and considerate of you to meet me. George had wanted to visit a bit with you at your monastery. I shall be a poor substitute for him, but I will do my best. On Thursday, April 22, I shall take the plane from Santa Barbara at 5 p.m. to San Francisco, where I shall stay at the St. Francis until the 17th. This hotel has always been the favorite of mine. If it is more convenient for you I can leave the monastery earlier on Thursday for I always manage to find interesting haunts around.

I have planned this trip on my own as a kind of prelude to a longer solo Scandinavian excursion in the not too distant future. I have always felt at home with the Danes, perhaps a throwback to a long ago Danish ancestor.

California will provide me with a pleasant respite from my various volunteer programs that have a way of growing. It is good of you to invite me.

With Best Wishes,
Edna

We have another snow warning and my tulips are up. But then my grandfather Lane called these white fluffy particles at this time of year poor man's fertilizer.

March 27, 1976
Mount Cavalry Retreat House
Santa Barbara, California
Dear Edna

So delighted that you can visit on April 20-22. I shall meet you at the airport at 1:48 p.m. Tuesday. Stay as long as you wish on Thursday.

It will be good to see you and I think we shall have some interesting things to show you.

As ever,
Bonnie

April 11, 1976
Mount Calvary Retreat House
Santa Barbara, California
Dear Edna,

Just a note to reassure you that I shall be meeting the plane at Santa Barbara airport on Tuesday, April 20th at 1:48 p.m. I shall be in my white habit so you should have no difficulty recognizing me. It will be a joy to have you with us. Have a pleasant journey.

As ever,
Bonnie

April 16, 1976
Dear Bonnie,

Thank you for your note of reassurance; it was most welcome. This week in Boston, my favorite city, I saw the "Belle of Amherst," the most delightful one-actor show I have ever seen. The touches of humor were priceless, and the play flowed naturally without effort before my eyes. I have always loved the theater when it was good. My mother first took me when I was a baby.

In Connecticut, the earth grows greener and more beautiful by the day. Unfortunately, a capricious frost bronzed the magnolias in both Connecticut and Massachusetts.

Barring unforeseen catastrophes, I shall see you Tuesday at 1:48 p.m. It will be good to see you. Either Harvey or Mary, my best friend, whom you once met here, will drive me to Bradley Airport at five plus in the morning. Mary married a pediatrician, who has since retired. They have been very kind to me.

With best wishes,
Edna

April 25, 1976
Hotel St. Francis
San Francisco, California
Dear Bonnie,

Thank you for a beautiful experience. I enjoyed our morning walks together, the truly spectacular views, the tour about town, the studio at the monastery, the religious evening with your delightful young people, and the warmth of your hospitality. I have chuckled many times over the way you forgot me on my last day.

Please give my best regards to your good Brothers and tell them I appreciate their consideration for an intruder.

Tuesday, after five days of touring San Francisco and the surrounding areas, I am flying home. I was happy to find you well, and once again wish to congratulate you on the splendid honor that is soon to be bestowed upon you—one that is richly deserved after all you have given to others through the years; spiritual contributions are the finest of all and the most sorely needed.

I shall always remember your monastery—Mount Calvary—as a kind of Shangri-la, where love, beauty, and peace prevail. Episcopalians have much to give and we need it.

I hope I was not too great a burden—interrupting your arduous routine.

Yours sincerely,
Edna

April 27, 1976
Santa Barbara, California

[The following is a response to a $100 gift by Edna to the Order of the Holy Cross, Mount Calvary]

Dear Friend:

Thank you for your gift in support of our work. We will be praying for you and thank you for your prayers to us. May you have a blessed Lent and a glorious Easter.

This month, on April 8 at 5:30 in the afternoon at the Church Divinity School of the Pacific chapel, Br Jack Wilson OHC will make his life vows in the Order. Br Jack is an American from Alabama, and has been studying for the priesthood at CDSP for the past two years. The Fr Superior will be here for the Profession and will spend Easter with us at Mount Calvary.

Fr Bonnell Spencer has been busy these past several months with two new ventures. He has been priest in charge of St Michaels Isla Vista during the interim while they search for a new Rector, and he has been active in the Santa Barbara theatrical field. He played the Mayor in a recent production of Front Page, and again is playing the Mayor in an up-coming production of The Lady's Not For Burning. Fr Spencer's work at St Michaels is giving him an opportunity to put some of his liturgical theories into practice, with very affirmative results. While operating parishes is not one of the usual activities of a member of the Order, all of us enjoy the opportunity to be involved in parish life from time to time.

The Grandparents of Br Richard Gill and the Priors father both made extended visits to the house recently. It is a special joy to welcome our "other" family into our Holy Cross family.

Br Richard, as well as his work visiting in several Santa Barbara Nursing Homes has a growing ministry with families whose lives have been affected by the disease of alcoholism.

The Prior has been busy with missions away from home. Recently he spent four days at the Cathedral in Fresno and a series of missions in the Diocese of Western Kansas and the Diocese of Oregon.

Br Orlando made his first back-packing trip recently. Orlando is a native of New York City and the wonders of the great outdoors are an exciting new discovery for him. With two students from Brooks Institute he climbed in the San Rafael Mountains and is keen to go again.

Faithfully yours,
The Rev George Swayne OHC
Prior, Mt Calvary

May 1, 1976
Grapevine, Texas
Dear Edna,

It was delightful to have you with us at Mount Calvary. All the Brethren, as well as I, enjoyed your visit and we are grateful for your generous offering. I hope you can visit us again—either at Mount Calvary or one of our other houses.

Here I am unexpectedly in Texas. I have had to come here to supervise the final corrections of the breviary which we are editing. As this is the house that I founded, I naturally feel much at home here.

Again I hope we shall be seeing more of each other before long. All best wishes.

Love,
Bonnie

May 9, 1976
Dear Bonnie,

I was indeed surprised to learn you had been sent to Texas, but happy you could return to the house you founded—you never told me about this extremely extraordinary accomplishment. Please do tell us more about it. You surely are versatile as well as creative.

Tonight, my neighbor invited me to attend a concert at Saint James (Episcopal) in West Hartford. Her son Erik, a sixth grader, whom I befriended in his early years, sang in their choir. Their voices were beautiful—almost as lovely as those of the boys singing in the choir at Evensong at Canterbury Cathedral last spring.

I, too, hope that we shall see each other before long. You are always welcome to stay here if you wish; there is plenty of room and Connecticut is now in a burst of glory. I can always pick you up—I won't forget you.

All the best,
Edna May

May 22, 1976
West Park, New York
Dear Edna,

Now that I have got to West Park I have a moment to catch up on my correspondence. It was nice to get your card. The founding of Whitby House was not so very difficult, since we had many friends in the vicinity who were eager for us to establish ourselves among them. From the start they were generous with their support, so that the house was able to be self-sustaining from the beginning. Local people supplied us with the original building and two years later we were able to double its size and add a chapel which is widely admired. That addition we designed and built ourselves with a minimum of professional help.

I am glad you were able to attend the choir concert. Some of our churches still have a good tradition of boys' choirs, though I fear it is fast dying out. One unfortunate side-effect of them, however, has been the idea that this is the only possible type of church music, with the result that small churches, with a choir of four women and two men, try to sing music that would tax the capacity of the Canterbury Cathedral choir. But fortunately one of the results of the contemporary liturgical reforms with their emphasis on congregational participation has been the development of some common sense in this matter.

When I was looking forward to my stay here until July 2nd, it seemed a long time. But now I discover that, with meetings of the Order and the ten-day retreat I hope to make, I shall have only a week free and that the one immediately before my departure. So I fear, except for the trip to Williamstown, I shall not be able to go anywhere during this visit east. But I do hope we shall be getting together somewhere before long. Meanwhile all best wishes.

As ever,
Bonnie

June 17, 1976
Dear Bonnie,

You have been so busy at West Park and around that I delayed writing lest I become a bother. Perhaps you have a few minutes now.

Harvey tells me that unforeseen factors prevented you from reaching Williamstown-I am so very sorry; I had thought of you having a delightful visit, and the weekend was beautiful. If there had been one excursion within my power to preserve for you, it would have been that one.

Your account of the founding of Whitby House was most reassuring—faith, imagination, and work can surely accomplish miracles. You earned your doctorate. Life sometimes yields appreciation for labors well done.

With the help of my neighbor boy, Jimmy, I have made some progress with our flower gardens. Tomorrow I am taking my other neighbor boy, Chuckie, out to lunch. He is eager to go since I told him he may have whatever he wants. He has been most helpful.

I have been consoling myself with an old friend, Galsworthy, with whom I have long felt a certain kinship. At the same time, I am reading Martin's Adlai Stevenson of Illinois. It seems that we tend to elect the wrong presidents more often than the right ones. Stevenson's wit and power with words have always fascinated me. He was a true statesman. Years ago, I campaigned for him from door to door. At one house, I encountered a middle-aged woman, who gaily remarked, "I'm a Democrat, but I'm voting for Ike this time; he has such a lovely smile." At that I folded my tent and went along my way.

I am truly sorry that you have no time for me, but I understand and hope that you have a safe and rewarding journey on the second of July. What is your mission there—if it is all right to ask?

At least, I have my memory of Shangri-la.

With best wishes,
Edna

June 26, 1976
West Park, New York
Dear Edna,

Thank you for your letter. It is good to hear from you and I especially appreciated the page from The Christian Science Monitor. It confirms what I have thought, that Carter is not fuzzy on the issues and that his position is one I can heartily endorse. It is a most delightful miracle that he has been able to pull the Democratic Party together. Last fall I was afraid all the candidates would cut each other's throats and the Convention would be a shambles. On the other hand, I expected the Republicans to endorse Ford with no real opposition. How pleasantly contrary things have turned out.

I had a pleasant visit from Harvey and Ann the other day. When I found out that he did not go to the Reunion, I was very glad I had not. He was one who I most wanted to see.

My trip to the Caribbean begins Friday with a visit to our house in Nassau for a week. Then I proceed to Barbados, where I am giving a two-week course in Liturgies to the Summer Clergy School at Coddington College. After that I visit Trinidad to make contact with Associates and possible vocations to OHC there. Then to Guyana for the same purpose. I then return to Nassau to keep one of the brothers there company while the rest are on vacation. I have a busy vacation myself in the vicinity of Augusta, the first week in September, and then on to Minneapolis for the opening of our General Convention. I expect to get back to Santa Barbara by the middle of that month. So it will be a busy, and I hope happy time.

All the best,
Bonnie

July 17, 1976
Dear Bonnie,

I do not know if this will reach you or not.

How fortunate that you are having all those rich and varied experiences this summer. You must find Codington intellectually stimulating. Does it really remind you of Oxford?

I am inclined to agree with your political observations although I had wanted Church or Udall. I am delighted with Carter's choice of Mondale, whom I have always admired. If his subsequent choices show as much insight as this one, the national scene must improve. So many executives in all walks of life have failed us because they were unable to distinguish a knave from a saint. It gives me new hope to realize that our people really do want a leader with ideals, a man who demonstrates that the family unit is sacred and vital to the progress of this nation.

The clippings I am enclosing help me to understand Carter better.

All my life I have tried to understand people, and sometimes I don't get very far. My father was a man of rare understanding— fortunately for us for my mother was as proud as Lucifer, like some high spirited filly, but possessing a delightful sense of humor.

I was distressed to hear Father Drinan inject a religious prejudice into the proceedings of the Convention in an interview. I fail to see the importance of a particular creed as long as each one is sincere in his belief. Perhaps this is because I happen to be a product of a long ancestry of many different Protestant faiths. I was raised a Baptist according to my father's beliefs. I tried the Methodists (my mother's allegiance), but I reverted to the philosophy of my great grandfather Bangs and became Unitarian.

In the same way, I started as a Republican (my father's people supported this political stand in New York City from the time the party first began), but I chose to become a Democrat; although I always try to vote for the best candidate irrespective of his party affiliation. I shudder at the political corruption revealed in Adlai Stevenson of Illinois and realize the same shenanigans must go on in all states.

One day last week, I drove to the Williams Theater to see Shaw's Heartbreak House. It was a beautiful performance, and the actors must have been heartened by the warm, enthusiastic response of the spectators.

Monday I am going to New York City for a few days to visit a very good friend, a professor who is a deacon at Riverside Church (her father was a Baptist preacher). We are going to see My Fair Lady. Some years ago George and I saw this show on Broadway. On New Year's Eve we went to the theater early to capture tickets from someone who might be returning them at the last moment. George accused me of jumping into the arms of two young men who had tickets to sell— their dates had deserted them. I was so eager to get them, and we did. It was a glorious night.

Two of my neighbor mothers have taken up the practice of joining me in my nightly walks—whether this is for my protection or they really want the experience, I don't quite know, but it is good. By day, I walk round the Avon Reservoir and always thank God for the beauty of the earth—it makes pain more bearable.

I am glad you have a vacation forthcoming for they work you pretty hard.

May you have a happy summer,
Edna

August 3, 1976
Guyana, South America
Dear Edna Mae,

Since I was writing Ann and Hob when your letter reached me in Barbados, I asked them to thank you for it and the enclosures, which I read with great interest, and to share with you the news which I wrote them. I trust they have done so. Now I am at least getting around to answering you; I hope you will share this news with them. The Summer School went very well. Although I turned out to be the only teacher, I learned much from the group. They were already moving along the lines I recommended and helped me—and each other—perceive what was involved in their church life and worship truly indigenous. This is particularly important in these countries who received Christianity originally from their slave-masters and colonials overlords. In these days of indigenous rulers in both state and church the ultra-British culture of the Anglican Church links it with a past from which the best minds of the present are liberating themselves that they may become true and full human beings. It is disastrous for the church to seem to be opposing this, although many of the older generation—black as well as white—are frightened at the new responsibilities and are clinging for security to the past. Fortunately the live and influential leaders see the issue and are facing up to it. Again in Trinidad last weekend I stayed with a young priest who is doing creative pioneering along what I agree are the right lines. There I had a chance to speak to a group of the clergy who seemed eager to learn what is going on and why. Here I am the guest at the moment of the Archbishop, the last of the white bishops, who is elderly + conservative but nevertheless still providing keen leadership.

The miracle of Carter's unification of the Democrats is most enheartening. I am disappointed, however, to learn that McCarthy is running against him. I earnestly pray he does not take away so many votes that Carter loses key states. My hope is that his followers who failed to elect Humphreys and so gave us Nixon are now older + wiser and that McCarthy is unknown to the current younger voters. I shall be interested to learn by how much Ford gets the Republican nomination + how the Reagan camp reacts to it. If Reagan consents to be Vice President, Carter may have a hard time against the Republicans plus McCarthy. One can only hope, pray + vote. I trust you are having a good summer—your last letter sounded as if you were. My best to Ann + Hob, and of course to you.

As ever,
Bonnie

August 14, 1976
Dear Bonnie,

Your last letter was of great interest to me. I gained a better understanding of your mission and its wide need. Your work must bring you great joy. All good teachers learn so much from their students. How fortunate for them that you were their only teacher.

Harvey had read your letter to me over the phone, and I shared your last letter with him.

It is indeed unfortunate that McCarthy must assert his importance at this point, but his effect this time may prove less potent. I have never admired either Buckley; both impress me as arrogant egotists. I have worked all year for the League of Women Voters in the legislative area and am now circulating a petition among voters to urge the major party candidates for president to meet in public debate on the issues facing the country. I thought the League television forums where the presidential aspirants discussed the issues were excellent.

Perhaps this coming year I should become involved in nursery schools. It is with our children that the hope of the world lies. If only good nursery schools were free for all the children and the affluent mingled with the less affluent (children learn so much from each other). Little ones are eager to learn—long before the age of five. I have always urged mothers to read to their babes in arms. My two little boys, Andrew and Brian Sole, each day after lunch take to the living room with their books to read to themselves. Of course, they can't really read, but the three year old has memorized his stories and the year and a half one busily names all the animals and gives forth the appropriate sounds.

Unfortunately, the good Lord did not see fit to give me little ones of my own, but I have always enjoyed other people's offspring. George used to tell me that if I had had babies, I would have scrubbed them all away.

I am still disappointed in our governor; she is no leader, and I feel she is false. I worked hard, but not successfully this winter trying to find work for the good state employees she let go; and now we have a substantial surplus in our Connecticut treasury. Unemployment is a powerful demoralizer.

Since I feel a deep need to get away somewhere, I am planning to visit Scandinavia for 22 days beginning September nineteenth. I am going alone (I must become accustomed to it), but I expect to get along since it is a Four Winds Tour. I have always felt at home among the Danes, a most democratic people. I have been grateful for some Danish ancestry (1/8) even though it goes back about a century and a half.

Do keep well and happy.

We hope to see you before too long—if it is possible.

As ever,
Edna

November 22, 1976
Dear Bonnie,

Perchance you have received neither the letter of August 14th which I mailed to Guyana (the stamps on the letter you sent from there on August 3rd were very beautiful) nor the card I sent from Copenhagen on October 10. Mail has its own way of getting lost, I have discovered.

As I mentioned in my letter, I escaped to Scandinavia for three weeks on the 19th of September. The days in September and December are always a bit difficult for me. The trip carried with it a kind of welcome therapy—even though the tours seem to have a way of attracting light-headed individuals. I proved to be the only serious walker, but then, I am accustomed to tramping alone. However, in Norway I did find an English girl who enjoyed climbing mountains. We really need more Scandinavians over here—their cleanliness, industry, and cheerfulness were admirable. We had the best guide I have ever known—a young woman with a disposition of pure gold plus a delightfully contagious enthusiasm. The fjords and mountains of Norway never cease to fill me with awe. We found many beautiful Lutheran churches throughout Scandinavia, including a most unusual modern one in Helsinki. For the most part, I fail to be inspired by most of the modern architecture.

With great interest, I followed the progress of events at your conference in Minneapolis. How heartened you must be by the outcome. Don't ever lose your youthful enthusiasm; it is a joy to behold.

And the national election finished correctly! I hold great hope for Carter and Mondale. Now, may we see the end of the Nixon shenanigans. I was disappointed with the showing made by California and Connecticut.

May you have a happy Thanksgiving.

As ever,
Edna

December 15, 1976
Santa Barbara, California
Dear Edna,

Despite its Christmas wrappings, I have taken the liberty of opening your gift early, as I wanted to express my gratitude in time to get this letter to you (I hope) before the feast. The book is simply splendid. E.B. White is one of my favorite people and I always read his articles in The New Yorker with great pleasure. So there will be hours of enjoyment in this delightful book. Thank you so much.

I trust you have received my last letter and know that I did receive both your letter to Guyana and the postcard. It is always a joy to hear from you.

The remainder of my trip east was great fun, especially the week in Michigan when I got some real winter—much snow and cold, but with periods of sunshine and moonlight to give a postcard effect. I miss winter tremendously out here, so even that brief touch of it has been deeply appreciated.

Now I must get to work on the reading of the book I hope to write while the UCSB library is still available to me. I forget whether I have told you that I expect to be transferred to our house in Nassau next April. That ought to be good fun and I hope some interesting ministries will be opening up for me there. More of this later, and I shall give you my address there in good time before I go.

I hope you have a most blessed Christmas and that the New Year brings you much joy.

As ever,
Bonnie

P.S. Thank you also for your card and its interesting account of your trip. The election is most encouraging as it the care with which Carter is preparing for his responsibilities and the caliber of the persons he is appointing. If anything can save this country I believe he has a good chance.

January 1, 1977
Santa Barbara, California
Dear Edna,

Thank you for your Christmas letter and card. It is always good to hear from you. I am glad the pre-Christmas season was going well for you and I trust it continued through the feast, and into the New Year.

I am continuing my reading for the book I hope to write. I must get as much as possible done while I have the UCSB library available.

I go over about every two weeks and stock up with six or seven books. There also are several books in our library here that I hope to read before I leave in April. The book will be on the doctrines of creation, man, and the incarnation mostly. I think the time has come to cut loose from some of the traditional ways of putting things theologically, and I am surprised to find much endorsement of my ideas in the books I am reading, some of which were written a good while ago. Philosophically, I find Whitehead most helpful, indeed I expect my basic position as to the function of the universe will be derived from him.

I do not believe I have read any of Eric Fromm yet, but I have him down in my bibliography to read eventually. Thanks for the recommendation. Incidentally, in the field of psychology I find Frankl very helpful. One of the most encouraging signs, from my point of view, is the insistence in many writers on the need to restore meaning and purpose to our concept of the universe. This is just where I am at.

The New Year will have got well started before this reaches you, but I hope it is already bringing you joy and prosperity and that it will continue to do so. I am happier than every over Jimmy Carter, and trust things will begin to go better for our country and our relations with the rest of the world.

All best wishes.

As ever,
Bonnie

January 27, 1977
Dear Bonnie,

Thank you for your good wishes for the New Year. We are having a genuine old-fashioned winter with heavy snow, bitter cold and some treacherous ice—sparkling on the trees, but uncertain under foot and beneath car. I appreciate all but the ice since I have been driving only two years now. I first learned when I was nineteen, drove for some thirteen years and then ceased. George didn't want me to drive because he said my reaction time was too quick. However, after he went, I felt I had nothing to lose so I went to the AAA Driving School. They were excellent teachers. I now drive all over—except over ice—but sometimes I get caught when I am out—no accounting for New England weather.

I have been dipping into Whitehead—so I am sure to drown. I have always had the utmost respect for him. I know that you have a far better background in philosophy than I. Most of mine I have gleaned from the fine arts. My best teacher was a Fine Arts professor at Boston University. I was not a major in this area, but I kept coming back because I learned so much from him. His standards in both ethics and subject manner were beautifully high, and the classes were small.

Thank you for recommending Viktor Frankl; I have found him most rewarding. I first went to the library and then later bought The Doctor and the Soul as well as Man's Search for Meaning. The latter we are going to consider at The Book Discussion Meeting at our church next week Friday. I am responsible for heading the discussion on Bertrand Russell, especially his Conquest of Happiness. It is good for me that the participants are not the least bit backward. We have some lively times. I hope you won't mind if I ask you some questions about Frankl, Whitehead, and Russell next time.

This year I continue on our local board of League of Women Voters as their legislature chairman so I get to the Connecticut General Assembly as an observer. I hope this year in Hartford it is better than last year for I was somewhat disillusioned.

I am still serving as chairman of the McCusker Scholarship Program for the CSEA. To date we have been most fortunate in the caliber of judges we have selected. We award $500 scholarships on the basis of academic standing, social adaptation and financial need. The latter two are most difficult to evaluate. In 1976, we gave away 24 awards, and I hope we can do better this year. We give them a party in June; my faith is always renewed when I greet the winners, and their families—for they seem so genuine and unpretentious. We subsist on contributions alone; this is one area when the state employees really think of others.

On our last two Sundays we have had the sermon delivered first by a psychologist and then by a psychiatrist. The people came in droves and even crowded the chapel afterwards for a talkback. The speakers have been excellent. Do you think Unitarians have more problems than others?

I have sent you some cookies I made from scratch for your good Brothers. I know not how they will arrive, and perhaps I have done the wrong thing—I truly did not wish to upset your diets. I wanted to do something for them before you left Mount Calvary. Perhaps you can think of something better I can do.

If there is any reference you need in your research, I would be glad to send it to you in California or Nassau. I have access to many libraries and I always get lost in book stores.

Edna

January 30, 1977
Santa Barbara, California
Dear Edna,

Thank you very much for the box of goodies which arrived in fine shape. I wish you could have heard the exclamations of appreciation when they made their appearance at tea. You would have a better idea than I can convey to you how much they were welcomed.

We are disturbed at the kind of weather you and everywhere else in the country seem to be getting. Our weather is its usual delightful self—though with less rain than is needed.

I thought Jimmy's walk down Pennsylvania Avenue was sheer genius. Set just the right tone. He seems to be getting off to a fine start. We must not expect miracles, but I truly believe he will be getting the country moving forward again. Republicans, as Truman pointed out, function only in reverse. Jimmy rather reminds me of Harry!

All join in sending best wishes and thanks.

As ever,
Bonnie

February 12, 1977
Santa Barbara, California

Dear Edna,

Thank you for your letter. I trust you have already received mine thanking you for the cookies which were thoroughly enjoyed by the Brethren. They all want me to express their appreciation.

People cannot believe that I regret missing the winter you are having, but I do because I love snow and cold. At the same time, I fear the weather has caused much hardship and suffering, and that I regret. In this state, especially the northern part, we are suffering a severe drought which may, if it has not already, destroy much of the fruit and vegetable crop. That along with the destruction by cold in Florida and elsewhere in the southeast will, I fear, make food very scarce and expensive this winter.

I shall be glad to have you ask the questions you wish on the various philosophers, but I cannot guarantee to be able to answer them. I find Whitehead very difficult, but he has suggested some ideas—whether they really are his or not I cannot be sure—that I have found helpful in working out the position. I am trying to get ready for the book I hope to write.

I think the Unitarians are more willing to recognize and discuss our contemporary problems than some other Christian groups. However, I do find that, when Episcopalians are given some solid material to chew on and an opportunity to discuss it, they can be vocal also. In fact, there seems to be a most healthy desire on the part of laypersons to become better informed in theology and kindred matters.

I hope everything continues well with you.

As ever,
Bonnie

March 17, 1977
Dear Bonnie,

It was good to hear from you—both letters. We would have loved sharing our bitter winter with you, but we are worried about your western drought for that is truly serious. Here spring shows early signs of arrival—pussy willows, budding bushes, sprouting bulbs and spring peepers—fine nights in a row.

Your comments about Episcopalians and Unitarians were most interesting. Sometimes I think Unitarians are so busy following their heads that they forget their hearts.

I am sure Episcopalians have many lively discussions. My mother named me for her best friend who was a devout Episcopalian.

Tonight I witnessed via TV Jimmy Carter's meeting with the people in Clinton—another stroke of genius. I think you realized in the beginning that Carter had a warm, moral commitment to the people. People really do want leaders that can inspire them, and that is a most comforting factor. Both Franklin Roosevelt and Harry Truman gave us so much.

Our League of Women Voters has a deep interest in the U.N., especially in the problems of developing nations. We must help then, but we cannot expect them to achieve in one generation what it took us ten generations to accomplish. Today I spent hours at our state capitol defending the LWV position in favor of the Equal Rights Amendment for we have those in Connecticut who seek to rescind the Equal Rights Amendment the legislature passed in 1973. The ignorance and demagoguery abroad were astonishing.

Our CPTV has the best programs and no commercials. This winter they gave two excellent dramatizations from California—The Belle of Amherst which was really superior to the production I had seen in Boston, and Cyrano De Bergerac, an old favorite of mine. Last night they broadcast La Boheme live from Lincoln Center—superb.

Have you taken part in any more plays this winter? I would have enjoyed seeing you perform. I shall be eternally grateful to you for introducing Viktor Frankl to me. He is the best I have encountered in psychiatry; at least, I agree with him. How was he able to rise so high above those concentration camps? I would have perished promptly. I have recommended Frankl to others so your inspiration is spreading.

To be sure, Russell is both brilliant and controversial. He is a most lucid writer; his simple maxims for writers of prose should form the preface of all manuals on writing. What do you think of Russell's position regarding England's entrance into World War I? Do you mind reacting to the following quotation? "Throughout all politics, both for good and for evil, the two chief forces are the economic motive and the love of power; an attempt to interpret politics on Freudian lines is to my mind, a mistake . . . The desire to understand the world and the desire to reform it are the two great engines of progress, without which human society would stand still or retrogress. It may be that too complete a happiness would cause the impulses to knowledge and reform to fade . . . To a man of sufficient energy, pain may be a valuable stimulus, and I do not deny that if we were all perfectly happy, we should not exert ourselves to become happier. But I cannot admit that it is any part of the duty of human beings to provide others with pain on the off-chance that it may prove fruitful." "Fear is the main source of superstition and one of the main sources of cruelty. To conquer fear is the beginning of wisdom, in the pursuit of truth as in the endeavor after a worthy manner of life."

I hope you are well, and sometime I still hope to see you.

As ever,
Edna.

April 11, 1977
Santa Barbara, California
Dear Edna,

Your welcome letter came while I was away on a preaching trip and I have delayed answering until just before my departure for Nassau. My address there will be Holy Redeemer Priory, PO Box N-1930, Nassau, NP, Bahamas, WI. But I shall be in Barbados April 20-May

20 at Coddington College, St. John, Barbados, WI giving a course on liturgical renewal.

Yes, I also am much encouraged by Jimmy Carter's leadership. It is all I had hoped it would be so far. Of course the situation is terribly difficult, but it seems to me that he is facing it honestly.

I am glad you like Frankl. I find him most helpful. I have just read his The Unconscious God, which is very fine. I find all your philosophical questions quite acceptable. In my forthcoming book (if it ever comes!) I hope to deal at length with the problem of pain and suffering. There is much fuzzy thinking on the subject. But I fully agree with the passages you quote on that subject.

I hope you are having a blessed Eastertide.

As ever,
Bonnie

May 1, 1977
Dear Bonnie,

Thank you for your two addresses. As I remember, you enjoyed last year's experience at Coddington College, and I hope this year's stay is even more rewarding. I know that it will be so for your students. I hear strange stories about the mail in those Caribbean islands, but since I have never been there, I really don't know; I trust this letter arrive in time.

I have ordered The Unconscious God, but it has not yet arrived. This Friday, I agreed to lead our church discussion group on Frankl's Man's Search for Meaning. I wish that you were here to guide in my place; your enlightenment would be deeply appreciated.

Next week, I hope to spend a couple of days in Boston when the book market is more plentiful. I always stay at the College Club on Commonwealth Avenue—a safe and central location. This is where I roomed on my sabbatical.

Wednesday on the 25th of May, Ann and Harvey embark for a three week trip to Sweden. We all expect matters to move smoothly.

Saturday I spent a disheartening day observing the Appropriations Committee of our Legislature debate the availability of increasing welfare benefits 20% to the 1974 level—cost of living. After more than four hours, they defeated the motion so that these poor people will receive only a 10% increase. They can't possibly feed their children adequately on this budget, but these Conn. legislators (most of them) heartlessly disregard their needs. This is not Christian of me, but I hope these selfish legislators someday know what it means to be in want. Both the LWV and our Hartford Region Conference of Churches to which I go as a delegate, are working for increased welfare benefits—at least 20%; it should be 40%.

If you are allowed to tell me, what will your duties be in Nassau? What is your Priory like? Is it large? I hope you are well and happy. I still remember Shangri-la in California.

As ever,
Edna

May 13, 1977
Codrington College
St. John, Barbados
Dear Edna,

Your good letter has arrived safely and is much appreciated. I am glad to learn of your continued enthusiasm for Frankl and of your sharing it with others. It is too bad that the legislature is so unresponsive to the needs of those on welfare, but as few of the latter vote and most of the taxpayers do, one knows where the interest of the legislators lies. But when enough voters like you demonstrate your concern, they may come to think differently.

I am sorry to learn that Hob has had to have an operation. I hope it has come out well and that he and Ann are able to get off alright on the 25th. I know how much they are looking forward to it. Please give them both my best.

I am not sure yet what my duties in Nassau will be. Here at the theological college in Barbados I am principally giving a course in liturgies. I am also getting in much reading for my projected book. Nassau is unfortunately very deficient in theological libraries. But I hope to have a week in New York at the seminary there in June and another ten days or so at a seminary in Sewanee in July. I also have a number of books I purchased waiting to be read in Nassau and will probably buy a few more. But in any case I am going to have to call a halt soon to my reading if I am ever going to get at writing the book. If I have nothing else I have to do in Nassau the reading and writing will keep me fully occupied.

This is a lovely spot, as I told you last summer when I was here. This time there is the additional pleasure and privilege of having the students of the College present and getting to know them. Most of the clergy of the diocese of the Province of the West Indies (the ex-British colonies) are trained here. They are a splendid group of men, a real hope for the Church of the future. I deeply appreciate the opportunity of making a small contribution to their preparation for the priesthood.

I hope all goes well with you.

Love,
Bonnie

P.S. I leave here next Saturday, May 21. So your next letter should go to Nassau.

May 31, 1977
Dear Bonnie,

Your letter was most enjoyable, and the stamps were as beautiful as those of last year. It took about ten days to reach here, but I hope this one travels faster.

Harvey's operation was most successful so that Ann and he were able to leave for Sweden on schedule—as happy as larks.

I have been busy with my volunteer jobs and my garden. This year my tulips were lovely even though some turned out to be red instead of purple. I wanted to paint them the way the gardener (Two, Five, and Seven) did with the roses on the Queen's Croquet Ground. Instead I returned the 21 errors to the nurseryman—flowers and bulbs intact. He was quite surprised but promised me purple ones next year. I am so fortunate to have Jimmy, the lad next door, to help me with the gardens and grass. In fact, I am singularly lucky to find such good helpers—efficient and cheerful—in all avenues—housework, painting, and car repairs. This winter someone (I don't know who) damaged a back fender when my car was parked, but the garage man put it back in perfect condition.

Our CPTV is going to run The Forsyte Saga—to my delight. I have always been partial to British plays performed by British actors. I once had a dramatics professor who maintained that the English made the best actors for their reserve enabled them to reveal emotions without divulging all; there was always a depth not yet plunged. This winter Upstairs Downstairs was superbly done.

I finally received The Unconscious God and read it. I agree with his views, but I found this book a little more difficult and shall reread it; I have it all marked up with red pencil—this to me is the joy of owning a book. I do so agree with his statement—"True conscience has nothing to do with the fearful expectation of punishment. As long as a man is still motivated by either the fear of punishment or the hope of a reward—or, for that matter, by the wish to appease the superego—conscience has not yet had its say." Once upon a time, I had great respect for psychiatrists (I have never been to one). Some of my friends have engaged their services. Today, I believe many psychiatrists are somewhat devastating to the individual. In contrast, Frankl seems so sane and logical. I do wish I could discuss him with you. During our church discussion, it was hard to get the members to probe deeply enough. I am in your debt for your recommendation of Frankl.

I am glad you are going to have access to good theological libraries. When you come to New York, would you like to stay in Connecticut for a visit? Ann and Harvey should return by the 16th of

June and I have plenty of room. I could even drive you to the Yale Library, which is only 30 miles away. The Hartford Seminary Library is not what it once was.

I should like to see you and talk with you. If Connecticut is not possible, I visit N.Y.C. on occasion and could see you there somewhere. I could even invite you to dinner if you would go.

I know that your book means everything to you and you probably have a full program—so please do what you most want to do.

Edna

July 7, 1977
Nassau, Bahamas [written from South Carolina]
Dear Edna,

Thank you for your letter. I am embarrassed that I have left it unanswered for so long. But when it reached me I was getting ready for a trip to the states, and decided to wait till I got there. But I have been so occupied, reading furiously for a week at General Seminary and then attending the Conference Week and Chapter of the Order, that I only now have a chance to write. I am at our house in South Carolina beginning a ten-day retreat. It is a perfect, quiet spot for it.

It is especially inexcusable that I have delayed so long when you were so kind as to invite me to visit you. But that was quite impossible this time. I arrived at West Park the afternoon before the big service at which the Presiding Bishop dedicated a shrine to our Father Founder. That afternoon I had to attend a relative's wedding in Kingston. Conference Week began Monday, with meetings morning, afternoon, and evening, including Saturday. Sunday was the Life Profession of one of our Brothers. Monday and Tuesday were chapter, the annual business meeting of the Order. Wednesday morning I left for here. So I trust you will understand why I could not visit nor write.

On the 17th I go to Severance for another few days in the library. I could, of course, spend another year or two reading for the book I want to write, but I hope by the end of the summer to have covered enough that I can start writing. Even professional theologians have a hard time keeping up these days, and I do not aim at more than a popularization of some notions that have been around for quite a while.

I hope your manifold activities are prospering, though I suspect the political ones are in abeyance over the summer.

Here I have a little one-room cottage all to myself. It is even equipped with air-conditioning. As I have no desire to emulate the asceticism of the ancient hermits, I find this most agreeable, since the weather here so far has been very hot and humid.

I get back to Nassau at the end of the month. All best wishes for a grand summer.

As ever,
Bonnie

August 29, 1977
Dear Bonnie,

I am very happy for you that you were able to do all you most wanted to accomplish when you were in the states this summer. I am sure your long list of commitments kept you busy and content. It was indeed providential you had your air-conditioned refuge in South Carolina for most of our summer in the East has been hot and humid.

I was sorry to hear about your ankle from Harvey; you didn't mention it. How were you ever able to walk with a fractured ankle? Please do follow your doctor's instructions. I hope you are able to get all the exercise you need.

Fred and Betsy—my favorite nephew and niece (they are George's) have acquired a new baby boy—bouncing and healthy, their third offspring. I was hoping it would be a girl because I think it is good for every family to have both boys and girls. Andrew, the first born, was deeply disappointed to learn he had a brother instead of a sister. Brian, the middle one, is quite precious with a delightful personality—warm and lovable as well as being intelligent. He reminds me of George.

He regards all the little animals as his friends. I miss my little boys; Michigan has the advantage.

This fall I am relinquishing my post as chairman of McCusker Scholarship Trustees after better than six years because I think I shall seek other fields of activity. I have worked in various capacities for the Connecticut State Employees Association for many, many years. I believe in unions, but I think the leadership often leaves much to be desired. The language at one Executive Board meeting was such that had I been a man I would have tossed one character out bodily. Today's language is often offensive and so unnecessary. Your Father Geyer of Hartford agrees with me.

It is not surprising that the SAT scores have steadily declined over the past 14 years. I have contended right along that education from the elementary schools up has been far too permissive, haphazard; the standards have lowered.

This Leonardo cartoon which I have always found most meaningful seems to be beautifully explained here. To me, the original was breath-taking. In my room, I have a copy on one wall and the Birth of Venus on the wall opposite. I find a bond of feeling between the two copies. I suppose you will think only Unitarians would see any such connection. But I like living with them just the same.

One of my most rewarding courses in college was Renaissance Art.

Last week Mary, her husband, and I drove to Williamstown for a couple of days—Chekhov's Platonov was well done but rather disappointing. We enjoyed the campus; it was truly beautiful, and I felt George was with me. I want an oil painting of Thompson Chapel and perhaps Griffin Hall. Do you think just one building would be better?

I am toying with the idea of a European tour in October, but I haven't decided which one yet. If I don't make up my mind soon, it won't be available. Harvey's pictures from Sweden are a work of art.

May your forthcoming book be the best of all.

As ever,
Edna

September 18, 1977
Nassau, Bahamas
Dear Edna,

Thank you for your letter. I particularly enjoyed the analysis of Leonardo's cartoon. It is one that I too have admired and I can readily appreciate your association of it with the Birth of Venus because both emphasize the earthy human qualities which are all too often neglected by "religious" folk. This is particularly strange in those who believe in the incarnation—that God manifested himself supremely in an earthy human nature. The trouble is that most incarnational Christians do not really believe in the human nature of Christ. I suspect that the desire to recover its integrity was one of the factors that led to the rise of Unitarianism.

The decline of S.A.T. scores is unquestionably due to permissive + haphazard standards. But I have a theory as to one of the contributory causes which I should like to try out on you as an educator. During the 60's, it seemed to me that a basically sound development started among the youth of this country—a serious questioning of assumptions as to the "good life" which deserved to be questioned. Inevitably many of the manifestations of this "revolt" were to us oldsters revolting. But I believe that underneath was a thoroughly constructive criticism of current, + and search for new, standards, which The Greening of America detected. If these could have been accepted and worked with, I think we and the young people could have mutually led us all into greener pastures. Unfortunately the backlash through the Nixon administration prevailed + forcibly crushed the "revolt." (Remember Kent State.) Force, however, was not enough. Appeasement had also to be used to defuse the situation. So instead of encouraging the constructive criticism of the standards and values of our culture and working with the young people to establish a civilization better adjusted to ecology + race, more equal distribution, etc., the young people were bought off from their social criticism of the establishment by being allowed to do what they wanted in school, etc. Hence the peculiar combination of "law + order" + permissibility which has prevailed. I have found Paulo Freire's Pedagogy of the Oppressed (Herder + Herder, 1972) enlightening, though he writes for the situation in Brazil. I shall be grateful for your comments on all this if you feel inclined.

I hope you have a glorious trip to Europe. I did the Rhine trip from Cologne to near Rothenberg in 1932! All good wishes.

As ever,
Bonnie

November 5, 1977
Dear Bonnie,

It was good of you to write me before I took off on my European jaunt. I appreciate it; your letter was most interesting. We had too many one-night stands; although I was able to withstand the fast pace, there was little time for reflection, and there were so many pieces of art I was unable to see. We were only one night and one day in Florence. I gave up my lunch so that I could go by myself to see the Fra Angelico frescoes at San Marco, a beautiful, peaceful spot, and everyone there was most gracious. In Paris, there was no provision for the Louvre so two young nurses and I set off on our last morning to get something of an acquaintance with the Louvre—mostly Leonardo—an inspiration. Unable to secure a taxi, we walked there— it was well worth the effort. In the tour group, there were 32 of us— all ages and conditions. I was the only northeasterner, most were from the western and southern sections of our country. I think in the future, I need to find a tour that allows more depth of perception.

It was heartening to read your fine understanding of Botticelli, Leonardo, and Unitarians; your background is priceless.

I fully agree with your theory regarding our educational and political decline during the 60's. In my opinion, society should be well mixed—all ages and origins for we have so much to learn from each other. Many of the youth were absolutely right in their rebellion, but unfortunately, many opportunists who were shallow thinkers climbed on the bandwagon for ulterior motives and helped to discredit the cause first as many oldsters were ill prepared to wrestle with the problem and admit their mistakes. I don't know how the young can ever forgive us for Vietnam.

I ordered Freire's Pedagogy of the Oppressed but it didn't arrive until after I returned from abroad. I found it stimulating and provocative. It would take me pages and pages to respond. Perhaps in each letter I can react to different parts. And I hope sometime, I can discuss it with you in depth. I'm going to try it out on my friends. In the large sense, I agree with him; he is an idealist, and we cannot progress without ideals. There are, however, many pitfalls in the process. Our leaders, for the most part, are lacking in background, intelligence, commitment, and integrity. Too many of our people give up too easily, lack drive, insight, and true love for their fellow sufferers. I believe in the problem posing approach, communication, critical reflection with action. I do not quite understand his placement of authority. His treatment of the young at home and at school needs further delineation. I agree that education should persist from the cradle to the grave. I have always been somewhat amused by the catering to classes in American society. Money and social position have always seemed unimportant to me. Integrity and concern for others should remain paramount. If you have any guidance for me in reading Freire, I will welcome it. I am glad that the early Spanish settlers in most of North America did not prevail for our country would be in greater trouble today if they had.

Yesterday, I had a traumatic experience with a friend and her husband whom she recently divorced. I had taught at the college with both of them and didn't realize until much later that he was somewhat sadistic toward his wife. I shall never be able to understand how a man can hit a woman or how man and woman can love each other without respect. There is no human relationship worth its salt unless it is based upon respect. And these two young people have two beautiful children. Here divorce was the only solution, but it is a rugged outcome.

Harvey tells me you are moving to Cat Island for a month. I hope you have more opportunity for walking. Do take care of your health. We do worry about you.

I am sure your book is progressing. Do you have any more books to recommend?

All the best,
Edna

November 5, 1977
Nassau, Bahamas
Dear Edna,

Thank you for your cards. I am glad you had so pleasant a trip despite the pace. I also find tours that involve almost continuous traveling to be a strain. But I am a hopeless tourist anyway. I trust you are now home safely and rested up again.

I am to have a new experience. On Friday I leave with two of the Brethren for Cat Island. It is reputed to be one of the most primitive both in terms of living conditions and the cultural level of the people. I shall be interested to see how well I can adapt to it. My job will be mostly celebrating the Communions as there is no priest now resident on the island and there are 10 parish churches (most with only a very few members of their congregations). The island is very long and narrow and the many little communities are quite separate from each other. Incidentally there are historians who claim that it, and not the island now called San Salvador, was the place where Columbus first struck land.

I shall be there for a month. But if you write meanwhile please address me here in Nassau. My mail will be got out to me somehow. I should not trust the post offices on the island itself.

I plan to take my notebooks with me and reorganize them while I am there in preparation for writing the book itself. I have already drafted the prelude. I am getting quite excited about it. Your comments on Rothenberg, Rome and Versailles are quite interesting. My father painted a picture of that tower when we were in Rothenberg—which I like you found most delightful. I didn't see St. Paul's, but must admit St. Peter's impressed me. As for Versailles, I found it a bit excessive. If you wrote from Vienna, somehow the letter has failed to reach me. All best wishes.

As ever,
Bonnie

November 20, 1977
Dear Bonnie,

Your good letter reached me on the twelfth; our messages must have crossed en route. I did not write you from Vienna as I promised; I wanted to. I was in such a state of locomotion that I finally ended the tour without having written any letters whatever. Three fourths of the members succumbed to some kind of virus, but I was fortunate to escape it—plenty of vitamin C. The activity seemed to agree with me. In Florence, our guide was superb the best the whole area. In Venice, we all embarked on an evening gondola ride—with music; but somehow I sat in the wrong location so that I separate a man and his wife. I really didn't want to dampen their romance, but I didn't dare exchange seats with him (he was so big) for I was afraid we might both end up in the canal. (The water was quite dirty, and I don't know how to swim).

Versailles is excessive; rococo has never been a favorite of mine. When I saw the portraits and heard the stories, I was grateful that none of my ancestors were among the royalty.

I read that Cat Island is one of the loveliest of the Bahamas. Is it? How primitive is it? I do hope the natives understand sanitation, and I hope you are comfortable. How varied your life has been. I suspect nothing upsets your equilibrium.

In Connecticut, we have a new Episcopalian bishop who apparently is more liberal than his predecessor; that is good.

As I read Pedagogy of the Oppressed, I felt I had a glimpse of the reasons you turned to the Order of the Holy Cross. You have given so much. Freire's goals are true and good, but difficult to realize—everything worthwhile is exacting, I know. He does have a "creative mind and a sensitive conscience to the extraordinary misery and suffering of the oppressed around him." I like his faith in the people—that "men discover they are creators of culture, and that their work can be creative." . . . "I work, and working, I transform the world." "It is solely by risking life that freedom is obtained."—Hagel

The above, I believe but the attainment encounters many problems. Most settle too readily for security, the near at hand; they forget their visions. What do you do with man's greed, his lust for power? The true measure of man is the way he uses his power. I believe we should try, but we need better teachers—ones who are truly enlightened. Today's young are so confused—they have lost their bearings and surely need a mission in life. Our culture is too materialistic.

When you are guiding the young, there must be a place for authority—enlightened of course, but until they develop self-discipline, it must come from without. I began teaching when I was seventeen—in a one-room country schoolhouse (I had never been in one before). Some of my pupils were only a few years younger than I, but we got along. In high school I had enjoyed debating so much I thought I wanted to study law. I found I loved teaching—never a dull moment—so I went back to school to study. I have never regretted my choice of vocation, I have never been bored; the young have so much natural enthusiasm.

Do take care of yourself and have a happy Thanksgiving.

As ever,
Edna

I hope things become easier. Won't they let you have a little church of your own, or let you teach somewhere?

December 10, 1977
Cat Island, Bahamas
Dear Edna,

Your two letters and their enclosures arrived and are much appreciated. I have not answered before because it is difficult to get mail off this island. I shall take this letter with me when I leave for Nassau tomorrow and mail it there.

You seem to be getting what I hoped you would out of Freire. He is an idealist, and when the CIA engineered the overthrow of the Chilean government he and all the others working for the good of the people had to flee, if they could get out before they were imprisoned. Living in a third world country has convinced me their only hope is a break from and repudiation of US imperialism. They must move in the direction of communism. I only hope they can accomplish it, without falling victim to the imperialism of the USSR.

I agree completely in the need for authority which the young themselves recognize in their best moments. But especially at high school age, the essential in my opinion (and experience) is that they should have a full share in determining the regulations and in administering the discipline. This doesn't mean they are to have no guidance and they will in fact need restraint because they are such idealists that they are likely to aim too high and be too rigid. But if they are trusted they can be counted upon to see the issue and at least the direction in which its solution is to be found. I have great faith in them, provided the system is such that the best of them are encouraged to rise to the top and exercise real authority under guidance.

Cat Island is delightful. It is with real regret I return to Nassau. The people have been most cordial. Our house is far from primitive. It has inside plumbing (which has to be operated in part by buckets since the tank and pipes are not working properly). It has electricity (except the last week when the generator broke down). It lacks a refrigerator (which has not worked for us) and a deep freeze (which fortunately has). Most important of all, it is fully screened, for the mosquitoes here are legion. So it has not been too rugged for us. The people themselves for the most part do not have such luxuries. But they are able to grow sufficient food and raise vast numbers of thoroughly healthy and happy children. (This and the other out islands are known as the "Family Islands").

The weather has been superb, warm and sunny with only occasional and very brief showers. The cloud effects, especially sunrises and sunsets are superb. The ocean is a short block from our house. I have gone for a walk nearly every day and they have been delightful. You need not worry about my health, which is excellent, and I assure you I do not want a little parish. The Order is my life and I have never regretted it. With all best wishes and much love,

Bonnie

December 17, 1977
[Christmas Card]
Dear Bonnie,

I have not read this book, but it has had excellent reviews. I hope you find something of interest in it; otherwise, just give it away. I tried. You are a better judge of literature than I. Please say exactly what you think. My mother brought me up to "take it on the chin."

May you have a joyous Christmas.

As ever,
Edna

Summer 1978
West Park Monastery

PART TWO

1978 - 1980

January 8, 1978
Dear Bonnie,

Harvey told me you have moved back to West Park. How wonderful! Now you can be at home with your friends, who I am sure were most happy to greet you. Even the snow turned out.

I thoroughly enjoyed your last letter from Cat Island; it was one of your very best. Your descriptions of that island were warmly graphic. Since the children were happy and healthy, they must have had ample love, an ingredient absolutely essential to all growing youngsters. Sometimes I feel that our western world is too sophisticated; we become so embroiled with things that we neglect the attributes of the spirit. I agree with your conclusions about U.S. imperialism and the third world, especially Chile. Often I become discouraged with the apathy and ignorance of my compatriots, but democracy is the only form of government I want to live under—if only we could make it work better. I could love to know more about your experiences in the third world. You are right about student government. I have participated in it all my life—on both sides of the fence. In teaching local, state, and national government, we fail to give our students many more vital first hand experiences. We must help them to see the truth even though it is often shocking. There is so much of life that cannot be gleaned from books alone.

The other day I attended a most interesting workshop on the need for fiscal reform in Connecticut; it was sponsored by the Capitol Region Conference of Churches. Unless we somehow educate the voters, we are never going to succeed in this area in Connecticut. Even there at the meeting, we encountered so many who have no true compassion for the impoverished.

I am still struggling with the legislative program in Conn. for our local LWV. We need more members. I continue to grow impatient with the mushrooming criticism of President Carter. It does seem that we should give him more time. I suppose his rise to the presidency was so meteoric that everyone expected him to produce miracles in short order. It does seem as though we might send a few more statesmen to Congress.

On Monday, December 19th, I sent you a Christmas package airmail and insured to Nassau. Did you receive it? If not, I will begin checking.

Once more, I will extend an invitation to visit in Connecticut anytime and as long as you wish—if you are at liberty to do so, and if you care to. I know Ann and Harvey would be happy to see you. So should I.

Do take care of that cold (I hope it is not the flu) and have a happy fulfilling new year in 1978.

As ever,
Edna

January 21, 1978
West Park, New York
Dear Edna,

Thank you for your letter. First, let me deal with piece of business which you raise. I left Nassau before your package arrived. A couple of weeks ago I received word from one of the brothers there that a package had come for me, and that he had readdressed it to me here. I presume that was your package. It has not yet reached me, but the mail being as it is, it is really too soon to expect it. However, if you want to start the checking process, it might do no harm. I gather the brother did not accept the package but only readdressed it.

It is wonderful to be back at West Park, which is more home to me than anywhere else. Especially I am enjoying the weather. The two snowstorms this past week have been glorious. And I hope when the weather gets better to come over to your parts or to have you come over here. Finally, it is a real help to be near libraries again. Right here in our house I have found many books I was looking for, and others are available at SUNY and the General Seminary. I went to New York on Thursday to borrow three books from them.

Meanwhile my writing of the book progresses and I have started reading it to a group here. That is a help to me because it gives me reactions that enable me to clarify what needs it and to correct errors. So far the reaction has been good.

I find myself in full agreement with your political and sociological comments. I am not disturbed at the criticisms of Carter—they all come from the right quarter. All our decent presidents have been hated and maligned—witness FDR + Truman. I should be much less happy about Carter if most of his critics applauded him. We do have to make democracy work, for there is no alternative that recognizes human dignity. Unfortunately, all too often democracy does not recognize it either.

Trinity Church, Boston, is a great place. The former rector—Theodore Ferris—was my tutor the first year I was in seminary.

My cold is a thing of the past, I am glad to say. It hung on in the sinuses longer than usual + was a nuisance.

All the best and hoping we can get together before long.

As ever,
Bonnie

February 16, 1978
Dear Bonnie,

I enjoyed your letter, but I am very sorry that your Christmas package has failed to reach you. Ever since your letter arrived, I have tried to locate it. I seem to have been running around in circles. Finally, this morning, the Newington Post Office man instructed me to write directly to the postmaster at West Park. I did, but perhaps I need to write to the one in Nassau. I would gladly send more postage to Nassau if that is where the trouble lies. I sent you a box containing one book (a copy of E.B. White's <u>Essays</u>), three handkerchiefs and one pocket size black leather daily reminder. If you do not receive your Christmas present in a week or so, I will send you another one—different, in case the original makes an appearance one day. This is my first experience with a delinquent package and I fear I am not very knowledgeable.

Our recent great waves of white must have descended for your special benefit; they were indeed very beautiful and delightful for walking if you didn't plunge head over teakettle. We had drifts six to eight feet high. In the first storm, I was caught at Mary's in New Britain. The drive home—ordinarily of half hour's duration took me two hours for all the roads were a glaze of ice, brakes were a no-no, and I got lost. Once, I thought of abandoning my car, but decided to stay with the ship even though I was forced to sail through stop signs blowing my horn madly. With a rate of five to ten miles an hour, I reached home in one piece. Snow, rain, and darkness are negotiable, but ice is another matter.

I am so happy that you can be at West Park with all your friends—books as well as people. Your book will be a masterpiece.

At the annual meeting of the Capital Region Conference of Churches the other night Rev. Edward Geyer of the Church of Good Shepherd in Hartford (Episcopal) was elected president. I think he will be very good, and he has a lovely wife. The Conference is really trying very hard to have a healthy impact on our current General Assembly in Connecticut. We had a number of informative and worthwhile workshops that should prove helpful.

Are you planning to come to Connecticut the first week in May? I have been asked to attend the National Convention of the League of Women Voters in Cincinnati as a delegate from Newington May 1-5. If you are coming here then, I will not go to the convention. I have plenty of room for you.

I am disappointed with Congress. We surely need more statesmen there; at least Minnesota had the good sense to send Muriel Humphry to Washington. If only these senators and representatives would cease to exploit their positions. How do you feel about the Middle East impasse?

Edna

February 25, 1978
West Park, New York
Dear Edna,

Thank you for your letter. I have inquired about the package and our post master knows nothing of it. (He is not too reliable, but eventually he gets most of our mail to us.) I am convinced the trouble is in Nassau. The brother who first learned of the arrival of the package there should have kept it and sent it up with someone traveling here, but he was new in Nassau and did not fully realize how undependable the Post Office, especially the package service, is. I have known of packages being delivered over six months late. So I suspect yours is stilly lying around there. It may yet turn up. Don't send them any money for postage. I am sure that would do no good.

I have been thinking of you particularly during our blizzards and hoping you were coping all right. I have been delighting in them, but I do not have to shovel snow or drive in them. I am glad you have come through successfully.

I have been negotiating with Hob about a possible visit in May. I can easily avoid the first week. He has not yet suggested dates, so you might call him and ask that he put it later. You should definitely be at the conference of the League of Women Voters.

Thank you for the clippings which I have read with interest. I think we must recognize that the government, whoever is in "power" in the White House or in Congress, can really do nothing to control the vested interests. The President can try, like Carter, or do nothing, like Ford—but in the end the big corporations, including the Defense Department, will control policy and finances. I see no hope. But I nevertheless send best wishes.

As ever,
Bonnie

March 7, 1978
West Park, New York
Dear Edna,

Your Christmas package has at last arrived. Thank you very much for it. I appreciate all its contents, especially the beautiful handkerchiefs. I shall look forward to reading White's essays. He always has something worth saying. I am glad that all the trouble you went to in order to send me these gifts has not been in vain.

Thank you and all best wishes.

As ever,
Bonnie

March 24, 1978
Dear Bonnie,

Thank you for letting me know so promptly about the arrival of your wayward Christmas package. I finally located a woman supervisor at our local post office—a most cooperative individual who sent on all the necessary papers. For now we have to clear through New Orleans. They finally sent word that I would have to wait nine months before restitution could be made. Three months was much shorter. The experience has proved quite enlightening for me, but I am sorry you had to wait so long. In the meantime, I had purchased a replacement so I shall send it along as a spring package. Perhaps it will arrive by summer.

We still have snow around here; the last storm was the most beautiful of all, but I am ready for spring with its birds and flowers.

I am busy trotting over to our legislature to follow the capricious maneuvers of our lawmakers. I selected the areas of human services and appropriations, but I also observe other forms of legislation. Some of the testimony at the hearings is unbelievable. I am opposed to the expansion of nuclear energy and so were a number of others who were not connected with the industry. I thoroughly enjoyed the young, earnest people present—babies and all.

On the human services committee sits a forward looking, intelligent woman-senate chairman, who is doing her best to blaze new trails, but people drag their feet. We need well equipped family planning centers and havens for battered women. The young are so confused today in this world of tangled values. I believe in legal abortions if all else fails, for I deem it immoral to bring a child into the world unless you are prepared to love and care for him. Child care centers leave much to be desired and must be improved. However, mothers need to stay home with their little ones for at least the first three years, and we should be willing to subsidize those who are poverty stricken. I have been reading along these lines and find Selma Frailberg a superb authority. Babies have always held a certain fascination for me. We do need fine nursery schools for children. 3 years to 5. Then we could help to equalize the advantages of those who have and those who do not.

I have been asked to serve on a Special Ad Hoc Education Committee of the Capitol Region Conference of Churches. This is a subject in which I am vitally interested and there are some ideas abroad that truly worry me.

I have just received a call for jury duty—my first experience. I would be just like me to cause one hung jury.

I hope to see you sometime this spring.

As ever,
Edna

April 29, 1978
Dear Bonnie,

It was good to hear from you; I always find your ideas sound and stimulating. I would thoroughly enjoy a good discussion with you.

My jury duty was short lived for they released me in the beginning to pursue my obligation to the Conference of Churches and the League of Women Voters. When I began to serve, I sat around a great deal reading when I was not pacing the floor. I was chosen three times—the first failed because the parties settled out of court, the second, they selected a panel before I was reached for interrogation, and the third, they questioned me but then dismissed me because the case was going to continue into next week. That would interfere with my departure to the convention in Ohio; the judge, who possessed the kindest eyes, said they must not incur the wrath of the League of Women Voters. After all this, the clerk promised to send me a certificate of merit for my service, but I didn't do anything. Sometime I really would like to serve so that I would gain a better understanding of the court system which our league is planning to study this coming year.

Tomorrow I fly from Bradley to Cincinnati for the National Convention of the League of Women Voters—I will do my best to represent Newington and know I shall learn a great deal. I shall arrive back home Friday night May 5th.

Connecticut grows more beautiful each day—this is the season for poetry. Painters and poets have a special way of painting up the essence of life, and I know you have a rich background in both these areas.

I have invited "you all" for dinner—if you care to come. I do hope to see you when you reach Connecticut.

Edna

April 6, 1978
West Park, New York
Dear Edna,

Thank you for your letter and the enclosures. This is being written from Florida, where I am conducting some retreats. I left before your package arrived, but no doubt it will be awaiting my return on the 14th. The problem of the former package was not getting it to Nassau (difficult enough!) but expecting them to forward it somewhere else. I still consider it a miracle that it finally arrived.

I fear most people thought the show on Easter was a bit much, but I must admit I enjoyed it. A couple of days later it was gone.

It is grand that you have and are taking the opportunity to work with the legislature. It is heartening that there are some in it who care, even though the majority drag their feet. Sufficient and persistent stimulation will get action at last. The Communist set-back in France is probably a good thing. It may help the Communists to make a still further break with USSR and really move toward democratic socialism. That as far as I can see is the only hope on the political horizon, and I am not too sure even of that.

I agree completely with the need to care for battered women, even to making abortion available. And of course birth control should be encouraged. I like your idea of supporting a mother for at least three years. In fact, I myself believe that the right to life ought to include the right to a living and that one ought to be supplied for everyone. Rather utopian, I fear, but perhaps someday we can discuss the bind I think our present economic situation is in.

Jackson is right—there is no substitute for the Push for Excellence. But somehow children must be given the sense of being worth something, which they cannot have when they live in abject and hopeless poverty. I see his point about tax credit for private tuition— but it is hard on parents who want that education for their children to have to pay for that and taxes for public education also. There are no easy solutions.

All the best.

As ever,
Bonnie

April 15, 1978
    West Park, New York
Dear Edna,

The package arrived safely during my trip to Florida, so I found it when I returned last evening. Thank you very much. I shall look forward to reading the biography of Jimmy as I share your enthusiasm for him. And the handkerchiefs are lovely. I hope to see you next month. Meanwhile all the best.

As ever,
Bonnie

May 13, 1978
West Park, New York
Dear Edna,

It was so good to see you during my visit. I am especially grateful for the grand dinner you gave us.

I was glad to hear of the League of Women Voters' Conference. Your report confirmed my opinion that they are doing excellent work. And I know your contribution is no small one. It is also fine that you are working with the Conference of Churches. The cooperation of churches, especially in the social and political fields, is most important. They do not have the impact for good that they could have because they are so divided. It is not so much opposition to each other as lack of common policy and effort. So all you can do toward developing those is time and energy well spent.

Weather here is a little less pleasant than it was during the past week. It feels like rain but doesn't. So we get the disagreeableness without the benefit of the moisture which is still needed.

I hope I shall be seeing you again soon. Meanwhile all best wishes.

As ever,
Bonnie

May 22, 1978
Dear Bonnie,

It was indeed good to see you after two long years; you looked wonderful and your purple shirt was most becoming. I welcomed the two opportunities to talk with you "en masse" for it gave me a little better understanding of you as a person. I found your dialogue exciting and thought provoking. You have genuine dramatic talent—it was fascinating to watch.

I presume you remember Lynn Fontaine and Alfred Lunt, an illustrious pair. Not anywhere have I ever witnessed such magnificent, sensitive, timely response to each other. For me today's theater does not equal the Lunts, Katherine Cornell, and Helen Hayes. And my old dramatics professor used to maintain the English with their strong control of deep emotions have a profound impact upon the senses because they rarely let go completely.

I was intrigued with your national origins—combinations produce such interesting results. On my father's side Claes Cornelius Van Cott came to New Amsterdam in 1652. At the Holland American Society in N.Y. he is written up in the same book as the Roosevelts. On my mother's side Robert Lane emigrated from Derbyshire, England to Stratford, Connecticut in 1660.

Is there any Scotch in you? I would suspect so. (I don't mean the kind they pour in.) The Saunders were of Scotch derivations—strong and healthy.

I have always been somewhat amused by the American preoccupation with the subject of age. I have even been comfortable with all ages even as a child and make it a deliberate practice to mingle with all the segments; I have friends all along the line. I do not believe people were meant to be consigned to one particular level; crossing the line is far more exhilarating and healthy. The term "senior citizens" is strangely ludicrous and demeaning. The years should bring wisdom, maturity—a realization that true values can at last be understood and fully enjoyed without apology to anyone. I feel people should go forth to meet life—unafraid and eager to fathom its mysteries and vicissitudes. This is the way I counsel my young friends.

Hypocrisy and sham are ever to be shunned.

I have decided to return to my dancing, a favorite form of exercise. Recently, I took lessons for a year then gave it up because I questioned the worth of some of my teachers as well as the price tag.

I walk 3-5 miles a day and enjoy it as well.

The day you were in Williamstown, I called Ann to see if you wanted me to take you anywhere on Thursday—a walk around Avon Reservoir, a trip to the Wadsworth Athenaeum or something else. Since I didn't hear all morning, I concluded you had something far better to do. Thus you were able to visit with Ann and Harvey most of the time. I took myself around the reservoir alone. It was very beautiful. When I travel such places alone I carry a kitchen knife and a stick for protection. It was very beautiful.

I hope to see you again before too long. I missed you after you had departed.

As ever,
Edna

June 2, 1978
West Park, New York
Dear Edna,

Thank you for your letter. It was so good to see you and to have a chance to talk,-not to mention the delicious dinner you gave for me.

Yes, I saw the Lunts, once in Shaw's <u>Pygmalion</u> and Helen Hayes in Barrie's <u>What Every Woman Knows</u>. Also Katherine Cornell in <u>The Barretts of Wimpole Street</u>. There is nothing like them in the theater today. Alfred Lunt was a member of The Players, to which I belong, but I got into it only in time to hear his obituary. There is an outside chance, if I am stationed at this house again next year, that I may have a part in The Players' in-house annual performance, since they are doing a play in which I had a part in Santa Barbara.

When I was in high school, I did some tracing of my genealogy. I know of English, French (Huguenot) Dutch (New Amsterdam) Italian (Bonelli—from which my first name is derived). No Scottish or Irish so far as I know. One ancestor was Lofferty, but I understand the name is French—La Fertie. He lived in Ireland so may have had some Irish intermingled. His daughter, through whom we descend, was an illegitimate child apparently by an Indian mother—so I am particularly proud of having some Amerindian (probably Iroquois) blood.

Like you, I feel young as ever. One great help is having plenty of contact with young people—of whom we have a houseful. Today we successfully elected a Superior for the next three years, so things can settle down again. I hope to continue to be stationed here and that you can come over and visit us sometime.

Meanwhile all the best,
Bonnie

June 22, 1978
Dear [Foxy?] Grandpa,

It is good to know you are blessed with a houseful of young'uns, for with them one never knows what will happen next.

You saw some of my favorite plays and actors; it is good to remember.

I well understand your pride in your Indian ancestry. When my mother was a young girl, she thought she was descended from Indians, but she was disappointed to learn later that such was not the case. How often people have learned to be grateful for an illegitimate origin since it meant the inheritance of superior genes—especially among the aristocracy. We need to do so much more with genetics.

Last Saturday night I was asked to substitute as a delegate from my church to the Seventeenth General Assembly of the Unitarian Universalists Association in Boston—so here I am until Saturday, the 24th. It is being held at Boston University. I am learning a great deal about the Middle East situation from Noam Chomsky of MIT and John Nicholls Booth.

[The following in quotations is crossed out] "I am inclined to think we made a mistake when we helped to create the state of Israel. I don't believe any state should be controlled exclusively by any one religion. I have always had great respect and admiration for the Jewish people, but I think it would have been better if we had encouraged them to spread throughout the world with their enriching influence. In simple justice, we must provide for the poor Palestinians.

Last night we heard a comforting lecture by Jean Mayer, President of Tufts University, assuring us that we can prevent starvation and malnutrition in the world and that these means should never be used as weapons of war.

If it is convenient for you some weekend in July after the first week (from the 15th on), Dolores, a former student of mine, one of my best, a favorite, sensitive, artistic, and in her early forties and I could drive up to your part of the country, put up at an inn nearby and drop in to" see you and your monastery on a Saturday or a Sunday. We should like to take you and anyone else out to dinner if you are permitted to do so. She is a Roman Catholic. I mix very well with all religions. I remember years ago when my two sisters-in-law (both my brothers married Roman Catholics long before I was married, and I was the first born), looked as me, sighed, and said I would have made a good nun if only I had been born a Roman Catholic—but I would not have been suited to that vocation.

If you have more company than you know what to do with or you have other plans, do forget all about this excursion.

With all my best wishes for a happy summer,

Edna

I welcomed the two opportunities to talk with you en masse for it gave me a little better understanding of you as a person, although you are still something of an enigma to me. I have never known a monk before. You have genuine dramatic talent—it was fascinating to watch.

I presume you remember Lynn Fontaine and Alfred Lunt; an illustrious pair. I have never witnessed anywhere else such magnificent sensitivity, with a timely response to each other. For me, to-day's theater does not equal the Lunts, Katherine Cornell, and Helen Hayes.

I thoroughly enjoyed our discussions, especially the opportunity to "pick your brains." Beginning in high school my favorite exercise was being on debating teams. Over the years I have spent in various organizations, I have enjoyed working with males. When George used to tease me about it, I replied that men's minds have always held a certain fascination for me; and he, in turn retaliated—"That's hardly complimentary to them."

I have always been grateful to my ancestors for their bequest of health and stamina; I didn't inherit any money to speak of but what they have given me is far more important—money can't buy it.

Edna

July 1, 1978
West Park, New York
Dear Edna,

We shall be delighted to have you and Dolores visit us on a July weekend. We hope you will stay with us, not at an Inn. On Sunday morning, I have to go off to do supply work, so I shall be home all the weekends in July. If you got here on a Saturday, I could go out to dinner with you that evening. I will be back in time for the midday dinner on Sunday, so we could have that together at the monastery. Our accommodations are quite comfortable, and it will be a great pleasure if you can stay with us. We often have Roman Catholics and Unitarians visit us and both are most welcome. We try to make all visitors feel at home.

I quite agree with you about Israel. I am glad that Carter is taking a strong stand and that the country is beginning to grasp the Arab point of view. The Israeli state was a mistake from the start. No state should be based on religion. Of course, in that regard, one must admit that some of the Arab states, such as Saudi Arabia, are just as bad or worse.

Church conventions are rarely as well organized as political, but I suppose they serve a useful purpose.

I shall be looking forward eagerly to your visit. Let me know as soon as you can which weekend to expect you so that I can make your reservations.

All the best.

As ever,
Bonnie

July 9, 1978
Dear Bonnie,

How gracious of you to invite Dolores and me to stay at your monastery for the weekend. We accept with pleasure and plan to leave here Saturday morning the 22nd and should arrive sometime early that afternoon. We are happy that you will come out to dinner with us that evening and promise to make it special. We shall appreciate having dinner with you at your monastery Sunday at midday. I know you will enjoy Dolores, whose values are the finest. She received her doctorate from Columbia so she knows New York. I gave her Frankl's <u>Man's Search For Meaning</u> and <u>The Doctor and the Soul</u>, both of which she found inspiring and most helpful. You would be surprised to know the number of people I have helped with Frankl—thanks to you.

Your point on Saudi Arabia and church conventions are well taken. I surely hope the people give Carter a second chance in 1980.

Friday night this week I have to lead the group in play reading in our Book Discussion at our church. I promised to bring ten copies; I am contemplating Shaw's <u>Candide</u>. I surely wish you were here to select a proper play and lead the reading; it would be so much more effective.

I am still concerned about the course of events in the Middle East as well as the disastrous effect of Proposition 13 in California. I value your opinions on these matters.

We are looking forward to seeing you soon. If the weekend of the 29th should prove more convenient, just let me know.

With all my best wishes,
Edna

July 11, 1978
West Park, New York
Dear Edna,

It is splendid that you and Dolores can spend the weekend with us. I hate to postpone it for a week, but since you say July 29th is equally convenient for you, it would be better for me. On the 22nd there is the Profession of two Sisters which I really must attend, and I cannot get back here before 4 pm. On the 29th, however, I can be ready to greet you right after lunch. So unless I hear from you to the contrary, I shall expect you for the weekend of July 29-30. We can have a good time discussing politics, education and what-have-you!

All the best.

As ever,
Bonnie

August 3, 1978
Dear Bonnie,

It was good to see you once more, and I liked your purple shirt—that color belongs to you. (It is my favorite hue). Dolores and I returned home refreshed from our visit—having absorbed the peace and beauty of West Park. We both were uplifted by the spiritual atmosphere throughout. Dolores says she will never forget this experience. We enjoyed your brethren and I am always fascinated to watch your mind work; you possess a remarkable store of knowledge. Discussions with you are ever choice for you always reach the point directly as well as dramatically.

Your dining room is delightful, a spacious house hung out over the trees—reminding me of Hudson's Green Mansions.

The trip over and back was glorious. I did not realize you were so near—geographically.

Thank you for your kind hospitality. We were most comfortable and well fed.

I had an uneasy feeling we kept you from pursuing more important matters. I am sorry—I never mean to interfere with your schedule or your preference. You were most generous with your time and consideration.

Ever yours,
Edna

August 12, 1978
West Park, New York
Dear Edna,

Thank you for your letter. It was a joy to have you and Dolores with us and I am glad you enjoyed the visit. Br. Ronald and I are especially grateful for the dinner. We are always happy to share the beauty and the spiritual atmosphere (which is always more noticeable to others than it is to us). We hope that sometime you can be with us again.

I assure you did not keep us from more important matters. As it was, you recall, I went right ahead and deserted you Sunday morning to do my supply work in Poughkeepsie. Other than that I had nothing to do except visit with you and nothing I would have enjoyed more. We feel that making our house available to others is the least we can do in gratitude for all God has given us. The guesthouse is an important element in our ministry.

I am also grateful for the beautiful book on Rome. The Pope's death makes the pictures especially timely. Paul VI was, I believe, a great pope—in fact, I think he gave practical expression to John XXIII's vision, as the latter never could have done himself. The relationship is very similar to Johnson's and Jack Kennedy.

All best wishes.

As ever,
Bonnie

August 29, 1978
Dear Bonnie,

Your last letter was reassuring for I did worry about our visit to West Park—lest we inconvenience you. Our dinner with you and Brother Ronald was a pleasant experience; I still remember the beauty and peace at Holy Cross. And you looked wonderful.

I have just returned from a week's trip to Vermont and New Hampshire, favorite areas—Manchester, Stowe, and Woodstock in

Vermont—Whitefield, Jefferson, Lancaster, and North Conway in New Hampshire. A friend from N.Y. City and a friend of hers went with me in my car, which behaved beautifully. Her friend and I did all the driving without any untoward incident. Two days after I returned, however, I drove alone to a wedding in northern Connecticut, an unfamiliar territory, and promptly got lost after leaving highway 86. Fortunately for me, I encountered a trooper whom I hailed for direction; and he kindly escorted me to the church. Sometimes I think I do have a guardian angel. When I was seventeen I got lost in the middle of NYC but came through unscathed.

My brother Charles thinks I should buy a new car, but I intend to keep mine another year for it is in good condition—under 50,000 miles, and I have a reliable garage mechanic. Like my mother, I have no mechanical sense whatever. Whenever I am confronted with problems where I am not proficient, I search out the most trustworthy individuals I can find so I think I have a good attorney and a good broker as well. Thus far I have been blessed with good health so I am deeply grateful to all my ancestors; it is the best present they could have left me.

I hope that Pope John Paul will be forward looking so that much needed reforms will take place. He certainly should have deep sympathy for the poor and the unfortunate.

I also hope that Americans will not be carried away in the wrong direction over Proposition 13. We do need tax reform so that the levies are fair to all, but we must pay our share. We have been allergic to taxes ever since the American Revolution.

I am co-chairing a local League of Women Voter Committee on ways to finance education in Connecticut so that all children have equal opportunity. For the LWV in Connecticut I have been auditing the meetings of the Human Services Reorganization Commission.

On September 12th we have a democratic primary to nominate a governor.

May you realize all the best.

Ever yours,
Edna

September 15, 1978
West Park, New York
Dear Edna,

Thank you for your letter and the interesting clippings. I find my faith in Carter undiminished—but the Democratic Party is more and more of a disappointment to me. I hear Ella Grasso was renominated in Connecticut. I suspect from all I hear that means a Republican governor will be elected. Whether that will be good I have no way of knowing. Here in New York the vehement opposition to Carey, even though he won handily, will do him no good. Again I suspect the Republican—an arch conservative—will be elected. That means the restoration of the death penalty and most of the efforts at aiding the downtrodden will be stopped or reversed.

I envy you the trip to Vermont, though I should prefer to make it about a month from now when the color will be at its height. On Monday I leave for a conference in Colorado Springs. That should be a pleasant experience.

From what little I have been able to learn about John Paul I, I find myself hopeful. He certainly was a dark horse and obviously no one in the news media was prepared for his election. That it was engineered by Cardinal Benelli, the leading conservative, raises some questions, but the conservatives also elected John XXIII. They are usually very stupid and undiscerning people—which is why they are conservative, of course. So Benelli may be fooled—or at best John Paul may be the most conservative of those who were electable at all—and still he could be quite forward looking. Another point to give pause is that he is something of a theologian and his training was all in the old school. That also might keep him from moving. But on the other side, he is chiefly known as a pastor, and if he approaches the problems that face the papacy pastorally, he cannot fail to turn into a progressive. That is what I am counting on. I think the Third World cardinals, who had more than a controlling block of votes, must have felt that way about him. There really is only one direction the Roman Catholic Church can go if it wants to survive. I am quite confident that under John Paul it will move in that direction.

Our major Episcopal conference at Lomberth seems to have come off satisfactorily—issuing nice compromise statements on <u>faito accompli</u>. We have the Bishop of Kumasi (Ghana) and his wife visiting us. I visited them when I was in Ghana and it is a joy to see them again. We also have four of our African novices spending a few months with us here. They are fine men and I am more hopeful than ever about the growth of the Order in Africa. We just clothed our first Spanish-speaking novice. So we continue to move in an international direction.

I wish you every success in your political ventures. It is good to have people like you watch dogging our representatives.

All the best.

As ever,
Bonnie

September 29, 1978
Dear Bonnie,

Your last two letters were thoroughly enjoyed—they were warm and most interesting; your knowledge and insights are indeed rewarding. If you wish and if you have the time, I would be happy to drive you to Vermont to see the glories of Vermont for one day or several days. I can bring friends or so can you. You are the only monk I have ever known and I want only to do what is right for you. Indian summer is very beautiful. I would want you to select the route. Anytime in October is good, but the season is progressing so rapidly that the early part would probably be the most scenic.

It is wonderful you had the opportunity to attend the conference in Colorado Springs. Years ago, I spent a summer in Boulder, Colorado at the University of Colorado. It was a rich experience. At six in the morning I used to rise for my riding lessons. Since I was not a very good horsewoman, I always hunted for the animal that was the shortest so that the trip to the ground would not be so far.

Edna

October 14, 1978
West Park, New York
Dear Edna,

Thank you for your letter and the clipping. I was at a conference the week that the Camp David breakthrough occurred and we saw no newspapers or TV, so I almost missed it entirely. I am glad Carter was able to accomplish it. It is characteristic of him to tackle the real problem personally <u>before</u> there was any assurance of success. He is a very sincere and courageous man, so much so that I fear this country will not want him in office long. We really do not want intelligent and honest presidents—witness our rejections of Stevenson and Humphreys.

We are having a Fall Color Weekend—about 25 guests. A few minutes ago it was raining—hardly a helpful contribution. It has stopped now and perhaps it will clear up for the projected walks in the woods. I go down to the Sisters in Newburgh, so will get out of it. I am sorry I cannot take you upon your invitation to tour Vermont, but I must keep working on my book. The final draft is nearing completion—two chapters to go. Next week I hope to start feeding the first chapters to the typist for the good copy.

I hope your work for a soundly financed educational program is successful. Nothing is more important for the continuance of democracy.

I suspect the Conclave meeting today will have a hard time selecting the new Pope. They may have to fight it out between the liberals and conservatives. I hope for the sake of the church the liberals win. All best wishes.

As ever,
Bonnie

November 14, 1978
[Dear Bonnie,]

Someone sent me a copy of Holy Cross, which I found both interesting and enlightening. Thank you. What is the background of your new Prior? I did not understand him.

Our little ones at church are delightful, but the older ones—those in the Liberal Religious Youth group need to cultivate a greater sense of responsibility and reality.

Do you in your work participate in activities to improve the quality of family life? Here, our foundations appear to be crumbling. On our Ad Hoc Education Committee for the Conference of Churches in Hartford Region, we seem to be on a merry-go-round in trying to find a role church people can play in an effort to improve quality of public education. Apparently I am cast in the role of loyal opposition to two of our Christian women and one Roman Catholic priest who are determined to tax the American citizens to support private and parochial education. I want very much to have the churches help families realize their mission, parents guide their offspring and child care centers improve their facilities. It is so hard to get people to realize that the first three years of a child's life are the most important. Values are established in the home, and it is extremely difficult for the schools to build on a wobbly foundation. I keep reminding the good Roman Catholic priest that our values are very similar even though we are on opposite ends of the religious totem pole.

The elections throughout the country were indeed interesting as well as confusing. There were some bright spots, however. I agree with you that the average voter does not understand the political process; he does not care enough to recognize intelligence and honesty. I did not vote for Ella Grasso, who is a deceitful woman, but I was unhappy with her opponent Ron Sarasin. The Republicans should have chosen Lewis Rome, who ran for Lieutenant Governor and they waged a weak, unimaginative campaign. Chairman Bickel should resign. Lew Rome was intelligent, honest, caring, modest, and liberal.

I think it is good that a man who was not Italian was elected Pope. He seems to be strong, intelligent, and caring, but I doubt that he will sanction the much needed reforms in the Roman Catholic Church. You know far more than I about these matters. How do you feel?

Do you think <u>Jesus</u> by Michael Grant is worth purchasing and reading?

I am going to send little Brian—age three in Michigan to nursery school. Of all the Soles, he is most like George—intelligent, creative, a natural with wildlife and people. At Sunday school when his peers were beset with tears and wails, he mounted a table and proceeded to regale them with the tale of his two bunny rabbits living in his barn. Suddenly, all was quiet, those little wet things on shiny cheek dried and complete attention was given the impromptu story teller. Someday he, too, may go to Williams.

With the brilliance of autumnal colors and the glorious weather there was a pervading sadness.

May you have a very Happy Thanksgiving.

With all my best wishes,
[Edna]

December 9, 1978
West Park, New York
Dear Edna,

Thank you for your letter and the card from Boston. I am surprised to see how Trinity Church is now decorated. It used to be very stark.

I do not know Michael Grant's Jesus. Had the book come out before I wrote mine I should have read it, for it is on the same subject as two of my chapters and seems to deal with it in the same way. Of course, I do not know if we reached the same conclusions.

As always, I have enjoyed your clippings. I am surprised at the high percentage of professors without foreign contacts. There is so much traveling today—but perhaps the professors are too old to have been caught up in it. Even at the undergraduate college level, a year in Europe or elsewhere is frequently part of the program. So the next generation of professors may be better equipped.

Thank you for telling me about Brian. He certainly sounds like a boy who will profit from any help he gets.

Fr. Rodel Miller, our Prior, grew up on a farm in the state of Washington. The Order's ministry is quite various. Some members do a good deal of work with children or youth in summer conferences, parish missions, etc. Some also participate in Marriage Encounter meetings.

I fear I tend to be on the other side of the support of the private schools question. I think it hard on parents who want their children to have private schooling, especially for religious reasons, to have to pay taxes to support public education and then pay tuition in addition. Somehow to me it seems fairer if a share of the tax money proportionate to those tax payers went to the private schools. It must also be remembered that the private school are saving the state an enormous expense. When California attacked the private schools some years ago, it was pointed out that if they closed it would cost the state millions of dollars to provide education for their pupils. In the light of that the voters defeated the attacking legislation overwhelmingly. One real problem in the USA is that freedom <u>of</u> religion seems often to be interpreted as freedom <u>from</u> religion. A fair proportional support of all religions seems to me a better expression of freedom of religion than the refusal to support any.

I am very pleased with Pope John Paul II so far. I do hope he will be able to begin a better rapprochement with Communion which as a Pope he should be able to effect. I expect also he will do much traveling. As Pope he should be a <u>world</u> figure.

All best wishes for a blessed Christmas.

As ever,
Bonnie

Christmas 1978
West Park, New York
Dear Edna,

Thank you for the magnificent scarf and the useful engagement book. I shall find the scarf very comfortable when I take my walks. The doctor urges me to walk two miles a day, and I must admit I feel better for doing so. On the cold days that will be coming, the scarf will be a blessing.

We are going to have a white Christmas. It is snowing hard—the kind of snow that means business. No doubt you are getting the same storm.

I have spent the 24th checking the typescript of my book, and so have left the decorating to others. We have enough willing hands and the whole house looks very festive. We have already had an elaborate First Vespers, and we shall soon be gathering for the Midnight Mass. Christmas Day will include a joyous time with each other, including a dinner with all the fixings. My brother is here with us, which not only means much to me, but he is also very popular with the Community.

I hope you are having a blessed Christmas and I am most grateful to you for adding so much to the pleasure of mine. May the New Year bring you much joy and prosperity.

With much love,
Bonnie

December 31, 1978
Dear Bonnie,

Your letters were most enjoyable. This year at least your Christmas present reached you on time. I am happy that you liked your scarf for I wanted you to have one to warm you on your winter walks. I hunted all over creation and finally found the only one in all of Boston; the search was fun. How wonderful that your brother could be with you at Christmas. It was good to hear about your festivities.

I sent my little boys in Michigan some puppets so I hope they will make up stories to dramatize; daddy will have to construct a stage for them.

The other night Ann and Harvey came to dinner along with Dolores and two very good friends of mine, who were married in the home I shared with Florence, my favorite sister-in-law, while my brother was in the service. We missed you.

I want so much to read your new book. When will it come on the market? I have just purchased <u>On Being a Christian</u> by Hans Kung.

I understand your concern for private schools. I know many of them are superior to many public ones, partly because they are not forced to accept all the problem pupils and the classes are smaller. Public education needs to be upgraded; during the past 20 years both the schools and the home have been far too permissive. Standards must be upheld, and education must be provided for the underprivileged from 2 to 5 years of age. In a classroom, even one problem child is a threat, let alone 50 percent of the class. In so many places, the administration is weak and self-seeking. I know we graduate teachers who should never be permitted to enter a classroom, who were selected for principals. I have often complained.

[in margin] "it was not my "A" girls, but my "C" boys" who got the principal jobs.

I believe strongly in the need for religion but I do not believe it should be supported by public monies. There will never be one creed—and that does not bother me. I have good friends of many different faiths and find them inspirational and helpful. I feel our choice depends chiefly on our backgrounds and temperaments. The world needs more religion rather than less, but most of us do not practice our beliefs. Sometimes I hope I have an opportunity to discuss these issues with you at some length.

Our state legislature opens Wednesday; I hope they show some degree of wisdom. I shall be there to watch.

Mary and her husband have invited me to drive down to Venice, Florida the eleventh of January to stay for two weeks. If all goes well, I shall probably try it.

Edna

January 11, 1979
Dear Bonnie,

This is just a short not to tell you that I did not leave for Florida today because Mary and her husband are needed in Lancaster,

Pennsylvania now. Mary's sister, who still lives at the old homestead must be taken to Philadelphia by ambulance for an operation, and her only brother must have a serious heart operation as soon as Mary's husband, can find a competent surgeon. Mary has a wonderful, loyal family, who need her now: Mary and her husband have invited me to fly to Florida to stay a bit sometime in the future, but I have not made up my mind about it.

I do hope they keep you warm enough at West Park for your weather must be as bitter as ours.

Sunday Dolores and I are traveling to New York City to see John Wenner's exhibition of paintings. He and his wife took me to Williamstown this past summer to choose a setting at Williams for a painting he is doing for me.

I received another copy of your Holy Cross, which I find interesting. Thank you.

The clear, crisp quality of the air is invigorating, but you must dress warmly.

Edna

January 17, 1979
West Park, New York
Dear Edna,

Thank you for your letter, the interesting enclosures, the birthday greeting and now the card that informs me you have not gone to Florida after all. I am sorry to learn of the illness of your friends that prevented the trip.

You may be assured that your scarf is keeping me thoroughly warm when I am able to venture out on a walk. In fact on several occasions it has been too warm. We seem to be having a mild winter on the whole—the snow comes and goes.

I agree entirely with your concern for proper education for the under-privileged, especially at the pre-school level. I am also concerned, however, for those who consider religion to involve much more than morality, that they should have opportunity to give their children spiritual training supported by the money they pay in education taxes.

I learned of a heart-warming thing today. In Augusta Prep—a very posh private school in Georgia—a black biology teacher has been hired and is off to an excellent start. Thank God things are changing in that area.

I visit my old school in New York on Monday last and found it flourishing—Trinity School—founded 1709.

My book is at Doubleday's. Too soon yet to hear their verdict on it. All the best.

As ever,
Bonnie

February 9, 1979
Dear Bonnie,

It is good news that your book has reached your publisher, and I am sure that it will be appreciated. I am currently reading <u>Jesus</u> by Michael Grant and <u>On Being a Christian</u> by Hans Kung so I am getting ready for yours.

There are many superior blacks that should be duly recognized, but we need to work to bring forward the best for when the unworthy rise above the others, they do great harm to their kin. We should have brought this to pass two generations ago. In our country, strangely enough, we have been slow and inept in assimilating newcomers.

I respect and understand, I think, your position on financial aid to private schools, but I cannot agree with you. I know that your own education from beginning to end has been far superior. Both you and Adlai Stevenson were able to weather excellent private schools without losing compassion for the less fortunate, but I doubt most accomplish this feat. When I was growing up, my neighbors, whose home was my second one, had an uncle, a graduate of Wesleyan, who taught at Choate. Many of those boys who were very wealthy spent very little time in their own homes and looked upon Choate as their true haven.

I spent most of my life teaching in public institutions—I had the best of two worlds—the children and the college students. I often had children from both sides of the railroad tracks in the same classroom, and they learned much from each other. I have seen youngsters who had nothing and came from nothing reach some beautiful heights in human relationships. It gave me great faith and boundless hope. I believe children from different faiths need to live and work together that they may better understand each other. Perhaps my interpretation of the spiritual is different from yours, but in my books, the spiritual side of life is the most rewarding. It does not have to be tied to a particular creed. I still feel that God's best creation is a fine person. The public school is an American institution. Without it our country would be more backwards than it is. Through my mother I have lived in this state of Connecticut for more than 300 years. I believe some of the more enterprising settlers traveled west, and this made our nation more democratic.

This year I have been clerk of my church, but will terminate this task in April. I am still carrying on my commitments to the Conference of Churches in the Capital Region and the League of Women Voters. I am auditing a course on the Legislative Process at the Law School of UConn. Most of the members of the class are law students. It is fascinating and I am learning a great deal.

On the seventeenth of this month I am planning to fly by way of Atlanta to Venice, Florida to visit Mary and her husband for two weeks. I find I need to get away for a bit.

With my best wishes,
Edna

February 26, 1979
West Park, New York
Dear Edna,

Thank you for your letter and the enclosed card, which is a beautiful statement of true Christian humanism.

You make quite clear that in discussing public aid to private schools we have in mind different institutions. I certainly do not think Choate should be funded, but those posh boarding schools are an infinitesimal proportion of the private schools. Those I have in mind are of two classes. The biggest are parochial or parish schools. The Roman Catholic schools of this type definitely include all classes of society and exist for parents who want the Catholic faith to be a fundamental part of education. But do not forget that in addition to the Roman schools many Protestant groups maintain them as well—Lutherans, Episcopalians, Adventists, Disciple of Christ, etc., etc. These schools cater to the class represented by the congregation, but it should be noted that at least the Episcopalian schools have been pioneers in integration. For example, all the Augusta private schools now take blacks because they could not refuse the blacks graduating from the Good Shepherd parish school on the grounds that they were inadequately prepared academically. Note also that were these private schools to close, the appropriation for state education would have to be doubled. This was demonstrated in dollars and cents when the Masons tried to eliminate parish schools in California. They were attacking the Catholics, of course, but forgot the large number of Protestant schools. Their efforts were overwhelmingly defeated, fortunately. It does seem unfair to me that parents of children in these schools, which save the state so much money, should have to pay the full expense of the parish school in addition to taxes to support the public schools.

The second type of school I have in mind is one like St. Andrews, Tenn., was in my day. It took boys from all classes who a)either needed a home as well as a school because of family deficiency or b)needed a better education than was available in some of the (deplorable) southern public schools. Only a half dozen or so boys paid "full" tuition and even that did not cover expenses. Again the parents were paying taxes for public schools as well. (Today I fear St. Andrews is close to being a posh school—so there may no longer be any schools in this class. But the parish schools still abound—but may not be able to service without public aid.)

There are today many different interpretations of what the spiritual life entails, and many Christian, Jewish, Buddhist, Moslem, etc., schools of thought hold firmly that what one believes (i.e. a definite, specific Creed with its concepts of salvation, grace, etc.) is the essential foundation of spirituality. Humanist and humanitarian morality may not need this foundation, but most of the genuine adherents to all the great world religions consider it essential. It is difficult to teach this as an optional appendage to a secular education. Hence the desire to incorporate it in the school.

Friday I leave for South Carolina to make a four-week retreat. If you wish to write me before the end of March, address me:

Holy Savior Priory-Tower Hill
Pineville, SC 29468

After March 30th, send letters here at West Park.

I hope you had a good visit in Florida. All the best.

As ever,
Bonnie

March 15, 1979
Dear Bonnie,

When I returned from Florida on the fifth, your letter was waiting for me. It helped. I had a lovely, peaceful experience in Venice, a welcome change from the rigors of Connecticut. But when I entered my doors, the quiet loneliness hit me afresh, even though my brother and his wife had met my plane at Bradley and had taken me out to dinner. Now, I am once again busy with my various volunteer activities.

I appreciate the explicit candor of your last letter—I think I understand you a little better. Later on I will write more about those particular topics. I am planning to visit some parochial schools in Hartford.

(This was my first visit to Florida in the winter time.) The sea air is truly beneficial, but I missed the hills and mountains. The people were friendly and most helpful—even on the planes when I was laden with various bags. Mary, who is one of my best friends, was most gracious. Her husband is not well, but she takes beautiful care of him, and he never complains. It was good to be free to walk all over without skidding about.

Last night at our church Council meeting from six to ten-thirty, we had quite a discussion. It seems that our art committee has seen fit to decorate our foyer and corridors with some hideous modern pieces of sculpture. In my books, art must be beautiful, not just meaningful. So much of modern art is worthless. The decision was to permit the art committee to remain autonomous. I do not believe committees should have the right to do exactly as they choose without the approval of the governing body. I think some Unitarians carry "doing their own thing" too far.

I am expecting to tutor some Russian Jewish immigrants in the Hartford area.

President Carter surely has proved himself in the Mid East. People really expect too much of him; I believe he is doing his best. I have never quite trusted Begin.

I am so glad that you were able to go to South Carolina where the weather has been kinder. I sent you a card from Florida, but you probably took off before it arrived.

Are you coming to Connecticut this spring? I hope so, for I should like to see you again.

Edna

March 25, 1979
West Park, New York
[South Carolina]
Dear Edna,

Your card and letter have duly arrived and I am grateful for them. Thank you also for the clippings. The budget could be balanced tomorrow if they would cut the military expenditures by 1/4. But of course the military establishment has too great a hold on the government for that to happen. If the budget is balanced it will be at the expense of education, social services, welfare, foreign aid, and the like. Those have less political clout.

I have only glanced now and then at the headlines, but I do know that the treaty is scheduled to be signed tomorrow. Although only a beginning I think it is a significant achievement. Perhaps its chief importance is that the US has for once not backed Israel implicitly and has forced her to make a few concessions. There are many more she must make, but Carter has made them easier the next time.

I am glad you enjoyed Florida. The weather here in South Carolina since I arrived has been mostly wet and cold. Today is clear with a typical blustery wind—March as one expects it up north. But the situation is perfect for my retreat and I have been able to keep the silence without interruption. I find it a very helpful and prayerful experience.

I am not sure whether I can get over to your parts this spring, but I shall try, and hope to see you if I do.

As ever,
Bonnie

PS I have a few appointments down in the area and will be home for Easter.

April 24, 1979
Dear Bonnie,

By now you must have returned to West Park, and I am happy for you that you could enjoy a restful, revitalizing experience in South Carolina.

I think I shall be glad to see the end of April for I have been far busier than I care to be. Somehow I don't seem to be able to refuse to help. No one can be more foolhardy than I. May holds forth more promise, and it is perhaps nature's most glorious month. Our local League of Women Voters seems headed for a merging with Hartford, and I think this is disgraceful. If a city the size of Hartford and a town as typically American as Newington are unable to find enough willing and able women to run the show, we are indeed weak. If we merge, I have decided to give up my league activities and place my time, money and energy elsewhere.

Saturday I drove to Meriden to attend the annual meeting of the Connecticut Valley District of the UUA. Somehow I could not agree with the speaker from Springfield, Massachusetts, a man who is Commissioner of Community Development and the City Planner. He feels that only regional bussing will enable us to homogenize the participants in our educational system. I think it would be better to move more of the impoverished to the suburbs where they would live in the neighborhood of the school. Somehow we must bring the home and the school closer together. We in the suburbs look the other way when urban problems rear their battered heads. But then in this country, we have never been very considerate in assimilating newcomers to our shores; I don't know how long it will take us to learn.

Peter Roby is a black boy I had in my class at the lab school years ago. He was most promising—bright, charming, a natural with people, artistic, athletic with a sense of drama and a lovely voice. Since I was worried about the youngsters he might meet in the junior high school, I interested Mr. Robinson who ran a private school and was also chairman of our Board of Trustees over the four state colleges. As I was chairman of the Advisory Council to the Board of Trustees at the time, he knew me and believed me so that he took Peter and gave him six years of schooling free. I knew Peter needed the masculine discipline Mr. Robinson could promise. His father tells me that he mixes well with all and does not segregate himself—that is how it should be. I hope someday Peter becomes involved in government; it needs him. I am very proud of him—and so would George be.

I agree with you—military expenditures are not the answer; we must find ways of making and keeping the peace. We cannot protect ourselves from atomic weapons. I hope to see you this spring. You are always welcome to stay here—if you wish.

With all my best wishes,
Edna

May 13, 1979
West Park, New York
Dear Edna,

Thank you for your letter and the clippings. It will be interesting to see what comes of SALT II. The fight will be horrendous. But Jimmy won on Panama and possibly will pull it off again. But the Senate's record of confirming treaties down the years has not been good.

The problem of equalizing schools is not likely to be solved because the parents of children in the better ones have political clout and those in the slums have none. I am glad Roby has so good an appointment. It underlines the fact that the division of opportunity, especially in the north, is no longer between blacks and whites, but between middle class (including skilled blue collar) of both colors versus the unskilled and poverty-stricken.

I hope things have eased up for you by now. The difficulty is that the number of people with both interest and time is very limited. So the load falls on a few overworked volunteers. But the work is so important it is to be hoped that they will keep it up.

Like you I am not impressed by Jerry Brown. I think it is still almost certain that Jimmy will get the Democratic nomination. But whether I want that or not, I really do not know. I dread to think of the kind of Republican who might beat him. But again, maybe that would be a good thing. Republicans produce depressions like Democrats produce wars. It might be better to have the depression with a Republican taking the blame and get it over with, than to go on hovering on the edge of one while suffering from inflation. It's all a mess.

I seem to be getting busier and busier so I doubt that I shall be able to visit your parts this spring or summer. Meanwhile all the best.

As ever,
Bonnie

June 10, 1979
Dear Bonnie,

It is always good to hear from you. I do hope that you are taking adequate care of yourself. The last time we met you looked as fit as a fiddle.

I have terminated some of my activities and am casting an eye about for new causes to pursue. The League of Women Voters in Newington voted to merge with the city of Hartford so I severed all my connections with them because I feel that under the circumstances I can help another cause more effectively. I sometimes find that an active protest brings a certain clarity to a situation. I found the legislative work fascinating, but I can contribute in this area to Connecticut Citizens Action Group and Common Cause as well as the Religious Coalition for Abortion Rights. If we could only make sure that all the little babies born would be wanted and loved, half our problems would disappear. So many people do not realize the spiritual need love fulfills. I have likewise finished my duties as clerk of my church. At the Annual Meeting I tried valiantly to persuade the members to amend the constitution to give the clerk a vote on the Council, but I failed. We needed a three-fourths approval, but only 60% voted in favor.

I am still, however, working on the Ad Hoc Education Committee for the Hartford Regional Conference of Churches. Father Geyer, whom I like, is chairman, fair and most considerate; I feel at times he doesn't quite know what to do with me (He is not alone there.)

I found myself caught in a position where I had to request that an additional paper be submitted to answer Father Fanelli (Roman Catholic) in his contention that private schools should share in tax funds. Thus, I volunteered to prepare the paper. When I was on my sabbatical at Boston U, I wrote a paper on the subject—30 pages long, but I have been asked to cut it to five so I shall have to condense it and bring it up to date this week. We talked at great length about values. Although Father Fanelli, a fine young, sincere man, and I come from different religions segments, I feel that our values are very similar. Do you think I am being obtuse? In all my years of teaching, I never had any problems concerning religion. Once I had a principal who told me I included too many Jewish children in my programs in the auditorium. I looked at her dumbfounded, said nothing, and carried on as usual. I never questioned a pupil's religious affiliation when I selected him for a job.

I agreed with all you included in your last letter. You have a clear, concise way of stating your position (even when I don't agree with you.)

Please tell me how you feel about the activities of Pope John Paul II. To me, he seems forthright, caring, and courageous. His warmth is so reassuring. During WWII, he was truly Christian and brave. I wish he were not so conservative, but given his background, he probably must be thus.

Jimmy, my helping boy next door, and I have been gardening so that the premises are greatly improved. This activity is reputed to be therapeutic. I am getting a bit of competition from a bunny rabbit I rescued in early infancy.

For September 6th through September 27th, I have signed to take a Caravan tour through Britain. I plan to go alone, but I always feel safe on a conduced tour, and with Caravan I can cancel or postpone without losing more than fifteen dollars. I have been to Britain a number of times beginning in 1937, but this small island always holds something new as well as many fond memories, and it is not because 3/4 of me is British in origin—sometime in the past of long ago. Perhaps I shall then have something more interesting to relate to you. I probably bore you as I prattle on and on.

I am disappointed that you will not be coming this way either this spring or summer—I had a sad feeling you would not be. Perhaps you will have some free time this October—I hope so.

With my best wishes,
Edna

June 22, 1979
West Park, New York
Dear Edna,

Thank you for the letter and the enclosure. I am afraid I agree with the article. Jimmy will be renominated and is no longer electable. The fault lies with the Democrats in Congress who have been determined to eliminate him. The result will be a Republican in 1980—probably Reagan. God help us! The really horrible part is that he will probably be able to appoint a couple more justices to the Supreme Court which will be reactionarily conservative for the next 10-20 years. If the constitution can survive that it will be a miracle!

On the other hand every President elected in an even 20 year since 1840 has died in office. 1980 may be a good year not to be elected!

I think you are wise in expending your energies on specific causes to which you can make a real contribution. The religious question turns on how much specific doctrine parents want their children to learn. Some religious groups believe that doctrines not accepted by other groups are of the essence of Christianity and therefore are not satisfied by a generalized religion inoffensive to Jews or Christians of any stripe, and a few moral principles. If they have to pay for public education, freedom of religion seems to me to mean that their money should go to support schools that teach the religion in which they believe. It is not freedom of religion to be forced to support schools that teach somebody else's concept of religion or none at all. The latter is freedom _from_ religion, not freedom _of_ religion.

John Paul II is very conservative in doctrine and I fear will take a conservative line in practical matters such as contraceptives, abortion, clerical celibacy, etc., that have in his mind doctrinal significance. However, he is an intelligent man and has been kept out of touch with contemporary RC thought because he has been behind the iron curtain. His visit to Poland showed him to be a brave and progressive man in terms of issues he understood. As Pope he should gradually become aware of what is happening elsewhere and I cannot but believe he will grow in the office. I think before he is through he may surprise us with the things he tolerates or commends.

I do indeed hope you have a happy visit to Britain. I am sure a caravan trip will be quite safe. The Irish revolutionaries concentrate on big stations when they want to cause trouble.

I still have not found a publisher for my book and I become less hopeful with each rejection, naturally. I have now taken it to the main Episcopal Church Press, but I was rather disappointed by the editor's reception of it. He said all the necessary things, of course, but I got the feeling they were just formalities and he had already made up his mind that he was not interested. Oh well, time will tell.

I hope you have a good summer and shall hope to see you after your return in the fall.

As ever,
Bonnie

July 2, 1979
Dear Bonnie,

Wednesday I received your good letter. I am concerned about your publishing problem with your book because I know how much it means to you; with your wealth of background and experience you have so much to give to others. Today it seems that people's literary tastes have greatly deteriorated; in fact, most expressions in the area or arts are somewhat impoverished. I cannot bear to think of your book going unpublished. Is there some way I can help? Do you know that Stinehour Press in Lunenburg, Vermont? George and I used to stay with the owner's mother in Whitefield, New Hampshire. Mrs. Stinehour was delightful and a devout Episcopalian. Her son does fine work. I dropped in last summer to visit with her, and the business was prospering. How many pages will your book cover?

I agree with you about those Congressmen in Washington—they are unbelievable. True statesmen are indeed rare. To be sure, Regan is far, far from being good presidential timber. Neither do any of the other candidates seem at all worthy. I always worry about appointments to the Supreme Court.

I should like to ask you a question. Please do not feel constrained to be diplomatic if you reply because I truly want to know. If you and I were teaching in the same school system how would your values differ from mine? Are there not basic values important to a democracy and common to our various religious faiths, values that must be maintained in our public schools? Are not the public schools the best place to teach true respect for different beliefs? Will not tax support for all private schools lead to a proliferation of numerous varied denominational institutions of learning and so lead to greater divisiveness and misunderstanding? We not only need cooperation and a workable unit in this country, but world understanding and good working relations with other nations as well. There is no reason why the young could not be released one half day a week to practice their religious studies in their respective churches. I think many do not realize the importance of value formation in the home and in pre-school years. Foundations plus heredity make real difference.

I liked what you said about John Paul II. I think the Roman Catholic priests should be free to marry. Since they so often represent the very best, they should make excellent husbands and fathers and could set a good example for their people. Life for them should also be more normal.

Edna

July 14, 1979
West Park, New York
Dear Edna,

Thank you for your letter and the enclosures. I also was encouraged by the Weber ruling, and I hope the Child Care Program turns out to be all it claims to be. I agree with Good that Carter can get the nomination if he wants it (and I'm sure he does) but I am not so sanguine that he can beat a Republican if that party chooses a reasonable moderate.

Thank you for your information regarding the Stinehour Press. The difficulty with outfits like that is that they have no access to the national market. My book is at present being considered by Seabury, and I have yet to hear if they will accept it.

When you ask how I should run a school differently from the neighboring public school, I find it impossible to answer. For I assume your question means how would a church school differ, and I should not attempt today to run a church school. That may surprise you in view of my insistence that parents who want their children to go to parochial schools and the like should have their share of school taxes go to those schools. The difference in Catholic schools is that they teach Christian doctrine—ie. specific affirmations about God and his activity as well as morals.

Only Roman Catholics and a few radical sects are able to run schools for only their own religious personnel, and therefore theirs are the only church schools of this type. Other "church" schools draw their students from a wide range of church affiliations and hence can teach only a general Protestantism which turns out to be respectable morals and the American way of life—and hence is little different from public schools. I therefore should not be interested in running one. Their justification, if any, is that they offer a better education, smaller classes, etc. I think the question whether they are justified is debatable—but it is true that public education in many (most?) places is deplorable, and perhaps capable students should have a better chance. I recognize, however, that draining off this groups will help keep the public schools inferior. However, if private schools are justified on the grounds of better education, parents who want them for their children should get some assistance from the school taxes.

That is a different question from church schools. If I could run one of the latter, and St. Andrews was one in my day because most of the students and all the faculty were Episcopalian and it was understood that doctrine as we held it would be taught—I should not want to run one today. I agree with you that in a pluralistic society, a pluralistic education is preferable. But I still think that parents who believe otherwise and want their children educated by their church should get state support. Though I do not agree with them, I insist they have a right to exercise their belief and preference without the financial disadvantage of having to support two educational systems.

Released time for religious education will rarely work in the form which is legally permitted. A successful arrangement was worked out in Urbana-Champagne, Ill., whereby every religious group could send teachers to the school to teach the students assigned to them by their parents. The instruction was given in the classroom. If parents did not want religious instructions of any kind for their children, they had a study period. The one atheist family took the mother to the Supreme Court, you will remember, on the ground that their child, who was the only one in the study hall, was embarrassed and discriminated against. So the whole scheme was thrown out as unconstitutional. This was particularly significant because, while religion cannot be taught on public school property, atheism can. Several high school students in various parts of the country have told me their biology teacher had said, "You can believe in God, or you can believe in evolution, but you can't believe in both." (see P.S.)

Letting the students to go to their various churches for religious instruction on school time does not work in most instances because the only person available to give the instruction is usually the minister. (If the instruction could be given at the school, regular and competent teachers could conduct the classes in many instances.) The minister, even if he is good at teaching children, and many are not, is usually too busy with other parish administration, visiting the sick, etc., to do a good job of preparing and conducting the classes. So the time released for religious education is largely wasted. I think it is better employed teaching other subjects at the school. I am content with the situation because I am skeptical about the value of intellectual presentation of religion to the young. I think they should participate in the adult fellowship of worship as their means of experiencing the religious faith and life, supplemented by personal counseling as they need it when problems arise. Religion must be lived not taught. The intellectual side, if they are interested, can be developed by reading, by special instruction provided by the parish from time to time, by summer conferences and by courses in religion at college, of which there is an increasing number of good ones. The point is that, when the youngster <u>wants</u> to learn about his religion, means can easily be provided. But required courses only antagonize most students and teach them very little. When one has a living faith, one wants to learn more about it. Until then, religious instruction is at best a bore.

I fear this letter is rambling and incoherent because I am arguing on two sides of the question at the same time. So let me repeat the points. 1) I am not in favor of private schools that have as their chief reason for existence the teaching of a specific religion. The question of private schools as a means of better secular education is another matter on which I am not prepared to give a final verdict. 2) I recognize that some religions urge parents to prefer a school that explicitly teaches that faith and practice and I believe those parents have a right to put their children into such schools and to get assistance from the school tax that all have to pay. Otherwise they are forced to pay twice for the education of their children and this is especially unfair because the private schools are also relieving the state of the expenses necessary to education those children. So although I do not myself encourage church schools, I think they should have public support.

I recognize that this self-contradictory position is not very logical. But as I grow older I am increasingly convinced that logical solutions are among the principal causes of social maladjustment. There is a large irrational element in life and the attempt to eliminate it in the interest of pure rationality is disastrous. Both the rational and the irrational must be integrated into the suprarational. This is the truth perceived by those who assert that God is not just omnipotent omniscience of pure reason, but is beyond rational and irrational, beyond good and evil, beyond being and non being. He is the One to whom there is no other. This is the ultimate mystery and life partakes of it.

I fear my answer to your questions makes up in length for what it lacks in clarity. Forgive me.

I hope you have a happy and restful summer. I am still hoping to get over to your parts in the fall.

As ever,
Bonnie

P.S. I realize you will answer that you have always taught religion in you classes, but remember by religion you mean morality grounded in God conceived primarily as the source of morality, whereas by religion I mean the specific doctrines about God held by the more theologically oriented forms of Christianity and other world religions, and the various practices of worship, sacraments, prayer, church organization, etc., derived from them. These cannot rightly be taught in public schools because there is not agreement on them. But those who hold them are not happy when a least common denominator is taught as an adequate form of Christianity.

August 5, 1979
Dear Bonnie,

Your most thoughtful answer to my question regarding the difference in values in private—including religious schools—versus public schools was deeply appreciated. I have read it many times and on each occasion I find a new clue, but I still have many questions.

I do not advocate teaching atheism although I maintain atheists have a right to exist. The lone child in the study hall should not have been embarrassed, a right not to have minded. When I was very little, I was taught to stand for what I believed even if I stood alone—and I often did. I was brought up in my father's faith—he was a Baptist but I attended the evening services with my mother, who was a Methodist. However, I evolved into Unitarianism. I do not understand the biology teacher's contention that God and evolution are in conflict. I believe in both. It is most important that the schools teach the young to respect all religions—there is no one religion for all.

Your idea concerning "the value of intellectual presentations of religion to the young" seems very sound. It is true that in the past, for the most part, released time for religion was not efficiently used. Is it possible to find a way?

I agree that public education in many places could be greatly improved. We are suffering from low standards, many inept administrators, as well as numerous inferior teachers. The large cities are in deep trouble but siphoning off the superior students to private schools via the route of tax subsidy for all schools will only increase the deprivations in the public sector. Children learn from each other. Even in a class of thirty with half to three fourths of them representing the minorities, the underprivileged, the learning will be impoverished. I know you care about the unfortunate. I also know that a class of superior students from superior backgrounds can easily outstrip the under privileged. In our society, how can we best raise the lowly—help all realize their highest potentiality? Our minorities face fearful odds. As a teacher, I found my greatest joy was to see those down under rise to the top. As a society, our standards are too low, our commitments too limited, and our faith too weak. We have lost our integrity. In greeting our opportunities we have forgotten our responsibilities.

I want so much to discuss with you—"Both the rational and the irrational must be integrated into the supranatural." This is the truth perceived by those who assert that God is not just omnipotent omniscience of pure reason, but is beyond rational and irrational, beyond good and evil, beyond being and non-being. He is the One to whom there is no other. This is the ultimate mystery and life partakes of it."

Under separate cover I have sent copies of Father Fanelli's paper and mine. If you do not have the time to react, or if they bore you, just toss them in the waste basket. I do not want to burden you.

I do hope your book is published soon. And I hope to see you in the fall.

Will all best wishes,
Edna

August 20, 1979
West Park, New York
Dear Edna,

Thank you for your letter and the papers. I particularly appreciate Fr. Fanelli's. I find myself in complete agreement with it and he has put it better than I could. My only additional comments would be, first, that it is the quality of private education not just the religiousness that I believe justifies its existence and support. There are other values than those which you recognize (as there are others than those I recognize) and many of these values are such as cannot rightly be taught in public schools because they must not be forced on those who do not hold them. Second, private schools are better equipped to handle certain types of students. For example the public school not only has to gear its level to the average student, but it is neither allowed to separate the superior (or inferior) students into special classes (that would be "discrimination") nor can it refuse to advance to a higher grade those who have repeatedly failed a lower one. In that situation many potentially good students do not find sufficient challenge to do their best work. Third, there is a double penalty on private schools. Not only are parents who choose them forced to pay taxes for the public school and tuition for the private, but the private schools relieve the state of the expenses of educating those children. When California a few years back considered taxing private school property, the church schools simply announced that if that were done they would close. The state would then have had to spend millions of dollars to provide buildings, teachers, etc., to absorb those children. When people understood the financial situation the proposed taxations was overwhelmingly defeated.

Incidentally, your argument that private schools are only for the privileged classes is quite unfair. Any private school worth considering does all in its power to provide scholarship for students who cannot afford to attend but who would profit from doing so. They are particularly eager to include blacks and other deprived minorities—in the South as well as in the North. If the state gave them their rightful share of the education tax money they could and would do more along these lines.

I don't want to discuss your paper by letter because it would be too difficult to do justice to it. If I get a chance to visit in your area this fall I shall bring it with me and perhaps we can discuss it in detail.

I hope you are having a happy summer. The early part of this month was terribly hot and humid here, as I suspect it was in your area also. The cool weather we have had the last few days, not to mention the much needed rain, has been a welcome relief. All best wishes.

As ever,
Bonnie

My book is still at Seabury's and I have not yet heard whether they are going to accept it.

September 18, 1979
Dear Bonnie,

With the preparation for the trip and everything else, life has been so hectic that my letter is long overdue, although I have thought of you often. It has even been difficult to find enough time to rest.

Our Caravan group is too large—38 from all over the US. They are all considerate but quite different from each other. In York, we had a bomb scare and two of our number have met with accidents. Otherwise, it has been quite interesting. All of your churches and cathedrals are inspiring—warm and comforting; I have always been drawn to them. I like the old ones best for they are the product of great love and care. For modern architecture, Coventry seems to be the finest. The west window, that magnificent glass screen with its translucent lace-like pattern of saints and flying angels is a marvel. I have never seen anything like it elsewhere. John Hutton was the designer. I have some booklets to share with you—but perhaps you already have everything. I enjoyed your last letter even though I share a different viewpoint. I always appreciate your candor. I expected that you would agree with Father Fanelli. Public schools do not need to gear their level to the average student. I did separate superior students from the others; I used to group them according to their ability in each grade. Sometimes, I had children reading at levels from grade one to grade eight in one grade. In our country, we are supposed to be born with equal opportunity, but we are not born equal; each has something special to give, however. It is dishonest to tell a child he is good when he isn't. We have to learn to live with ourselves. To be sure, there are many, many problems with the public schools, but they can be solved. I still believe that private schools for the most part do cater to the privileged. It has been my observation that the inclusion of the disadvantaged has been merely a token. If they receive government subsidy, I fear they will accept only the best, leaving all of the difficult problems in the public schools. In my past, I have had to deal with situations no private school (even parochial) would tolerate; but I never gave up.

I do hope to see you when I return. There is so much I want to discuss with you. I have faith in you.

Edna

October 1, 1979
West Park, New York
Dear Edna,

Thank you for your letter from Stratford and the postcards. I agree with you that Wills is one of my favorite cathedrals. Its most interesting feature is that reverse arch that had to be put up in to hold the main arch up.

I presume by now you are safely home and I hope you are getting a good rest from what must have been a very strenuous trip.

I visited Coventry in 1973 and liked everything except the tapestry that depicts Christ as a bumblebee. I had such a good talk with some of the clergy there and was much impressed by the work of reconciliation in many areas that they are attempting. But perhaps the most impressive feature was the ruin of the old cathedral which I had seen in its glory forty years before.

I am still hoping to get to your parts in the near future and trust we shall be able to get together to discuss the public v. private school situation. Apparently there is considerable difference in what is permitted in various areas. I have been told that in some places the separation of good from poor students is absolutely forbidden. Perhaps I have been misinformed, but I don't think so.

I forgot whether I told you I saw the production of Othello in Central Park, New York—a truly magnificent performance. I have never seen Cymbeline, and envy you that.

Seabury still has neither accepted nor rejected my book. When I called them three weeks ago they were still considering it. I go to New York on Wednesday for the rest of the week and shall get in touch with them while there.

All the best.

As ever,
Bonnie

October 17, 1979
Dear Bonnie,

It was good to receive your letter a few days after I returned. It helped. The night I came back I learned that Mary, one of my best friends, had lost her husband the night before. Unable to sleep, I completely unpacked and put everything in place. The next two days I did whatever I could to help Mary. I knew what it meant. With the jet lag plus a few hours sleep each night I felt like Alice down in the rabbit hole, but I survived. Fortunately, Mary's sister, Betty, who lives in Lancaster, PA, is staying with her. It had been a happy marriage and Mary did everything she could.

I am glad you feel the same way about Wells. My greatest concern with my British tour was the mad rush through all those glorious cathedrals. I am sure some of the men in the group came to please their wives for after a few turns through some of the cathedrals, they no longer wished to enter any more. We were never given time to sit and meditate. I often stole back myself. For the first time, I visited Winchester cathedral and found it truly beautiful; I also enjoyed the city of Winchester.

I agree with you about the tapestry at Coventry.

I brought back many maps, booklets, and books which I can peruse at my leisure; you must know all about them, but I have much to learn.

You have never told me about that production in Central Park. That I envy you.

The tour director, with whom I disagreed on occasion, told us that very few New Englanders join their tours for they prefer to travel independently. One other woman from Massachusetts and I were the only New Englanders. I do feel that independent touring is more satisfying. George and I used to have a marvelous time on our own. However, I am grateful for the experience.

London was more crowded and hectic than ever; I do not understand how the British manage to live with such high prices on their wages. The separation of the good from the poor has been a common practice in Connecticut. It would be exciting to discuss with you the problem of private versus public education.

I do hope to see you before too long. I should be happy to have you stay here if you wish—you may bring anyone you choose. I have plenty of room.

I feel sure your book will be published.

As ever,
Edna

October 31, 1979
West Park, New York
Dear Edna,

Thank you for the delightful luncheon. It was such a pleasure to be with you again and very kind of you to alter your schedule to make it possible. I was pleased to learn that you were visiting the parochial schools and discovering they were not one-class affairs. Some of the affluent purist schools are, to be sure,—though even they have a token integration. The clientele of the Roman Catholic parochial schools is more like that of the public schools.

I was not able to ask about the Episcopalian parish schools at the consecration because I was not in the area where the diocesan clergy vested. But I did ask my hostess afterwards and she said that the wife of the Dean of the Episcopalian Cathedral in Hartford would be able to inform you on the subject. I am sorry I do not have her address and phone number but no doubt you can find it without too much trouble.

I was sorry we could not discuss your paper in more detail, but I think we did cover the substance of it. I am sure we both have the same objectives but we differ on the priorities in reaching them. I rejoice that you are giving so clear an exposition of your convictions, which need to be taken fully into account in the final decision, and that you are willing to listen to and investigate those of others. May the right solution be found.

All the best.

As ever,
Bonnie

November 8, 1979
Dear Bonnie,

It was so good to see you again—even if it was brief; I always enjoy being with you. I had hoped to have an opportunity to talk with you on a one to one basis, but I guess this is never to be. You looked wonderful, and I am happy about your doctor's report, but do be prudent about the stairs.

I called Mrs. G (who has a very pleasant voice), who after consultation with her husband, told me there were no Episcopalian parish schools in the vicinity of Hartford, but there is one in New Haven—St. Thomas Day School. Thank you for your help. I plan to continue my visits to private and public schools in both Hartford and New Haven. I find the experience stimulating and rewarding; the children give me an emotional support which I have missed. It has been heartening also to meet some of the fine people I found in the parochial schools of Hartford.

Last Friday I saw <u>Old World</u> by Aleksei Arbuzou at the Hartford Stage. There were only 2 characters—Rodion Niolayevich and Lidya Vasilyvna, and their repartee was delightful. The horseshoe arrangement of the theater is most appealing—for one can see and hear from any angle. Good theater always gives me an illusion of walking on air. I must go more often.

You allusion to dreams intrigued me. How do you analyze them?

I fear Kennedy's entry into the presidential arena may have disastrous results. I think he should have waited until 1984. As a people in government we are so poorly informed.

Whatever can be done in Iran and Cambodia?

Have an enjoyable Thanksgiving.

I deeply appreciate your understanding.

As ever,
Edna

November 23, 1979
West Park, New York
Dear Edna,

Thank you for your letter and the clippings. Somehow I have the hunch that Carter will be renominated. It is hard for a party not to run the president for a second term and at the same time not to appear to have repudiated their own policics. I don't think Kennedy will run on an independent ticket if he is not nominated, and I don't see how Carter could. My fear, if Kennedy is nominated, is that his Roman Catholicism and the drowned secretary will prevent his election. I don't believe any Republican can beat Carter, on the other hand, except Ford, who is such a nincompoop he might easily get it.

This Saturday I am moving down to the Convent of the Order of St. Helene to be resident chaplain for the Sisters. My address will be for the winter: Convent of St. Helena, Box 426, Vails Gate, NY 12584. Letters sent here will still reach me, as I expect to visit here each week, but they will get to me quicker at Vails Gate. I shall have a little cabin to myself there, such as I had in South Carolina, and expect to find it very pleasant and helpful.

I shall be interested to hear what you think of the Episcopal school in New Haven if you visit it. I know nothing about it, so I cannot tell what type of student it might minister to.

This week has been very busy with preparing to move and Thanksgiving. I shall be glad when I have settled down next week.

All the best . . .

As ever,
Bonnie

December 4, 1979
Dear Bonnie,

What an interesting and comfortable change your new abode will be. I am so glad that the stair problem will be eliminated, and I hope your cabin will be warm enough. The Sisters will love having you.

I am planning to visit St. Thomas Day School in New Haven later this month and promise to relate all the details. It will be my first experience with an Episcopalian school.

So far my house has been put in order by an economical chimney sweep (I paid him more than he asked, in the name of justice), landscape gardeners (who were too high) but efficient, and painters as well as paper hangers who improved the interior. (The living room and hall are now a peaceful blue—April sky). I waited six months for a painter to renew the whole exterior. Now it is too cold so that I engaged a new painter who promised to perform in June.

On our famous or infamous panel two of the members objected to my contention that mothers should remain at home to nurture their little ones during the first three years. It doesn't matter whether it is father or mother who oversees the progress, but the very young should have consistent supervisions. Unfortunately today—too many do not realize that love is more satisfying than material advantages. I realize many mothers running single parent homes have no choice, but society should make it possible for working mothers to have more time with their little offspring. A caring mother is more important than two cars in the garage.

I agree with your views about the coming presidential election. I think Carter's stance on the Iran affair is admirable and shows real leadership. Somehow I am not sure Kennedy would measure up in a truly tough situation. It if comes to a contest between glamour and character, I choose the latter.

I trust you are duly settled and happy.

As ever,
Edna

I hope to make a flying trip to Boston or NY or both before Christmas.

December 16, 1979
Vails Gate, New York
Dear Edna,

Thank you for your letter and the clippings. I particularly enjoyed the interview with Bishop Walmsley. I think he will make a fine leader of the Diocese of Connecticut. The present bishop is a good man but his illness has taken its toll on him and it is time for a change. I was so glad I could be at Bp. Walmsley's ordination.

The Iranian crisis, ghastly as it is for the hostages, has been a life-saver for Carter. He has indeed shown amazing fortitude and patience. It is just what we should have expected because it was just that which accomplished the Israeli-Egyptian treaty. But then it was functioning in secret so people were not as aware of it. This time it is giving leadership to the entire country and commanding both admiration and response. I am still hopeful it will get us through the crisis.

I fear you are right about Kennedy. I agree completely with his assessment of the Shah's regime. But this was not the time to air it, especially as the doing so was a deliberate attempt to undercut Carter for political reasons. Even the Republicans see the hostage issue is not one to play politics with.

I suspect that the Shah's residence in Panama will have little, or even adverse, effect on the hostage situation at first. But it does give the basis for a graceful backing down when the pressure on Khomeini makes that necessary.

Enough of politics. I hope you have a most blessed and joyous Christmastide.

As ever,
Bonnie

December 31, 1979
Dear Bonnie

With your natural ebullience, wisdom, and understanding, you are sure to have a promising new year ahead. I am so glad you were able to be present at Bishop Walmsley's ordination. I agree with your estimate of him.

With all my best,
Edna

December 28, 1979
Vails Gate, New York
Dear Edna,

Thank you for your Christmas gifts. (The rural Post Offices were exceptionally slow this year, so I received it just this morning.) The scarf is perfect—wonderfully soft and warm and just the color I needed. The appointment book is much appreciated and the Christmas ornaments are a delightful touch. I have hung one on the Sisters' tree which makes me feel more part of that. The other I have hung in my cabin—on a lamp in lieu of a tree—to give a little Christmas flavor to the room. So I am most grateful to you for all your gifts.

I have had a very happy Christmas in both my families. I went to West Park on Sunday the 23rd and stayed there over Christmas. It was a joy to be with for all the worship and feasting. Then on the 26th I came back to Vails Gate with all the Brethren who came down to participate in our joint Boxing Day Folliew in which several of us perform. I did the Polonius speech to the King and Queen and then the scene between Hamlet and Ophelia. I had misgivings about the latter, but one of the Sisters wanted to do it, and the audience being very charitable, we got away with it. So everyone had a good time. I must admit I am glad to be home (here) again. I feel more centered in my cabin than I do at West Park, where I occupy a guest room.

I hope you are having a glorious Christmastide, and that the New Year brings much blessing and joy.

Love,
Bonnie

January 13, 1980
Dear Bonnie,

Your last letter at Christmastide was most enjoyable. I could feel your happiness through the lines. I wish I could have heard both of you in Hamlet; I know it was good. I pulled my copy of Hamlet from the shelves to reread. You deserve a cabin of you own. I still am blessed with wonderful neighbors and friends as well as two brothers and a sister in law who are always supportive, [but I wish you lived closer * written in margins]. Recently, I have been asked to serve as one of three on a trial board for the Connecticut State Employees Association. The case is somewhat involved. In my early college days I was chairman of our judicial board so I presume my past is catching up with me. When I was young and naive, I thought I wanted to follow law, but I have had much more fun spending my time teaching the young. This month, I shall also participate in the legislature process for the Permanent Commission on the Status of Women in Connecticut. Our legislature convenes in February. I expect to do more for the Capital Region Conference of Churches this year.

What do you think of the Hans Kung controversy? I own his <u>On Being a Christian</u> and find it challenging.

The aggression of the Russians is alarming. I wish all the nations would boycott the Olympics this year. I do hope our country moves wisely amidst all the international crises—I always felt that WWII could have been avoided if the leading nations had been more astute. We never should have allowed Hitler to gain all that power. What course do you think we should pursue now?

Edna

January 27, 1980
Vails Gate, New York
Dear Edna,

Thank you for the birthday card and your letter. I had a very pleasant birthday party here at the convent. I also celebrated my 40th anniversary of life vows on January 6th. With those milestones behind me I am settling down again to the business of living.

I am glad to learn of your involvement in the trial board and the judicial process. You have much to give in those areas. The work is frustrating, for one never accomplishes all that should be done, but it is the people who keep pushing who move us in the right direction.

I fear the Pope has allowed himself to be maneuvered into a disastrous position. The problem is at the heart of the Roman Catholic system. One basic element in it is the claim to infallibility. Its contention is that the Church has through the magisterium and the Pope an absolutely certain understanding of Christian doctrine and practices, formulated in detail. This makes it extremely difficult for it to adjust to changing times and cultures. Today, if the insights of modern knowledge are given their true weight, the formulations of the faith must be entirely revised, the more so because the philosophical basis of scholasticism has long been abandoned. Vatican II opened the door to modern knowledge. The council was held in opposition to the Roman curia and they have been trying to stop the process of rethinking ever since. Under John Paul II, unfortunately, they have a doctrinal conservative who is letting them get away with it. But it is too late. Either the curia and papacy will destroy itself by losing its credibility, or John Paul will learn to listen to the thinkers in his church and charge the personnel of the curia so as to make it more open to reality. We shall see.

I still have confidence in Carter and the people of this country to continue the mature response to the situation in Iran and Afghanistan. The expulsion of the press from Iran has been a good thing. The press was keeping up a focus on the hostages that prevented any possibility of negotiations for their release. The deprivation of the students holding them of a nightly appearance on television has isolated them to the point that their influence is greatly diminished. I have not yet heard the outcome of the election, but once there is a government to negotiate with, I think things can move faster. Carter's offer to give aid to the government in exchange for the releases of the hostages is a move in the right direction. So is the pressure on the USSR over Afghanistan. Carter really seems to be getting the breaks at least.

I agree that the Olympics must not be held in Moscow unless the USSR gets its troops out of Afghanistan. It would not surprise me if they do so sufficiently to satisfy that demand, if they can find a means to bolster up the government sufficiently to survive. But if they do not, I hope the Olympics can be held somewhere. The athletes have been working for years in preparation. They are at their peak now—another three years, or even one year, might be too late for many of them.

I too wish we could get together more often but I am tied down now by my responsibilities here. All best wishes for the work you are doing.

With love,
Bonnie

February 12, 1980
Dear Bonnie,

Your letter was again most enjoyable and very enlightening. I am happy that you had such a delightful birthday party—it was due you, and I am sure they loved doing it. The 40th anniversary of your life vows was extraordinary—how much you have given and sacrificed; it makes all the gifts from others seem so small. You enthusiasm for living is ever warm and comforting.

Your explanation of the meaning of the Pope's position is most lucid—even to a mere layman. I appreciate your breadth of understanding.

Last night I attended the 79th Annual Assembly of the Capital Region Conference of Churches in Hartford. We had the election of officers and board of directors. I am going to be one of the many directors—not a laborious task, but it should prove interesting. For the first time we elected a Roman Catholic for president—Rev. Francis S. O'Neill. He appears to be fine and understanding, but I did not appreciate the words on "The Future of Ecumenism" by the most Rev. John F. Whelan, the Roman Catholic Archbishop. I never seem to be in tune with that man. Our group received a citation from the Commission on Regional and Local Ecumenism of the National Council of Churches. We represent both ends of the spectrum—the Roman Catholics on one end, with the Unitarians and Quakers on the other. Most represent the Baptist, Congregational, Episcopal, Lutheran, Methodist and Presbyterian Churches.

What does Ecumenism mean to you? I would appreciate your reaction—I like the way your mind works.

Sundays at my church after the service a group of us discuss Great Decisions 1980, a Foreign Policy Association document. Last Sunday we discussed The World in 1980. I volunteered to lead and am afraid I am going to be caught next Sunday too, since no one else volunteered for the Mid East and the Gulf. It is next to impossible to cover all that material in an hour, but it is fascinating. To deal with today's problems we surely need voters with a deeper, broader background.

In my books, Kennedy still does not measure up. Somehow I question his maturity, understanding, and integrity. There are no quick easy solutions to the problems we face today. The legislative branch of our government is surely out of control.

It would be rewarding for me to be able to discuss these issues with you, but I know you are very busy.

Do take good care of yourself with all these flu and intestinal germs floating around.

Edna

February 22, 1980
West Park, New York
Dear Edna,

Thank you for your letter. Your involvement in the Regional Conference of Churches should be most rewarding. Ecumenism means to me honest and open dialogue between the churches, really facing the issues that divide us, not politely brushing them under the rug, and cooperation in work and worship as far as is consonant with the positions of the churches involved. The worship should be at the interparish level whenever possible—congregations visiting each other for their regular Sunday worship, not just holding occasional ecumenical services attended only by those already committed to it. We need to learn to understand each other, and appreciated each other, at the grassroots level.

What we do not need is schemes for organic reunion. We have far too much executive machinery as it is. Intercommunion, when churches can conscientiously participate is a much more hopeful road to the diversity in unity, which is the real goal. We must include the best of everybody's insights, not settle for the least common denominator.

Your group that discusses the issues in foreign policy sounds much fun and I am sure is doing a good work. We do not know nearly enough in that area and too rarely do any solid thinking even on the letter we do know.

I have never been enthusiastic about Teddy Kennedy and have become less so as the weeks go by. I am certain he can never be elected if nominated and I do want to see a Democrat in the White House. I earnestly hope New Hampshire knocks him out of the running, so that the party can get together behind Jimmy and go to work for the election.

I am rejoicing in the snow we have at last had. A little renewal we have had today should make it last a bit longer. I had the bug, whatever it is, early in January. Since then I have been feeling fine.

All the best.

With love,
Bonnie

March 4, 1980
Dear Bonnie,

It was good to receive your letter last Monday. The meeting of the Officers and Directors of the Capital Region Conference of Churches was held the next day so that your explanation of ecumenism was most timely for it—gave me a much clearer understanding of the topic. You explained it beautifully with a sincere and fair concern for all. It was very fine preparation for my year's work with this group. I believe it is most important that the different faiths work together for the good of all. The new president has a delightful sense of humor that should prove to be a useful safety valve. I always feel that a genuine sense of humor enables us to weather many a crisis with some degree of sanity.

I am reading a biography of Clementine Churchill by her daughter, Mary Soames. It gives me greater insight with reference to the British character during World War I. She was an extraordinary woman—how fortunate Winston married her—it was a beautiful marriage.

Recently, I purchased <u>The Unheard Cry for Meaning</u> by Viktor Frankl. I have not read it yet, but I am looking forward to it. I think he is the best psychiatrist, and I shall always be deeply grateful to you for your introduction to him.

The results of the primaries in Mass. and Vermont were surprising. Of all the Republican nominees, John Anderson seems to be the most intelligent but I want Carter to win. The Mid East problem still haunts us—I wish the Israelis would give more consideration to the Arab needs. I hope Carter finds a solution to the rate of inflation lest it should hamper his progress. Surely the economists do not agree. Who is following the best road?

How have your Brethren at Mt. Calvary fared during those recent dreadful storms? I often recall the snow was beautiful while it lasted—March may bring you some more; the blizzard of '88 descended March 11th.

I am sorry the flu paid you a visit; it has assailed so many around here more than once; be careful.

May we have a promising and early spring.

Edna

March 21, 1980
West Park, New York
Dear Edna,

Thank you for your letter and clipping. I fully agree that a sense of humor is the <u>sine qua non</u> of sound human relations, in religions and political as well as all other fields. I must be on the look-out for Frankl's book. He is by far the most satisfactory of the psychiatrists.

After Illinois, the picture has become pretty clear. Kennedy may yet do fairly well in New York because of the Jewish vote. I was delighted to see in today's paper the Vance has come out strongly against settlements in Arab territory. I plan to go up to West Park next Tuesday to cast my vote for Carter. My sympathies are mostly with the Arabs, even with the Moslems in Iran, despite the hostages. It is too bad about them, but in any war there are prisoners. From the Iranian point-of-view that is what the hostages are and I fear they have every intention of holding them until they win the war. I am proud of the way Carter and the American people have kept their heads so far. I earnestly hope they will continue. Reagan would get us into another Vietnam.

I fully agree about Anderson, and he might have a chance of beating Carter. But his failure to carry even his own state is ominous. My greatest terror is Ford, surely the stupidest man ever to get into the White House. If he could have got the nomination without serious opposition, I think he could have won. But the Reagan forces have gone too far. (I hope) to accept his candidacy, and the liberal Republicans like Anderson have got his number. He did well to decide not to run.

As you recall our Santa Barbara house sits on an out-jutting of rock, so it is not in danger of mudslides. I hear, however, there is a possibility of a washout behind the house. Apparently nothing happened in the recent heavy rains.

We seemed to have had a bit of snow while I was in Florida, but at present we are getting a torrential rain. Water in any form is welcome.

May your Holy Week and Easter be blessed.

Love,
Bonnie

April 5, 1980
West Park, New York
Dear Edna,

Thank you for Frankl's <u>The Unheard Cry for Meaning</u>. It is most kind and generous of you to give it to me and I look forward eagerly to reading it. I also appreciate the card—Wells is one of my favorite cathedrals.

New York and Connecticut were a disappointment. I had so hoped they would convince Teddy that he does not have a chance. Now it is up to Pennsylvania. I am quite sure he cannot take the nomination from Carter. What I now fear is the possibility of Anderson running on a third ticket. That could easily divide the liberal vote and give the key states to Reagan. I never really thought he had a chance of election. But now I fear it may well happen and that will be an utter disaster for the country. I do hope Anderson keeps out of it.

I have had a particularly helpful Holy Week. The Sisters have been keeping silence most of the time so I was able to make a five day retreat. Today I go up to West Park for the Easter Vigil that begins about 4:30am, so as not to have to travel from here (Vails Gate) for it. I shall return with the Sisters after it because I preach and celebrate here Easter morning.

I hope your Eastertide is full of joy.

Much love,
Bonnie

April 21, 1980
Dear Bonnie,

Your good letters were most welcome, and I am happy that all goes well for you.

Somehow I seem to get more and more involved with various ventures—"Fools rush in where angels fear to tread".

I have promised to teach Sunday school for seventh and eighth graders during the next six weeks. It took me all afternoon to scrub the classroom and another to decorate it. Some black youngsters waiting for their parents who were attending some Psychic Rally were most helpful and quite refreshing. My topics include beliefs about God, death, and religion. I am posting some of the quotations I found helpful in Trinity Church in Boston as well as some pictures form Renaissance art, which has always been inspirational to me.

Today the most confused mortals seem to be the adolescents. I believe in freedom, but it must be coupled with responsibility. In my class is a delightful girl, whose mother tells me she is leaning toward

Episcopalianism. I will not interfere with her inclinations for everyone must choose for himself. If I get beyond my depth, I will call on you for help.

Sunday I was elected to serve as a delegate to our UU Assembly in Albuquerque for a week—June 13 to 20. Fortunately, I have an alternate in case I needed. I have never been to New Mexico.

Tomorrow I consented to pitch hit for the secretary at the meeting of the Board of Directors of the Conference of Churches. That is one task I never enjoy but sooner or later I always seem to land in that spot.

The article on the Middle East seems quite logical to me. How does it appear to you?

I worry about Carter. I voted for him and will again if he is nominated. Both foreign and domestic policies are really too complicated to be understood by most. I agree with you about John Anderson and hope he decides not to run as an independent.

In one issue of <u>Holy Cross</u> it mentions the possible closing of some of the houses of the Order. Are financial problems this serious?

I hope for all the best for you.

Edna

May 11, 1980
West Park, New York
Dear Edna,

It is fine that you are teaching the Sunday school class. I think your friend has hit upon a real problem. Unitarianism is almost exclusively intellectual and rational. These capacities do not really begin to develop until the late teens. For the little I know of Unitarianism the emotional, intuitive, irrational unconscious side of human personality is neglected. As that makes up over 9/10ths of us, and is the area that children operated in, I should think there would be real difficulties. In the traditional church these are met by sacraments which can be acted and appreciated before they can be rationally explained and understood. When we used to minister at Letchworth Village, a home for retarded children, we soon learned that anything beyond the simplest stories were a waste of time, but the celebration of the Holy Communion was immediately and manifestly meaningful to them. One long step forward the Episcopal Church has taken recently is the authorization of small children to receive Communion. Their obvious comprehension is a joy to behold. Actions speak louder than words, not only in the moral sphere, but even more in the spiritual.

I must admit I find it harder and harder to keep up my enthusiasm for Carter. If I thought Anderson had a chance I should vote for him. But I know he will only succeed in throwing the election to Reagan. I am totally discouraged.

I am glad you are elected to the Assembly. You will love Albuquerque; but if you get the chance, be sure to go to Santa Fe—that is even more delightful.

The Israeli problem is insoluble because no politician can afford to lose the Jewish vote: witness Carter in the New York primary.

We just had a good meeting of the Order. Things look more hopeful than the article you refer to painted them. We are not out of the woods by any means, but I think there has been renewed determination to avoid closing any of our main houses. The West Park monastery is expensive to run, especially with the price of heating oil, but by closing off most of it for the winter, I hope we can manage. At least a substantial portion of the Order feels it is a primary obligation.

All the best.

Much love,
Bonnie

May 30, 1980
Dear Bonnie,

It is always good to hear from you and you were most helpful with my Sunday school problems. I think you are right about Unitarianism—that it neglects "the emotional, unconscious, intuitive, irrational, unconscious side of human personality." But there must be some way to integrate the intellectual and the rational. Perhaps that is why art (the sense of the beautiful), has always meant so much to me. I just cannot understand living without emotions—strong feelings—caring, but I need the guidance of the intellectual. I liked your description of the little children receiving Communion. I could see them in my mind's eye. I agree with you that actions speak louder than words.

In my recent endeavors, I am trying to infuse some emotion—I have never been able to teach without it, and my emotions are stronger than those of most people—always have been. I am using the arts, especially painting and literature for a deeper understanding of our problems. I am also trying to relate our religion to the problems of the day. Surely religion should deepen our understanding, our search for meaning, and our need to help each other. And, in my books, there is no one religion. Out of a class of twelve, I draw from none to eight on a Sunday, but I am not giving up—shades of my Dutch ancestry. In order that the young and I might reach a better understanding I invited them to my home one Saturday evening; eight came. I thoroughly enjoyed the experience and they seemed comfortable and happy. We discussed art quite a bit. Somehow I must motivate them to gain a broader view of the world around them—both emotionally and intellectually. The most sophisticated member of my home group was an eighth grade girl—an Episcopalian friend of one of my Unitarian girls. We both survived happily.

One Sunday our LRY group (older teenagers) presented a program for our Sunday service; it was a disgrace—poor quality in both material and performance. It could hardly have been called intellectual. Education should not descend to mediocrity. However, the young always give me a lift—and there is something quite young about you.

Perhaps after our federal elections this fall, a Middle East solution will have more opportunity. You are right about the power of the Jewish voters in this country. I expect to encounter trouble in this area at our General Assembly because I do not think Begin is playing fair.

Carter's performance is discouraging, but Reagan promises a disastrous four years. I wish our American voters cared and could see more clearly. Carter needed to study history more analytically and not try so hard to please everybody—that is impossible. He should never have authorized the reserve mission, and he ought not to have downgraded Cyrus Vance. We face a crossroads today that is widely different from any we have ever met before.

I am glad events at home are looking up. Your West Park monastery is very beautiful and peaceful.

Are you coming to Connecticut some time? I should love to see you again—and time has a way of fleeting by.

Edna

June 13, 1980
Holy Cross Monastery
Dear Edna,

The integration of the intuition and emotional with the rational is the key to the whole process of self-realization. The important point, however, is that the irrational and unconscious makes up the major proportion of our personality and operates prior to it both in our life history and in our moment to moment experiences. I think that our culture (and often in the name of Christianity) has allowed the unconscious as inferior, if not actually evil, and has exalted reason over the passions. So it has served to strengthen the dichotomy rather than unite the personality. It is not enough to use the emotions as an aid to reason. We need to get over our distrust of them to accept them and sanctify them. That is why I think it is important for religion to be able to minister to our unconscious and intuitive nature without always having to go through reason. As you say art is an expression of this direct approach. But again I think we tend to over rationalize our approach to art. (I myself I am so caught in that tradition that I find modern art difficult.) We need to see reason as the servant of our total personality, of which the major part is unconscious.

Of course you are correct in saying there is no ONE religion. I am counting on the great religions of the east to save us from the over rationalistic over moralistic over pragmatic religions which most modern Christianity has degenerated into. And the anti-rational reaction of the fundamentalists is no answer. We need to recover the whole personality.

All the Best,
Love, Bonnie

June 30, 1980
Dear Bonnie

It was good to find your letter when I arrived home from Albuquerque. Thank you for providing me with intellectual guidance. I read Frankl's Unconscious God and I had underlined specific passages. I have reread your letter many times and I respect your judgment. You have stated your position very well. Will you give me some examples of the integrations of the intuitive and emotional with the rational? I agree that the emotions are extremely important and should not be put down. Life without the emotional side would be dull. We need the wisdom of the heart. As I read your words I tried to sort out my own personality, but I am finding it difficult to label my various parts. Can you recommend some additional material for me to read?

I am most interested in your theories, but I need more explanation. I find that I do not enjoy modern art and do not feel apologetic about it either. Our present day civilization has many shortcomings and so does our art.

Re the Conference I attended part of it was stimulating, but other events left me in dismay. In particular the discussions on homosexuality and Israel were perplexing. One topic dear to my heart was the plight of our American Indians. La Donna Harris a Comanche and president of the Americans for Indian Appreciation gave a most insightful talk. She was warm, sensitive, and understanding. Her people need help. The day after the conference we were able to take a trip to Santa Fe. As you said it was unique and more beautiful than Albuquerque We also visited on the Indian reservations and I met many children there. I thoroughly enjoyed the conference and came away with many more questions to study back home.

Re home I have found someone to paint the outside of my house and with the help of the boy next door I have my garden back in shape.

As ever,
Edna

July 18, 1980
Dear Edna,

It is always hard for me to recommend books, but some which I have found helpful may be to you also. John V. Taylor, The Go Between God is the best thing I know on the Holy Spirit, who in my opinion is the intuitional aspect of God. William Johnson's Silent Music also deals with this aspect, as do James Hillman's Insured and Morton T. Kilsay's The Other Side of Silence.

Carl Gustav Jung on the other hand is the psychiatrist who is most positive on his dealing with the unconscious and religion. His Modern Man in Search of a Soul might be a good introduction to him. Finally the whole area of myth and symbol is most important for it is only through them that the deepest irrational truths can be expressed.

The matter of homosexuality in the ministry and education is complicated by two factors: First the word has two meanings. Basically it means a person whose sexual attraction is predominantly to members of the same sex. As such it is simply the opposite of heterosexual. But unfortunately the word has taken on a quite different tone. To call a man homosexual does not imply he is promiscuous and molests little girls. The word does to most people carry the implications of such misbehavior. This is most unfair, since there are plenty of chaste homosexuals who have deep, abiding and faithful love relationships. Second there have always been homosexuals in the ministry and education. In the past, however they have been at great pains to conceal the fact. Today many homosexuals do not consider their sexual bias a sin, a disease or an unfortunate affliction. It is how they are made and the way they are intended to love. They are offering themselves what they are. That raises an interesting problem. Do we ordain or employ homosexuals if they lie about it, but refuse to when they are honest?

It will take a long time for society to adjust to the fact that homosexuality is a normal condition for a considerable number of people and that they should be given the opportunity to live normal lives in terms of it. In our culture the whole weight of religion, society, and accepted mores has been against it for so long that the injustice and prejudice against them is even deeper than that against blacks and women. But at least we are aware of all these problems and that is a step toward solving them.

I am glad Bush is Reagan's VP nominee. I fear they will be elected. But the condition of Reagan's age and the fact that every president elected in an even 20 years since 1840 has died in office makes me more concerned than ever about the Vice President, mere superstition of course, but intriguing. I shall still vote for Carter and pray.

I am glad you are getting your house painted. I have discovered an unusual talent as I have been helping the Sisters by laying flagstones for their walkway.

This week I got definite news that my book God Who Dares To Be Man is on the Seabury Press fall list. We are hoping it will be out before the originally projected date of January 1981. I hope you are enjoying the summer.

With Love,
Bonnie

August 9, 1980
Dear Bonnie,

How wonderful your book is being published. I like the title and will buy it once it comes out. Your best wish did come true.

Finally I found two copies of the books you recommended at the Hartford Seminary. They are Images and Silent Music. I have ordered the others. I like to own books so I can make notations. I started Silent Music and find it challenging. I certainly thank you for your recommendations. Now I have enough to keep me busy all summer long with Anatomy of Illness by Norman Cousins and several biographies. Next letter I shall have some questions to ask you about the books you listed.

I appreciate your point of view about homosexuals. I know there have always been homosexuals in the ministry and education, but I can't believe they should be I do not want them to lie or hide in the closet. It is best they call themselves what they are. I am sure many are harmless that way and cannot help it, but I think some are bent that way through circumstances. To me their situation is tragic and chastity is probably the only way out. I feel deeply sorry for them and believe they should have access to any other kind of occupation. I was once given a young man who had tendencies that way to supervise as a student teacher. They gave him to me deliberately and I did the very best I could. It was the hardest assignment I ever undertook. I gave him an A and I have always had a reputation for being a hard marker. He earned it and did everything he could to excel. I wrote a confidential evaluation but I could never bring myself to write him any other reference. I never referred in any way to that particular trait. And we worked together very well, but deep down I never felt so sorry for anyone in my life.

At the assembly after I had spoken in opposition to homosexuals in the ministry a woman I had met in several of the workshops, but had never seen before Albuquerque, came to me asking for a few words. When I stepped out to consult wither she told me she was a lesbian and a teacher with two grown sons. At present she was living very happily with another woman and felt under these circumstances she was a better teacher than she was before she divorced her husband. I was dumbfounded and felt very bad. I told her I was sure there were all kinds of homosexuals. Some of the others in my group wanted to know what she said, but I would not tell anyone I do not want to hurt her. I know you will keep these two cases in confidence. She appears to be a very intelligent understanding person . . . At that point I would never have known. When I took my position on this issue I was thinking of attitudes and understanding the teacher must build and the minister must counsel. I frankly do not know how any homosexual could do this for the rest of us. I could never counsel homosexuals. During the past few years I had occasion to do some counseling regarding sexual matters. I bought a highly regarded text on the matter. I was astounded at some of the ideas and read it as fast as I could and then got rid of the book. Some of the techniques recommended for homosexuals were used by normal people. It was horrible. Sex is meant to be beautiful, natural, wholesome, not ugly and promiscuous. Years ago I found a sixth grader boy hiding a pornographic magazine in his desk.

The next day I marched the whole class down to the art museum for a lesson on nudes (paintings, and sculptures). I am sure they returned with a new respect for their bodies. I have always tried to build the best attitudes in the young. I don't like to see them short changed.

I am voting for Carter and praying also. I think he will win.

I do hope your cabin is air conditioned and that you are not laying flagstones in the heat. It is a real art and the Sisters are lucky.

My house has finally been painted and it looks better than ever. Two little girls born in Portugal have been helping me pull weeds. They are priceless children.

As ever,
Edna

August 22, 1980
Dear Edna,

This afternoon I mailed the index made from the page proofs to Seabury Press so the last major chore of the book has been accomplished. We are running well ahead of schedule, so I am hoping the book may be out before Christmas. I shall keep you posted. I do hope you find the books I recommended helpful. The problem of relationship with the irrational and the unconscious is one of the vital issues of the days. The books on the subject are innumerable.

Well Carter has the nomination and the indications at the moment are that Kennedy will make a sincere effort to get him elected. I still doubt that it can be accomplished, since I fear Anderson will draw off enough votes in the key states so that Reagan will have a plurality though not a majority. Thus he will win easily on the electoral vote. His enthusiasm for an arms race with the USSR is horrifying. He may well be the lost president of USA but I really have not the slightest hope that he can be defeated.

My cabin is air conditioned and I have turned it on a few times when the humidity and temperature get unbearable. But for the last two weeks the weather here has been excellent-rarely up to 80 then only in the middle of the day . . . As long as the nights are cool I have no complaints.

I have been making the retreat with the Sisters. So far it has been good, but not exciting. The conductor's lectures were helpful but not conducive to prayer.

All the best.

As ever,
Bonnie

October 1, 1980
Dear Bonnie,

Thank you for your promise to keep me posted on the progress of your book. I know your wisdom and insight will prove helpful to many.

Most of the books you recommended have come through to the bookstore of the Hartford Seminary Foundation. Tomorrow I shall collect the last one. While I was there, I could not resist Arnold Tonybee's An Historian's Approach to Religion. I sincerely appreciate your book list I am by no means through all of them; I am reading carefully and meditating along the way. They are different from ones I have read before and seem to give me a little better understanding of you. Jung's Modern Man in Search of His Soul is my introduction to his work and I need to live with it awhile.

I truly believe Carter will win eventually. It seems that many will make their decisions at the eleventh hour. I feel Anderson will lose as time progresses. You do need, however, to take my hunches with a grain of salt, for I am afraid I am something of an optimist. In my youth a good friend of mine used to shake her head and accuse me of viewing the world through rose colored glasses. James Buckley, who is now trying to represent Connecticut in the Senate is the last person I want us to elect. Christopher Dodd, who is very different from his father, thank goodness, is far superior-much more intelligent, liberal, and understanding. I am grateful his father had the good sense to marry his mother.

I have agreed to serve on the Policy Council of the Religious Coalition for Abortion Rights in Connecticut. It bothers me that so many who oppose are supporting political candidates who agree with them on this one issue alone.

On Sunday my good friend of thirty years is giving a special concert in memory of her husband, who died a year ago this September. Music always meant so much to him. She was wise to spend this past September in Switzerland with his brother and sister.

The Capitol Regional Conference of Churches (on whose board I remain) is having a fall assembly on The Electronic Church. Bishop Morgan Porteus is speaking on the future of Ecumenism. He should be good.

According to the Holy Cross Bulletin you were busy this summer with supplying work in the various parishes of the Hudson Valley. Your parishioners were fortunate.

As Ever,
Edna

October 17, 1980
Dear Edna,

Thank you for your letter and the clippings. I am a little embarrassed about the list of books I gave you. It was off the top of my head. I had not expected you were going to buy all of them. I do hope they will not prove to be a disappointment.

I am not as hopeful as you about Carter's election though things do seem to be improving for him. One hopeful sign is that I find many people do not take Reagan seriously. They think he is just a bad joke. I agree of course but it will be no joke if he gets into the White House. He may well have five appointments to the Supreme Court. God help the country if we get six Renhquists on it. And I do hope you succeed on keeping Buckley out of the Senate. The so called "Christian" political pressure groups are a great danger. I hope they will not prevail. Bishop Paul Moore gave a superb speech about them at the New York Diocesan Convention. It is printed and distributed. If I get a copy I shall send it to you.

I have just received a most encouraging comment on my book from one of the prominent persons to whom we sent page proof copies. The three others wrote me they would comment, but the last I heard they had not. A couple more like we have on the back of the jacket may be a real help in commending the book.

I have just returned from a pleasant trip to Tennessee, South Carolina and Georgia, visiting old friends and the school I ran for eight years.

All best wishes for your many interests and enterprises, especially the political one in this important election.

As ever,
Bonnie

November 13, 1980
Dear Bonnie,

You were quite right in your forecast of election results. I was too optimistic. Churchill, however, is so right to have said: "In a democracy people expect simple solutions to complex problems and most feel any change must offer improvement." It is most discouraging, but I have not given up hope. At least Hartford and New Britain favored Carter. We did trounce Buckley with Christopher Dodd. We also did rather well with our choice of Congressman and our Ct. state legislators. I hope Mondale becomes head of the Democratic Party. I fear the electronic church and Jerry Falwell in particular. Certainly the moral majority is most ignorant. I think our Connecticut Legislature will be reasonable. Did you read Barbara Tuchman's The Decline of Quality in the New York Times magazine on Nov. 2nd. I feel her observations are most astute. The article also helps to explain the election results. Our Capitol Regional Conferences of Churches voted to support the Jewish people in their movement to prevent reprisals such as took place in France. I volunteered to serve on this committee. Another large problem faces our state as the legislature is considering changing our tax structure by implementing an income tax.

A recent attempt at cross burning at Williams was discussed at the Alumni Dinner. I trust the College will prevent further incidents.

I also had occasion to take my black colleague with me to Vermont for a few days, where we did not encounter any racism. She is a college professor and administrator hoping to become a college president in the near future. She is most capable.

Since Halloween I have been under the weather with a flu-like illness and so have laid low. If you should become so afflicted be sure to take to your bed for the duration. These things are quite virulent this year.

I am still immersed in your recommendations. I prefer Jung to Hillman, about whom I have some questions. I find Taylor quite interesting and provocative. I am not yet ready to discuss ideas in detail, but I am getting there. Your comment about your book is most encouraging. I hope it will be widely read. I am also happy that you had the opportunity to visit your Southern friends. In general the South is noted for its hospitality.

As Ever,
Edna

November 24, 1980
Dear Edna,

Your letter and the enclosures are much appreciated. Now that elections are decided via TV I guess it is pretty hard to defeat an actor. The real tragedy is the Senate. I understand McGovern plans to organize a counter force to those ultra conservative groups. I have written him asking that I be put on the mailing list. So far no answer. I do hope he and Mondale, Church, Bough etc. will be able to come up with a progressive policy that can pull together those who are working for human rights and dignity for blacks, Hispanics, women and other deprived minorities, not that women are a minority of course. I congratulate Connecticut on defeating Buckley. It was the only bright spot in the election. I dread the next four (eight) years, but there is little we can do about it.

If Jung were the only dissenting voice in Roman Catholicism he would not be particularly significant. Other sound theologians have been condemned and persecuted before. But I was recently at a conference where ten Catholics were present, all members of important monastic communities and their unanimous contempt for John Paul II was astounding. As one put it: "When he speaks he puts his 19ᵗʰ century foot in his 16ᵗʰ century mouth."

I had not heard of the attempted cross burning at Williams. That kind of thing has not been characteristic of the student body in the past. Quite the opposite. The college came through the struggles of the 60s with flying colors and at least the black white relationships seemed good to me the last time I had any evidence. That was when a class elected a black as their alumni president for the first five years.

I am afraid Williams alumni gatherings are characterized by money, status, and drinking. After all only alums who consider themselves successful turn up. The rest disappear into the woodwork. Nevertheless the Alumni Association does an essential work for the college, raising, I think, 10% of its annual budget and giving substantial capital gifts at the 25 and 50 year reunions. I am glad they are including widows, for their help is necessary for reaching our goals. So that aspect of the work is constructive even if get-togethers are not, except in so far as they keep people who like them interested in the college.

I am glad the Conference of Churches is urging a change in the tax structure so that the principal burden does not fall on the poor. It will be an uphill battle especially in the present political climate, but winter is the time to get the seed in the ground so that it can germinate as soon as spring comes.

I am sorry to learn that you have had a bout of flu. It is good that you are recovering again. I hope by now you are fully well. I have not had it yet, nor have I had a flu shot. I must try to get the later. Jung of course is much more significant than Hillman. I suggested the later only because of his tie up of dreams and the spiritual life. I shall be glad to receive your comments on all the books when you are ready.

All of my book including the dust jacket is now in press. It will still not be out until January because even if it is finished in December printers will not mail the copies during the Christmas rush. Of the five people I asked to make a comment on the page proof copy, four replied with statements that are being printed on the back of the dust jacket. Three are from Episcopalians, a seminary dean, an ex-dean who has just gone to be chaplain of Princeton and a professor of theology, who disagrees with much that I have said, yet commented it is an interesting and clear light on the Gospel. The fourth is a Roman Catholic lay professor of theology at Fordham. He is a prominent process theologian and the book takes off from that position. I have not read what he said, but word from him should be very helpful.

I hope you have a good Thanksgiving. I go up to West Park tomorrow to stay until Friday. My brother is there so it will be a natural as well as a religious family affair. Then the next weekend I go to New Jersey to give a talk at a retreat for various religious orders. After that I have, at present, a free schedule for December. I shall commute back and forth each week between Vails Gate and West Park, but otherwise I shall stay put unless something unexpected turns up. I hope all goes well with you in your preparation for the feast.

As ever,
Bonnie

December 17, 1980
Dear Bonnie,

Your fine letter arrived the day before Thanksgiving. It was most heartening and timely. It is almost unbelievable that a man of Reagan's caliber could be elected president. His appointments to date are most unfortunate, especially that of Alexander Haig. On TV he had a look of Satan and the grin of a Cheshire cat. I don't believe Reagan will last more than one term. So our only hope will rest with some humane, intelligent leader in Congress.

The work of the Committee on Racism and Prejudice initiated by the Jewish Foundation and supported by organizations representing Blacks, Hispanics and our Conference of Churches in the Capital Region has been fascinating. The Blacks are truly frustrated by the past federal election but they must continue to fight and outwit their radical conservative brothers. We have come a long way, but not far enough. The housing problem in this area is critical and the suburbs are shirking their responsibilities Busing would not be necessary if we provided for the minorities in our suburbs. I have believed that large cities were inherently evil. It was not intended that the unfortunate should be huddled together in crowded ugly ghettos. Crime is inevitable when we permit this. We also need free nurseries for their poor children from the ages of two on. Otherwise these youngsters will never catch up. And it is dishonest to give children grades they do not earn. It is every child's birthright to be wanted and loved.

Thursday we have another meeting to plan for our February Forum on Strategies and Policies for Change relating to Prejudice and Racism. The Forum will be held on Feb. 12th at the Beth Israel Temple in W. Hartford. It will be an all-day affair with national and local speakers. This will not be the end but a beginning.

Your analysis of the Williams Alumni gathering is most perceptive. I shall continue to do my duty there as I see it. In January I shall look for your book at the shelves of the Hartford Seminary Foundation Bookstore. Your recommended book list should prepare me. You have opened new vistas to me and I am trying to proceed carefully without

135

getting lost. William Johnston's Silent Music book is quite revealing and very different from anything I have ever read. The rational is very strong in me, always has been. I am reluctant to give up my controls I think I would have to return to the market place quite often. I agree with St. Theresa when she says "We should desire and engage in prayer not for our enjoyment but for the sake of acquiring this strength which fits us for service." I agree contemplation and actions may not be opposed. I am still pondering over "The Road to Ecstacy" and a "Perilous Journey".

I have sent you a Christmas package that I hope arrives in time, and if the size is wrong, please let me know so that I can send the correct one or something else if you prefer.

As ever,
Edna

December 18, 1980
Convent of St. Helena
Vails Gate, N.Y.
Dear Edna,

Your Present has come. Of course I shall not open it until Christmas Day, but I wanted you to know that is has safely arrived. I am most grateful to you for remembering me.

Here is the flyer on my book. I trust that we are at last approaching its appearance, but the process has been so long I shall not believe it until I see it.

I hope you have a blessed Christmas and that the New Year brings much joy.

As ever,
Bonnie

no date given but in the envelope with the 12/18/80 letter:

Dear Bonnie,

Thank you for your hospitality on the 23rd and 24th. I had a distinct feeling that I had become something of a nuisance. I have never meant to be a bother. Forgive me for coming—I just thought I would probably never see you again.

Your present prior is certainly an improvement over your last one, who looked at me as though I were a Jezebel. During my whole life no one has ever regarded me that way. Being an only daughter I was carefully protected by my parents and brothers. During my youth I have always been accorded respect.

I have never known intimately any man but George. In that department, I have been somewhat naive and ever fastidious. We had a beautiful marriage based upon respect and trust, truth and love. Our relationship provided the most fulfilling experience in my past. He was ever gentle and understanding. The interlude of the twenty-five years was too short.

I concluded that one of two conditions existed—either he knew nothing about women or he had known only the wrong kind.

Edna

December 26, 1980
Vails Gate, New York
Dear Edna,

Thank you for the lovely pair of gloves. They fit perfectly and are just what I needed. Thank you also for the engagement book and the pair of birds, which are now located on the Sisters' tree. I also received your welcome letter just before Christmas. It crossed one from me, so by now you know that you can get my book at a special price from Holy Cross Publications, West Park, NY 12493. Just in case my letter went astray I enclose another flyer.

I fully share your distress at Reagan's cabinet appointments. My fear is that so many of the "humane intelligent leaders" were eliminated from Congress, that it will be unable to oppose him. I am glad your committee on Racism and Prejudice is trying to meet the challenge. The most important thing is for the various groups to pull together, as they have failed to do so in recent years.

I am glad you are enjoying Johnston's Silent Music. You have put your finger on the main difficulty of overemphasizing the rational. It is the way we try to keep in control and thereby resist the deeper influences, not just from the unconscious, but from the Spirit, who works in the depths of our personalities. When we recognize further that the presuppositions of our rationality are often prejudices inherited from our culture we can see how dangerous it can be to trust solely in our rational judgment.

I hope you are having a glorious Christmastide and that the New Year brings much joy.

As ever,
Bonnie

December 29, 1980
HAPPY BIRTHDAY
Dear Bonnie,

May your new year help you realize all your fondest wishes. One is on its certain way—the publishing of your book.

I have sent to West Park for two copies. Thank you for the flyer and it is a very good picture of you. It is fitting that you should share some of your wisdom with others.

As ever,
Edna

PART THREE

1981 - 1984

January 9, 1981
Vails Gate, New York
Dear Edna,

Thank you for the birthday card, note and clipping. I agree that Bishop Porteus message is the best. He is a really fine person. I am sorry to see him retire, but his successor is a good man too. Our diocese of Connecticut is fortunate in its bishops.

Thank you for your order of my book. The publisher tells me that the printer expects to ship the copies on January 16. I do not know how long it will take them to arrive, but I hope I shall be pleasantly busy toward the end of the month helping mail out the orders. On Monday I hope to have a conference with my editor where to send review copies and how to handle promotion. The response to the advance sale flyer has been encouraging.

I am greatly enjoying the snow. We have just enough to be beautiful and fun shoveling without being too much of a chore. I have a path from my cabin to the convent to take care of. I can do it in about 15 minutes.

I hope the New Year is bringing many blessings to you. I trust the change of governor in Connecticut is for the good. I wish I could think the same of the White House, but I have grave misgivings. Those of us who want to see decent government again must work hard to develop a viable program. All the best.

As ever,
Bonnie

February 16, 1981
Dear Bonnie,

Your books arrived expertly packed with a most artistic jacket, exquisitely designed with lovely colors and a most meaningful detail from Michelangelo's "Creation of Man". Thank you for the autograph.

The statements on the jacket and your Foreword from Bishop Moore are most supportive. By now you must have received many accolades.

I have read your book from "kiver to kiver". For the most part I did my reading at night before going to sleep. That is my favorite time for reading and meditation. Meditate I surely did. I also reread much and underlined many passages. It is most informative, stimulating and challenging.

You are indeed a scholar. You write beautifully, as well as clearly and succinctly, while expressing your thoughts most logically. Your many years of varied experiences in living have been truly productive.

I found your chapter on sin most rewarding. I have never been able to accept the doctrine of original sin even when I was only twelve. I agree that "The violence of nature is inherent in the evolution of man" and that "God or the universe is not to be held accountable for the evil that mankind accomplishes". I find your comments on suffering and pain reasonable. I believe that Jesus could be truly man only if he had a kinsman father and mother. Also I agree: "Because Jesus was living a human life, he was not following a prearranged script."

"Self-determination means that we go from one occasion of becoming to another, influenced by past decisions but not fully determined by them." Your chapter on incarnation was fascinating.

In your chapter on redemption you explain much I have always questioned. Your chapters on Mission and Liberation give me hope. Your definition of love and its importance especially on page 155 are sound to me. Your chapter on Consummation shows great insight, especially the last pages. I do not believe in a final judgment day—haven't since I was twelve. I think I need to take a course in religion—one where we have discussions with real give and take.

These few comments come from one Unitarian layperson who was brought up in the Baptist Church by her father, but who went to the Methodist Church Sunday nights with her mother.

Furthermore being descended from a variety of Protestants the influence included French Huguenots and Congregationalists. Thus I do not begin to have your depth of religious background, but I do my own thinking and I do not rightly know where my unconscious ends and my conscious begins. I have always revered the truth as far as I could find it since I was two.

Our forum on Racism and Prejudice was both provocative and productive. Best of all we will continue to strive in these areas.

Our new governor is a nice man, but I don't think he is a leader for reform either. At present the Legislature is ignoring the need for tax reform, but we will not give up. Our executive director of the Conference of Churches of the Capitol Region is resigning, so now we have a new search committee charged with finding a successor. I was elected to the committee by the Board, after the others had been nominated by the Executive Committee. I was also voted chairman by the Committee as no one else wanted the job. All my life I have tried to undertake those necessary jobs that no one else would do. So if you have any advice to offer, please pass it on.

I know you enjoy the snow and some exercise is good for you, but do use discretion in your shoveling activities. May life hold all faith, hope and love you want.

With all my best,
Edna

March 5, 1981
Vails Gate, New York
Dear Edna,

Thank you for your letter and the penetrating and encouraging comments on my book. You have summarized and appreciated many of the points I most wanted to make. Others are also writing in appreciations so I am becoming quite happy about it. The publisher was very slow in getting out review copies, so none of them have appeared yet so far as I know. I expect to see the editor-in-chief of my publishing house next week and shall try to put a bit more steam in the promotion.

I rejoice to learn of your continued activity in the field of human rights and social justice. It is extremely important that all who are concerned about these matters keep hard at work in order to counteract the indifference of our present government. And I do hope some definite and practical proposals can be agreed upon. The last election showed that the liberals were in total disarray and without a real program to advocate.

It is good that you were willing to accept the Chairmanship of the Search Committee. It is a real vocation to pick up the jobs and responsibilities that no one else will undertake. I am afraid I do not have any advice to offer as to a suitable choice for Executive Director of the Conference of Churches, since I know neither what the job entails nor who might be available to do it. But I trust you will find the right person without too much difficulty.

I have been slow in answering because I had a bout with the flu—very much lighter than most + now completely over. Curiously enough, although we have had warm weather ever since you wrote referring to snow, it is now snowing as I answer. I do like it, even in March.

All best wishes + keep up the good work.

As ever yours,
Bonnie

March 29, 1981
Dear Bonnie,

Somehow, I was hoping that you would be able to elude the flu, but I am glad it is over and that your case was lighter than some, for this year's type was quite virulent.

This season should be ideal for the promotion of your book—it must be widely read—you have put so much into it; surely it will elicit most provocative discussions—I should love to hear them.

My committee work has kept me running around; it has been most engrossing. We must adopt an income tax in the state for our system of taxation is most short-sighted and unjust. Our prisons are dreadfully overcrowded and inhumane; we merely punish without rehabilitating. Our social agencies are understaffed and underfunded. Housing in the urban centers is a disgrace, and the suburbs refuse to share the cities' burdens. Yet Connecticut ranks third throughout the nation in per capita income, while we are third from the bottom in taxing the rich. The state finance committee of the legislature held a hearing on the income tax in the hall of the House in Hartford. Father O'Neill spoke for the Capital Region Council of Churches. I arrived at six-thirty, but I did not get a chance to relate my piece for the Social Responsibility Committee for my church until eleven. The members of the Finance Committee were most patient; they had written the bill for the income tax. There was a certain metallic hardness evident in those opposing the tax. People do not seem to realize that prosperity is not always fairly earned; so many have all the cards stacked against them at birth. However, there were some affluent individuals who endorsed the income tax. Today in my church at the time of the moment of concern, I spoke for the income tax, but I could sense that there were many who did not agree with me. Be that as it may, we will forge ahead. Our Constitution State must not be caught napping.

I do believe that Reagan's honeymoon is waning; he surely aspires to the presidency. We have been busy protesting the sending of military aid to San Salvador. The bravado of the present administration is something to behold. I can't believe that Congress will continue to let Reagan's regime cut out our good programs so drastically.

On the 27th of April Your Bishop Walmsley will address the spring assembly of the Capital Region Conference of Churches on Ecumenism. I like your thoughts on the subject very much. Tuesday night those who are interested in continuing our coalition on racism and prejudice are meeting to evaluate our past forum and make plans for future activities. Elsa Cullen, a Quaker and a delightful woman is going with me. We hope to be able to fashion a model in the Hartford region for other state localities to emulate.

It is fortunate that I live in an area where there are many children—all ages and sizes, for I do enjoy them as I walk about. Children have a certain ingeniousness that is most refreshing. On one corner I have two little friends, French boys of three and five who are delightfully natural and always happy to greet me.

Florence, my favorite sister-in-law, is ever urging me to gather more fun out of life instead of pursuing one cause after another down the garden path.

Spring is budding; I heard peepers for the first time tonight. Surely, 'tis a season of promise.

It is always good to hear from you. Stay well and happy.

With all my best,
Edna May

April 20, 1981
Vails Gate, New York
Dear Edna,

Thank you for your letter. It is good to learn of all the worth-while causes in which you are involved and to which you contribute so much. Your sister-in-law is quite mistaken. There is no way you could gather more fun out of life than what you are doing.

A state income tax would seem to be most timely. Our present national government will do all it can to relieve the wealthy and put the burden on the middle income people. The state could balance things up by going after the wealthy. But I fear so just a policy has little chance.

There is no real solution of our social problems as far as financing the necessary programs goes without a drastic cut in military spending. There is talk of a constitutional amendment that would require a balanced budget. That would be a good thing <u>provided</u> it restricted defense expenditure to not more than one-third of the total budge except in time of openly declared war. Needless to say, the military-industrial complex would never let such an amendment pass. Without the proviso the amendment limiting the deficit would eliminate social programs altogether, which is, of course, the perennial goal of the Republican Party.

I have not heard from Seabury Press how my book is going for some time now. We had to take 2000 copies at cost—which allows us to sell them at the reduced price. We are getting in sight of having to dispose of half of them. They move slowly but consistently. Seabury sent out its official announcement of my book only the middle of last month, so probably the response to it, if any, would be just beginning. So far I have seen no reviews of it, but again, the review copies went out only last month.

I hope your Eastertide is full of blessings for you and prosperity for all your good works.

As ever,
Bonnie

May 9, 1981
Dear Bonnie,

Thank you for your encouragement for my path of causes. Ever since I began school at the age of five, I have taken life quite seriously; before that I was a mischievous imp with boundless energy and a vivid imagination. Perhaps I can help the cause of social justice both in my own church and in the Capitol Region Conference of Churches—I have been dismayed to find those who believe churches should remain philosophical but not socially and politically active. Whatever do they think religion is for?

In Conn—we are still pursuing band-aid taxation; reform has been postponed. I want all our churches to sponsor tax reform wholeheartedly.

Democratic leadership in Congress has certainly fallen by the wayside. I find it hard to believe that our senators and rep. can be so weak and stupid. We surely suffer from a dazzling Hollywood complex in this country; how easily we are duped by Reagan and his buddies. It will take a great shock to produce an awakening, but it will come.

Finally, I decided to attend the 1931 Class Reunion at Williams. I have invited Elizabeth to come with me. She holds degrees from Mount Holyoke, Bryn Mawr, and the University of Illinois. She has retired to New London, N.H. after teaching English at Albion College in Michigan. Her father graduated from Williams in 1902. It was through him that George gained a scholarship to Williams, for he was the principal of the high school George attended. Elizabeth's mother was always an inspiration to George—who lost his mother in England when he was only two, and he supported himself completely from the age of fourteen. He never lost the "common touch"; I have never known him to be obsequious. He had a rare understanding of people; he was more tolerant than I, more forgiving.

I am conscious of the fact that the honorary membership for Williams' widows is primarily a hope for financial support. I have just made a new will, but I have continued to bequeath to Williams one-fourth of my estate—as George wished. I mean to repay Williams for his four year scholarship with interest.

Your book still provides me with many thoughtful moments. I have included a check for two more books. Perhaps I can place them where they will be appreciated.

As ever,
Edna

May 15, 1981
Dear Edna,

Thank you for your letter and the order for my books. They were mailed to you Wednesday. A surprising number of people have written me to assure me they have found it helpful and stimulating.

I am so happy to learn that you are attending the 1931 Reunion and I shall look forward to seeing you there. It will also be a pleasure to meet Elizabeth. George talked about her father often and was most grateful for all he had done for him. No doubt you are right that honorary members are encouraged largely for financial reasons, but then the whole business of alumni reunions have that as a major purpose. But as wives attend the reunions all along, friendships are developed which we like to continue. And it is good to have those who have gone beyond represented by their widows.

George was a great man. After all, he put up with me for four years as his roommate. That took some doing. I have always counted knowing him one of my great privileges. And it has been a joy to come to know you also.

All the best. See you in Williamstown.

As ever,
Bonnie

Thank you for the clipping on Northern Ireland. It is terribly sad—and like you I see no solution.

May 28, 1981
Dear Bonnie,

You books arrived on Friday, so they reached this destination in two days—the same length of time your letters take—quite remarkable! Your supply should be exhausted by fall.

Thank you for appreciating George. Many have not realized his true worth. My life with him has been my most rewarding experience—he understood so much without the expression of words. I do believe sensitivity is inborn. I know he enjoyed knowing you for he always spoke highly of you. He said that you never had to study much—you just knew.

Elizabeth you will find most interesting and honest with a quick mind. She is a true product of her mother's Scotch ancestry—she has a fine sense of values.

What do you think of Billy Graham and his mission? Our Capitol Region Conference of Churches Board of Directors just voted to become involved with the Hartford area committee for the N.E. Billy Graham Crusade in May 1982. I abstained in the vote because I need to know more about it. I have some questions.

Our Conference held an all day Saturday meeting to determine what the CRCC future should be (goals and structure). We have as our guide and consultant, an ordained pastor in the Dutch Reformed

Church, and a man who has had a wide experience in working with religious groups at every level. He currently teaches at a college in Maine where he and his wife live on a farm. He appeared to be highly capable, honest, and perceptive. It was a most enjoyable day. We need this soul searching and evaluation before we can look for a new director. Thank goodness our board has grown more lively, the rubber stamp approach has bothered me for some time.

Mary and I were enlightened the other evening when we attended a banquet presented by the Men's Club of the Bethel African Methodist Episcopal Church in Hartford to hear Mayor Maynard Jackson of Atlanta, Georgia. We enjoyed the people.

Now I am busy gardening with a new helper, a bright, eager seventh grade neighbor boy. Somehow our ministry seems to specialize in boys—I hope this does not presage a war. I have promised six little boys, ages three and six, a tea party on my back porch. We have two new baby boys around.

I shall be happy to see your Fiftieth Reunion in Williamstown. Have a wonderful time with all your old friends.

As ever,
Edna

June 6, 1981
Dear Edna,

Although I look forward to seeing you next weekend, I am writing now because of your question about Billy Graham. We might not have time to discuss him at the Reunion with all the things going on and all the people to see.

I am afraid I have little use for Billy Graham on at least 4 counts:

1. His attitude toward the Bible is fundamentally that of a literalist, that is, he takes literally those passages he finds useful, and usually takes them out of context. In other words, his brand of rigid Protestantism is exactly what the Bible says and to question it in any way is to reject Christianity.

150

2. This is the kind of obscurant is biblicism that provides the basis for the "moral majority" and other fascist reactionary groups. Don't forget that Graham was the religious advisor of Nixon, though he jumped off the bandwagon when he saw it would be to his disadvantage to stay. His concept of Christianity is the direct antithesis of everything I hold theologically, politically, and morally.

3. He is a revivalist, that is, his show is aimed at an emotionalism over sin that will induce people "to be saved." Most of those who respond have a nice emotional binge, and that is that. Those who do not respond have been subjected to a major build-up of guilt feelings which are not relieved and can do much psychological harm.

4. The whole "crusade" rests on a huge public relations extravaganza out of which many people, including Billy, make a big billing.

I wish I could say that I think its religious value is nil. Instead, I very much fear that it does enormous harm.

It will be a joy to see you in Williamstown. Meanwhile, all the best.

Bonnie

June 25, 1981
Dear Bonnie,

It was good to see you once more—it has been a long time. You looked wonderful, all must be going well for you. Thank you for your consideration at the Reunion. I tried not to interfere with all your activities and your joyous reunion with all your friends. From my point of view, the activities proved most enlightening. I liked your prayer on Saturday night. We thoroughly enjoyed the seminar on American Culture. The final note—the service at Thompson Memorial chapel was beautiful, but inevitably sad—as are all partings.

I drove Elizabeth home to New London, N.H., stayed overnight, and then drove on to Barre to see George's only full sister at a Convalescent Home. From there, I managed to make Manchester, Vermont for a night's lodging at a favorable spot—The Weathervane.

The long drive home to N.H. and VT—was soothing and peaceful in its great beauty of landscape. All of my life when I have been torn and disturbed, I have found solace in the beauty of nature. Where ever I find the beautiful, I find God. It is man in the error of his ways who creates ugliness. Your religious background is far deeper and broader than mine so feel free to set me straight.

I deeply appreciated your evaluation of Billy graham and heartily agree with you. You are an excellent thinker and express yourself so clearly.

Our detailed study of the activities and goals of our Capital Region of Churches is nearing completion—in the first part, although we shall be unable to advertise for a Director until the end of October, I am grateful for the honesty and perception of our consultant, who has been most thorough.

We already have eleven applicants (without advertising), and one has worked with Prof. Paulo Freir. Thanks to you, I have read his book.

Elizabeth and I visited Arthur Carr, Chair of the English Department at Williams, and a liberal, a man she knew at the U. Illinois. His wife, his second, was related to the Barclays in Barre, VT. George was very fond of Grandma Barclay. If God had given me a son, I said I would have named him Barclay. George Barclay Sole would have given me another G.B.S. But then, I suppose he would have been sent to Vietnam. Veterans of this war have never been properly appreciated.

With all my best wishes,
Edna

July 10, 1981
Dear Edna,

It was grand that you could be at the reunion, and meet Elizabeth. I felt that George was well represented and that meant much to me. I am glad you had such a happy trip afterwards. You are certainly right about the beauty of nature, and I fear all too often man spoils it. It is a sin of which we moderns are especially guilty, since we exploit nature for our selfish gratification. Other cultures were content to work with nature and did far less damage.

It was wise that the Capitol Region Conference of Churches made a careful analysis of its activities, goals, and needs before starting to look for a new director. Not only does it help you to know what kind of person you want but it is also helpful to the applicants to have as clear a concept as possible of what the job expectancy is. Furthermore, I am sure it has helped all of your to clarify your objectives. So many institutions go on doing things that are no longer productive because they have always done them. A periodic appraisal of activities is always a wise policy.

I do not remember whether I told you we elected a New Superior the weekend before the Reunion. He seems to be doing a fine job. He has made a couple of changes in the heads of houses which are very wise. Already the tone of West Park House has perked up beautifully and the new Prior has not actually moved in yet.

I hope you have not been bothered too much by the current heat wave. I must admit I am enjoying my air-conditioned cabin. Have a good summer.

Love,
Bonnie

July 31, 1981
Walled Lake, Michigan
Dear Bonnie,

The heat wave has indeed been unbearable so that I am relieved that you have air conditioning in your cabin. Here I have an air conditioner in my bedroom and an attic fan for the rest of the house so that it is reasonably comfortable. We purposely planted shade trees around the house for protection. Nevertheless, I manage to embark on my daily walks, especially after sundown. Some of my good neighbors worry about me as I follow my itinerary after dark; I still carry my big stick.

I have been here in Walled Lake, Michigan to visit George's nephew, Fred Sole and his wife Betsy with their three sons, Andrew-8, Brian-6, and Mark-4 since Sunday and expect to fly back this Sunday. The boys have been challenging and most lovable—even when they were naughty. Somehow, children have always intrigued me and have never seemed to get on my nerves. I always enjoy their spontaneity and utter lack of hypocrisy. One never knows what they will say next. The Danes have a fine understanding of little ones—in their literature and in their sculpture—perhaps it comes in part from their warm nature. Brian is still my favorite although Mark is truly enterprising, original and colorful in his quick intelligence. Brian's face is ever quietly revealing for he misses nothing. All adults need to retain some of the spirit of childhood. I observe the essential ingredients of family life provided by Fred and Betsy and marvel that so many that grow from deprived backgrounds ever make it. Certainly the Reagan administration and its cohorts have no understanding of the reasons for crime. Do you think the Democratic plan to let the Republicans have their way is to show the American people that their ideas will not work? Congress has been amazing!

I still expect more violence here and abroad this summer.

I am happy that you have a new Superior at West Park; it should prove most helpful. How many of your books do you still have? Mary and I discussed your book in some detail the other day when she came to visit. She has read it very carefully and likes your chapter on Liberation the best. We find it inspiring.

August 3, 1981

P.S. I wrote this letter in Walled Lake, sealed it ready to post, but did not reach a mail box until yesterday at the airport after five, so I decided the results would be better if I mailed it from Newington.

The one missing ingredient in the family I visited was discipline, which Andrew, the eldest, sorely needed. When I had the temerity to exert it without physical contact upon Andrew as I helped him in his reading, which he was too lazy to pursue, it was not appreciated so I learned what I should have known before—outside a school situation (and even there quite often) disciplinary coercion, no matter how enlightened, is frowned upon. Thank goodness the two younger ones are naturally eager to learn. Once a teacher, always a teacher, I presume.

A virus caught me unawares and slowed my progress—even the anti-biotic would not help, but now all is serene again.

All the best,
Edna

August 24, 1981
Vails Gate, New York
Dear Edna,

Since your letter was written, the weather here has been quite agreeable. I have not had the air conditioning on all month. Even in July I used it only on the most humid days. I really do not like it, especially when it is a single-unit blower.

I am sorry to learn that the virus got you, but it is good that you have recovered and had the visit in Michigan.

The summer has passed quickly and pleasantly for me. A couple of weeks ago I visited New York to see the summer exhibits in the museums and to have a bon voyage luncheon with the former Superior. He is going to Africa to take charge of a new house in Ghana.

The Democrats, if they ever recover, will claim that they let Reagan have his way to prove that it would not work. (I hope they are right in that prediction.) But I fear the situation is more complicated. The combination of northern Republicans and southern Democrats, which misgoverned this country in the latter half of the last century and most of the first third of this, has been formed again. Unless their policy meets with speedy and obvious disaster, they may well be in control for the rest of this century. It may be, however, that domestically things will blow up in the cities next summer.

My chief fear, however, is in foreign affairs. As someone said to me today, Reagan has starred in too many Westerns. To me he looks like a ham actor getting ready to play Henry V. It would be hilarious if it were not so dangerous.

My book seems to be doing well, though August is always the doldrums of the book trade. We have about 1000 out of 2000 left at Holy Cross. I do not know how Seabury is getting along. In July they inquired how many copies we had, apparently with an eye to buying some back, but we have heard nothing more of it. We shall see.

There was a good review of it in <u>The Living Church</u>, the chief paper of the Episcopal Church. So far I have not seen other reviews, but they always take a long time to come out. I have received quite a number of letters from individuals saying how much they have enjoyed it, which is very gratifying.

I may be going out to California in December. My only niece is remarrying and I hope to attend the wedding. If so, I plan to visit Santa Barbara and also our house in Berkeley. It will be pleasant to get into those parts again.

I hope all goes well with you and that you do not over-exert yourself when you take up your busy schedule in the fall.

Love,
Bonnie

P.S. I am so glad an expert agrees that this Communism is rigged. The "Defense" Department has it going so as to foster their aggressive spending.

September 16, 1981
Dear [Bonnie],

How wonderful that you will have an opportunity to return to Santa Barbara in December-just the right time of year, and weddings are such happy occasions. I have very fond memories of Mount Calvary in Santa Barbara. Does your father's painting still hang there?

You were most considerate then—and duly appreciated. I came with some trepidation, but left with renewed hope. The beauty and warmth have lingered through the years.

I read in the last Williams Review that my former English professor had died. I heard him at a Quaker Conference ages ago and found him fascinating—his command of the English language was delightful and his espousal of liberal causes heartwarming. I was always proud of Williams that he was retained on the faculty, despite his controversial positions.

You most assuredly have pegged Ronald Reagan correctly and superbly. In the same way you have assessed the Democrat-Republican wrangle succinctly. You have an uncanny faculty of reaching a point swiftly and dramatically. Certainly today democracy is on trial in our country. Our educational system has failed to prepare the young for effective participation in government. The young have needed many more deep first hand experiences in that area.

The other day I held a tea party for the very young on my back porch. They were delightfully eager and refreshing. Since then they have appeared at my door frequently. They seem to enjoy my house (We discuss my pictures) and they are always ready for cookies and are reconciled to the water days when Tang is not forthcoming. Sometimes they do weeding for me—even the four year olds. I pay them, of course. Their spontaneous, natural reactions always hold charm for me. I find them uplifting. One little seven year old girl inquired one day as she looked over my living room, "You're not a millionaire are you?" Only the very poor would accuse me of that for my surroundings are simple indeed.

My fall schedule has begun. So often I have been pressed into the post of secretary—because no one else will do it; it is a chore I never enjoy but—Our Religious Coalition for Abortion organization has a difficult road ahead, but we will persist. Thank goodness some of our conservatives in Congress are opposing the Moral Majority that I dub the Immoral Minority.

As ever,
Edna

October 3, 1981
Vails Gate, New York
Dear Edna,

It will be pleasant to return to Santa Barbara for a visit. Dad's paintings are still there—four of them. I believe they hang now in the Order's sitting room. I am also hoping to get back three of his that I left at St. Andrew's.

Last month the professed members of Holy Cross who live at West Park went up to our summer house in New London, New Hampshire for a long weekend. The first thing I did was to get in touch with Elizabeth and I had a pleasant visit in her house. I am most grateful to you for bringing her to the reunion. I presume you have noticed that she appears in the picture in the Alumni Review with me on her right. Unfortunately, you, on her left, did not get into the picture.

I wrote out senators about the abortion legislation. Moynihan is opposed in its present form, at least, and has put me on his mailing list. A recent communication from him pointed out that Carter was the only president since Hoover who accomplished <u>nothing</u> in the way of social legislation. He had all the best intentions but simply could not carry through. How much it was his fault and how much the refusal of the Democrats in Congress to cooperate, I do not know. I fear some of the blame was his. Just after he was elected president a person from Georgia, who was sympathetic to him, told me that, although he promised big reforms when governor of that state, he actually accomplished nothing. Apparently that was his pattern.

I shall be dividing my time between here and West Park as before, since the House of the Redeemer proposal has been rejected—much to my relief.

All the best.

As ever,
Bonnie

P.S. After I had sealed + stamped the envelope, I remembered your question about my book. (Hence the messy sealing.) Holy Cross

Publications has terminated its introductory offer of $9.95 and now sells the book at its regular price of $12.95. It has been going rather slowly this summer but we are hoping sales will pick up again this fall. The two reviews which I enclose should be some help. I hope to find out how it is going at the Seabury Press later this month.

October 10, 1981

Dear Bonnie,

It is good that you are permitted to get away sometimes. I am so happy for you that you took the opportunity to get in touch with Elizabeth, and she is most fortunate that you cared enough to visit her in her home. I like her house—it is a delight. She is a gracious hostess, a fine woman, and very intelligent. The pictures of both of you in the <u>Williams Alumni Review</u> are excellent. It does not trouble me in the least that my picture was not included.

Thank you for your efforts to cast light upon the abortion issue. Help is ever needed.

Surely Carter and Reagan are widely different from each other. Sometimes genuine caring individuals forego the benefits of charisma and popular public relations programs in their sincere efforts to bring about needed reforms. Too many of us are hoodwinked by superficial trappings that the unscrupulous find advantageous to the promotion of their selfish desires. Not every charisma is authentic. Witness <u>The Emperor's New Clothes</u>. And surely many of our Congressmen are found wanting in the manly virtues; they are not true leaders. In the last analysis, the lowly voter is at fault.

In all probability, you are already familiar with the enclosed article by Raymond Baker. It rings so true to me. How often religion is misused and abused. It seems to be so difficult for us to understand and respect beliefs of others. Wars based on religion have been deeply bitter down thru the ages. The reviews of your book must prove most heartening for they are beautifully stated and well deserved.

With best wishes,
Edna

October 22, 1981
Vails Gate, NY
Dear Edna,

Thank you for your letter and the clipping. The letter is very much to the point. Again I fear part of the responsibility must be laid on Carter. He never really put the pressure on Israel that he could have to supplement the Camp David accord with real action in meeting the legitimate Arab demands. Unfortunately all American politicians have to fear the Jewish vote. They are a minority, but one which votes, as other minorities do not. I must even admit that Reagan is being a bit pro-Arab, at least in his remarks, than Carter was when in the White House. Carter's statement, along with Ford's, that we should begin to deal directly with the PLO is encouraging. But of course, neither of them expects to run for any office again, so they are free to speak their minds.

Religious fanaticism is a tremendous danger today, especially fundamentalists in this country who operate through the "moral majority" and other such organs. One of the problems is the enormous amount of free TV + radio time they get through Sunday sermons which they use for outright political purposes but which does not count as political time + their opponents get no compensating opportunity to answer.

The latest good news of my book is that the Library Journal has included it among the 40 best religious books of 1981 in their special issue with another favorable review.

I hope all continues to go well with you.

As ever,
Bonnie

November 8, 1981
Dear Bonnie,

Your views on the Middle East situation and the dangers of the so called "moral majority" are very sound—as usual. It seems that the fabric of foreign policy as well as Reagonomics is starting to fray at the edges. Perhaps people will begin to understand that there are no simplistic solutions to our many problems.

On my last trip to the Hartford Seminary, I found the October issue of the Library Journal but no special issue. I will try again. In the October number, I thought Schwarzer's review was exactly right in its summary. It proves that a long, thoughtful, caring life is essential in search of real and enduring truths.

I gave one of your books to The Rev. Jackson Carroll, who is Coordinator of Research at the Hartford Seminary; he said he would place it in their library. The other one I gave to The Rev. Richardson Libby, Jr., who is the minister of the Grace Episcopal Church in Newington. Will you please send me two more books? If the check for twenty-eight dollars does not cover all the postage, let me know and I will send additional funds.

In October, I attended the last Fiftieth Reunion of 1931 at Williams. I drove all by myself and managed to arrive just as darkness descended. I missed you. I enjoyed talking to some of your wives, especially Mrs. Crane with whom I agreed on the necessary criteria for raising the young. Unlike my father and older brother, I have never been an athlete so I spent my afternoon at the Art Museum instead of viewing The Game. I am sure that participants have far more fun than mere spectators. Your friend, Jim Reynolds made a fine host— he is positive that I inherited genes of independence and would have passed them on given the opportunity. I skirted around the cocktail parties with just a ginger ale. Your brethren were most loyal to their alma mater. Thus I feel I have completed my course in Williams Alumni Enlightenment. I would have enjoyed more contact with the faculty and students, but I can probably do that on my own sometime.

Last Wednesday Mary 1 and I took Amtrak to New York City for the day—not bad. We did the city on foot, but found it was most beautiful at night—with all the lights. We encountered a maze of people on the streets, walking in anything but an orderly manner. We saw My Fair Lady and sat enthralled. Good theater is ever good therapy. I must do this more often. It all had a revitalizing effect.

May you achieve all your goals,
Edna

November 13, 1981
Vails Gate, New York
Dear Edna,

Thank you for your letter and for your help in distributing my book. I gave your check and order to Publications and they promised to get the two copies out today. You more than paid for postage.

I have not seen the special issue of the Library Journal myself. I was told about it when I checked in at the Seabury Press last month. I did finally get a chance to read the review in the St. Luke's Journal and found it much more favorable that I expected. There has also been a supportive review in the New Review of Books and Religion. For all this I am most grateful.

It was grand that you attended the baton-passing of our 50th Reunion.

November 22, 1981
Dear Bonnie,

Your books came very promptly and expertly packed as usual. The more I become involved in the Capitol Region Conference of Churches, the Religious Coalition for Abortions and the Network Against Prejudice and Inhumanity, the more I realize people need to read your book. Thursday evening, Dr. Raymond E. Smith, an independent education consultant, talked to us about Holocaust Education. The meeting upset me. I have never been able to understand how anyone could enjoy hurting others. Somehow through education, we must begin with the very young and continue guiding them so that they will help others. History is filled with needless human misery. God is not dead.

Tuesday evening at our RCAR meeting, I had a long argument with two very young men from some Roman Catholic school in Cromwell, Connecticut; they may be planning to become priests. They had come to oppose our movement for pro-choice. The more I talked with them, the more I instinctively liked them—in spite of our differences—for I felt they were sincere and a cut above average. I told them that they needed to read more widely and promised to lend them a copy of your book. I did not implicate you in any way with any kind of movement. I have promised the other book to a fine Quaker woman—Elsa, who sits on out Board of the Capitol Region Conference of Churches. I like and esteem all the women on our board.

Thank you for your invitation to lunch at the Players, I have never been there. I should love to come for it sounds delightful and I should love to see you. There are so many topics I should enjoy with you because you know so much. Will you let me take you to the theater— either a matinee or an evening performance? Will you select the play? I can come to New York sometime in January. If that is not convenient for you—you name the month and date. I will need to plan ahead also for I would spend two days in the city in the winter and I would need to find a safe hotel that is convenient, perhaps you have some suggestions.

I am happy for you that you can spend most of December in California. Will you be there for Christmas?

Always with best wishes,
Edna

December 10, 1981
Santa Barbara, California
Dear Edna,

Thank you for your letter and the interesting clipping. I think McElvaine has diagnosed the situation very accurately. I am also most grateful for the distribution you are giving my book.

It is kind of your to suggest combining lunch at the Players with a play. The club is functioning best on weekdays, so I should suggest a Wednesday matinee. I know little about the current shows. I have looked through the New Yorker and, although I am not fond of light musical comedies, perhaps <u>The First</u>, a serious musical, may be the best. The only other two that sounded good to me, and that have a Wednesday matinee, are <u>Misalliance</u> (a show play) and <u>Mass Appeal</u> (about Roman Catholic priests). By January there may be other things available, and some of these may be gone. I am entirely content to leave the selection to you, not restricting you to those I have mentioned. As for the date, so far as I recall, all the Wednesdays in January are free for me, except the 6th. (Unfortunately, I do not have my engagement book for January with me, but if when I get home I find a conflict I shall write at once.) I am afraid I do not know anything about New York hotels. There is, of course, the Gramercy Park Hotel across the park from the club, but I know little about it.

I am having a most pleasant time in California, seeing relatives, brethren + other old friends and finding a gratifying welcome everywhere.

It will be grand to see you in January. It had better be that month, since I am away most of February and March.

Have a glorious Christmas.

As ever,
Bonnie

December 28, 1981
Vails Gate, New York
Dear Edna,

Thank you for your Christmas gifts. They are both very useful and much appreciated.

The three Wednesdays in January, the 13th, 20th, and 27th, are all still open for me in case one of them turns out to suit you. When I learn which you prefer, I may make some appointments in New York to go with it, but I shall hold off on them until I hear from you.

My trip to California was most pleasant. I got to my niece's wedding, visited Los Angeles and our houses in Santa Barbara and Berkeley, and saw many old friends.

I hope you are having a glorious Christmastide and that the New Year brings much joy.

Love,
Bonnie

January 3, 1982
Dear Bonnie,

All of your Wednesday dates are presently open for me; I have chosen January twentieth so that you will have ample time to make all your arrangements. I do hope we do not encounter blizzards— just in case, I have decided to take Amtrak to Penn Station on the Tuesday before (December 19th) so I will be there. I plan to return to Connecticut Thursday-late afternoon, the 21st. I may as well visit my favorite art museums. Thank you for your selection of Mass Appeal. (The reviews are good, and I trust your judgment.) I will also try your Gramercy Park Hotel. In my copy of New York by Dave Ashton, I have a beautiful picture of the park, and its surroundings.

On CPTV the other night, I saw your Bishop Moore being interviewed by Dick Cavett. I liked him—as we say in N.E. he was "all wool and a yard wide".

The first Sunday in December as I was going home from church driving in second along slippery roads in Hartford; I survived a most unexpected experience. All went well underfoot, but from a tall stately Elm tree in Elizabeth Park big limbs came crashing from above on the top of my car, smashing my windshield to smithereens, badly denting my top, bashing the door on my side and damaging the two posts supporting the top and the windshield. It was quite a surprise; and luckily I was not injured in any way. I am glad it did not fall on the small cars behind me or some small child walking along. A young man came to my car to help me out the other side, and then he took me to his girlfriend's house to call the Hartford police. From there he returned me to my car where a Hartford policeman waited. He in turn called AAA for a towing job. After waiting an hour and a half he drove me home to my door; he was not supposed to cross the city line to Newington, but he did—saying that it was a Hartford tree that fell on me. Everybody treated me royally, I am indeed fortunate.

I am now in the market for another car. My garage man, who is most reliable, has offered to inspect any possible purchase. I will buy a safe, sturdy one. The insurance company was eminently fair in my settlement. They were surprised to find my 1972 Ambassador in such excellent condition. It has a superb engine and I always felt safe.

I am very glad that you had such a wonderful time in California. It was due you.

I shall be happy to see you in New York.

You have a beautiful outlook on life.

All the best,
Edna

January 6, 1982
West Park, New York
Dear Edna,

The arrangements are excellent. I also expect to get to New York, on Jan. 19—you wrote Dec + [I followed you]—so there will be no difficulty in our getting together on the 20th. Let us plan to meet at The Players (16 Gramercy Park) at about 12 noon. The dining room opens at that time and we shall not be rushed eating and seeing the club house before we leave for the theater. I am glad you chose Mass Appeal. I know no more about it than what The New Yorker said, but I trust it will be good.

I am sorry about your accident but it was fortunate you were not injured. I hope you found a good car to take the place of the one you lost.

This month I am gradually moving up to West Park from the Sisters. You might begin to address your mail here—Holy Cross Monastery, West Park, NY 12493.

In case you need to get in touch with me at the last minute I expect to be at Alsalom Jones Priory the night of the 19th. The telephone is 212-926-1400.

I look forward eagerly to seeing you on the 20th. All the best.

Love,
Bonnie

The weekend before I shall be at the Convent- 914-562-0592

January 25, 1982
Dear Bonnie,

Thank you for a lovely day in N.Y. City last Wednesday. It was a memorable occasion. The Players club was fascinating with its many mementos and vital history enhanced my very personal tour. You surely support an excellent chef! And I liked your brother. It was good to know you better. The ride to the theater was fun. You chose the right play and your presence made it more meaningful. I thoroughly enjoyed our walk back to the hotel—puddles, ices, and snow—it had a certain frivolity. I appreciated your words of wisdom—I am still pondering. There were so many topics I wanted to discuss with you, but I didn't get there. After you left me, I missed you—I always do. I wanted to take a long walk, but I did not dare brave the city elements so I paced the corridors. The next day after I had walked way uptown, I had quite a time trying to corral a taxi on Fifth Ave. to reach my hotel for my bag and then Penn Station for the train. I finally walked to Park Ave. tipped a doorman to get one (He tried to induce me to rent a limousine for twenty dollars. I told him that I would miss my train first.) But he did succeed in flagging a taxi with a most helpful and honest driver who carried me to my destination most expeditiously.

Do take care on your projected trips and have a delightful time. You looked quite dashing with your bright red tie.

If you ever find another play that you would like to see, I can easily get the tickets.

As ever,
Edna May

February 14, 1982
West Park, New York
Dear Edna,

Thank you for the letter and the reviews of the play. Johnson's comes closer to my appraisal of it. I think Kauffmann is right in feeling that the priest's failure to have experienced love is not fully explored, but I felt is sufficiently hinted. Her criticism of O'Keefe is quite unwarranted, but Johnson's praise of him is a bit excessive. I agree with Kauffmann about the ending; I felt it did not quite ring true. But both reviewers seem to me to have missed the real point of the play, namely, whether it is right that one should have to lie about one's sexual activities in the past, and one's sexual preference if it is homosexual, in order to get ordained to the priesthood. That was recently a controversial issue in the Episcopalian Diocese of New York, and will come up again in our General Convention; I felt the play's presentation of the problem was forceful and timely.

I am glad you enjoyed your visit to New York so much and overcame the hazards of perambulation and transportation successfully.

My visit to Toronto was delightful. The Profession of Brother James Rober—my closest friend among the younger members of the Order-was a great joy, and I saw several old friends and made new ones. I anticipate an equally good time on my next trip—to the South.

All the best.

Love,
Bonnie

March 11, 1982
Dear Bonnie,

As usual, you write a reasonable and perceptive analysis succinctly expressed when you evaluate <u>Mass Appeal</u>. Upon reflection, I feel that Davis was questioning commonly accepted Roman Catholic practices—and rightly so. In my opinion, The Rev. Hans Kung's views are sound. I am happy that he was appreciated in Chicago in 1981. I believe that his convictions will prevail among American Roman Catholics some time in the future—at most, a century from now,—and surely when the present Pope is succeeded by a more liberal man, enlightenment will begin.

I liked O'Keefe; he was far better material for the priesthood than Father O'Shea, who left much to be desired. His dependence upon alcohol showed that he had not resolved his personal problems; likewise, he lacked a proper respect for the truth; he was not a leader. I admired O'Keefe for his daring to tell the truth even though it meant that he would lose what he most wanted in life. It is easy to tell the truth if there are not penalties involved. Of the two, the younger man was far more mature. Religion must face questions and honor truth.

Age and maturity are not always synonymous.

If you have time, will you react to the clipping I have enclosed? For the most part, it seems rational to me, but you are the philosopher. You don't need this because you will always be young in spirit—as you should be.

Finally, I found a car (second-hand) at Hertz—1981 Oldsmobile Cutlass with some 17,500 miles clocked. It is white-so it can be seen at night,-sturdy (I hope it can take a falling tree), and comfortable. I expect it to be with me for ten years—I have a curious penchant for acquiring things that last. And it was a good buy. Sometime when you are available, I will give you a ride in the car that is new to me.

In Connecticut, we are being plagued again by the Ku Klux Klan. In preparation for a statement we are making from the Capital Region Conference of Churches, I reread parts of your book (I often do)—especially the chapter on Liberation. You certainly see clearly and know how to express your thoughts. Thank you for writing the book.

I am so glad you had a delightful time in Toronto—I am sure you were a great joy to all of them.

Have a happy time in the South, where you will reach an early spring—congratulations.

Now I am off to a meeting of NAPI (Network Against Prejudice and Inhumanity).

Edna May

April 2, 1982
West Park, New York
Dear Edna,

Your letter was awaiting me when I returned to West Park. It arrived too late to be safely forwarded to Idaho.

Your comments on <u>Mass Appeal</u> coincide with mine. I felt it was a most penetrating play and I am very grateful to you for taking me to it, when I was in Chicago I had a chance to meet members of the faculty of the Catholic Theological Union there. They are, of course, much more progressive than the rank and file Roman Catholics and, although they did not say so for obvious reasons, they are clearly unhappy with the Pope. But as you say, someday things will change.

Incidentally, I found considerable enthusiasm for my book—<u>God who Dares</u>, including by one R.C. theologian (David Tracy). And in one library we asked the computer what other libraries had copies. To my amazement it took two computer screens to list them. In nearly every state at least one library has it! Today I got a letter from the Archbishop of the West Indies enthusing over the book. All very gratifying.

The article on the youthful spirit I find very interesting, indeed, I fully agree with it. There is really no reason why people have to suffer from the hardening of their mental and spiritual arteries, whatever their physical ones may do. The secret is twofold, I think: 1) keep open to new ideas; 2) keep contact with young people—not children so much as those who are beginning to think for themselves. My father was an excellent example of this. He never became set in his ways, either in general terms, or in his art. In his 80's he was still learning new techniques and adopted some modernistic trends. I try to do the same theologically and liturgically. I think the reception my book has had is some indication that I have not completely failed.

I am delighted to learn of your new car. I hope it turns out to be all you expect.

I rejoice that you are working on so many good projects to oppose the prejudices and injustices of our society, so many of which corrupt Christianity to claim its support.

May you have a blessed Easter.

Love,
Bonnie

April 27, 1982
Dear Bonnie,

It is truly most rewarding that you had the opportunity to stop at so many places as you traveled west, and how fortunate for them to have had you for inspiration. I discovered all this as I read your calendar of events in the Holy Cross. Which libraries in Connecticut have your book? I will check around here. Only a youthful spirit with a long and wide background could have written your book; you have indeed been successful in your mission. What happy, fulfilling memories you must have of your father. I am glad you recovered his paintings. I thoroughly enjoyed the page about Mount Calvary Retreat House. It is a most heavenly spot, and it holds very fond memories for me.

I do hope we can bring our search for a new Executive Director for the Capitol Region Conference of Churches to a happy close on May seventeenth. We received 71 applications from all over the country. All six members of our committee plus the past president have read all of them. We have interviewed 11, including three blacks, two of whom seemed outstanding to me. One, Rev., who has served eight years as Director of Programs for the Council of Churches of the City of New York, Interchurch Center, 475 Riverside

Drive, New York City, appears to have all the credentials. Surely, he was the best prepared for the interview. (I had sent each candidate a thick packet of materials to review before our meeting.) He was intelligent, sensitive, sophisticated, understanding, emotionally stable, and virile—my observation. I am now trying to find out more about him from different sources. Do you know anything about him? He is a Congregationalist, who was born in New York City in 1937. If necessary, I shall run down to the city to find out before our next meeting on May fourth.

We also interviewed a young black Baptist minister, graduate of Yale Divinity School, Mary l and I visited his church on Sunday. I have never seen a group of people who looked cleaner and better scrubbed. They were a warm, loving, caring, happy, rhythmical congregation. And the children were adorable. I do not believe we as whites really understand them and their needs. We have deep minority problems in this region.

We were also impressed with a Nathan H., a white man—Presbyterian, former Executive Director of new Commission on Regional-Local Ecumenism of the National Council of Churches and Assistant General Secretary, now responsible for ecumenical relations, development education and information for CODEL, Inc. 79 Madison Avenue, N.Y. City.

Do pray for us!

If there is some theatrical production you would like to see in New York City sometime in May or June, I should love to take you if you care to go.

Edna

May 7, 1982
West Park, New York
Dear Edna,

Thank you for your two letters. I am glad you found out the truth about one of the candidates before it was too late. As you say, it is necessary to check. The kind of person who makes a fine first impression is hard to resist, yet, as in this case, can be fatal. Unfortunately, I know nothing about any of the persons you mention or about anyone else who might be available, so I can be of no help to you.

I did not take the time to find out which libraries have my book, or even in which states they are. I merely glanced at the computer screen and was astonished at the number of entries.

I am much interested in the article from the <u>Hartford Courant</u>. It analyzed aspects of the situation I did not know. However, I cannot help but feel it is too bad England has allowed itself to be embroiled in this way over 1,800 Falklanders. It would have been so much wiser—and less expensive—to move them to New Zealand or Australia, or another sheep-raising country, if they were not willing to accept Argentinian rule. It is ridiculous for England to try to maintain sovereignty over those worthless islands at so great a distance.

I shall be going to Toronto again this month to attend the 50th anniversary of ordination to the priesthood of two of our Brethren. Then I hope to get to Williams as a member of the "Old Guard."

I fear May and June are too crowded for me to get to another play. Thanks for offering.

All the best.

As ever,
Bonnie

May 27, 1982
Dear Bonnie,

Let us hope the Falkland Islands conflagration does not escalate. It is a needless tragedy. In part, I blame our President Reagan with his bungling foreign outlook. How could we have elected such a stupid illiterate myopic individual! We seem to be blind to the devastating low regard for humanity in Latin America. While England is right as far as principle goes it does seem that the government its long history of diplomatic negotiation could have found a different solution. The present regime is ultra conservative.

Monday night our Capitol Region Conference of Churches brought an outstanding speaker, the Assistant Director of the Riverside Church Disarmament Program. I wish that half of Hartford could have heard him. I gathered information I have as yet not uncovered in my reading. Unless we stop this mad arms race soon, there will be no more life on this planet. The desire for power is indeed a great evil. Why does man use his brains for the wrong purposes?

Finally the seven members of our Search Committee voted unanimously for a man from New Jersey. We interviewed him again in West Hartford. I liked his wife. I tend to judge a man in part by the woman he chooses to marry. The Board of Directors approved our choice, but our candidate decided not to come. Thus, we must search anew for we cannot agree on the others. This time we are pursuing another route. We are enlisting suggestions from those we trust. We finally induced the Board to raise the limits of the salary. We have an additional problem in that our acting Director is also applying for the part, but I do not feel he is strong enough as a leader. Fortunately, our new Vice President has joined our crew. Now we are eight. Our staff seems restive and confused so we must meet with them.

The world is now very beautiful, and my car is functioning well. My walks are a true safety valve for me—two to five miles a day.

May life warm and enrich you in every way.

Edna

June 15, 1982
West Park, New York
Dear Edna,

The Falkland's affair seems to be over. England's veni, vidi, vici, is as boring to me as was Caesar's. If it brings down the Argentine Junta, that will be to the good. But its strengthening of Margaret's hand is unfortunate and the expenditure of such money, effort, and life to recapture islands England does not really want is too stupid for words. Israel's unchecked and uncondemned invasion of Lebanon is a greater grief to me. My sympathies, I fear, are 100% on the side of the PLO. After all the noise we made about the invasion of Afghanistan! Oh well, Jews have votes and Arabs do not.

I should have liked to take part in the New York rally last Saturday, but I wanted more to attend the Williams Alumni Reunion as a member of the Old Guard. There were 9 of us from 1931 and we had a glorious time. The college entertained us royally.

I am sorry that the candidate on whom you agreed decided not to come. That is really frustrating. I hope that by now you are reaching agreement on another and that he accepts. As you say, it has been an arduous search.

I fear I paid little attention to the Pope's visit to England. Neither he nor the Archbishop are my heroes. I am glad of the ecumenical aspects, but I fear nothing can come of them under such conservative leadership.

I shall be supplying in various parishes most of the summer, so I shall have to stick close to home, except for three weeks in Canada.

All the best.

Love,
Bonnie

July 15, 1982
Dear Bonnie,

How delightful that you were able to spend three weeks in Toronto; I hear that it is a beautiful city. I am so happy that you had such a glorious time at your Williams Reunion; it was due you.

Once more our committee members have agreed on a candidate for the position of Ex. Director of CRCC—although our Roman Catholic member is not for him. In her absence of one month, the priest authorized to take her place voted for our candidate. In all fairness, I shall present our vote to the Board on July 20th. I have bent over backward to be fair to all, especially the Roman Catholics. All admit I have been fair and honest. If the Board does not approve or if something happens to our candidate, I have another possibility-a Congregationalist from Maryland, one who once served a church on the Green in N.H. He is the only one I interviewed who said he found the material I sent him exciting. I do appreciate individuals who have a zest for living. The members of our committee have been faithful and industrious. We will march on fearlessly and fairly.

Friday night, I attended a wedding at a Covenant Church. Both the bride's minister and the groom's participated in the 8 o'clock ceremony. It was a beautiful church—my first experience there. The groom was George's great nephew—Thomas Sole, who graduated two years ago from West Point. (He ranked sixth in a class of 900; he was first during his last year.) They were married over a year ago by a Justice of the Peace so they all wanted a church ceremony. They have a beautiful 4 month old baby girl whom I adored. At ten o'clock I rescued her from her many admirers and carried her to the peace of the nursery where she could recover; she cried so hard for she had had enough. It is strange how people do not seem to understand how sensitive babies can be.

This week Thomas and Robin return to the state of Washington, where he is currently stationed with an engineering unit. He hopes someday to return to West Point to teach. I could not resist reminding him that fathers were just as necessary in rearing children as mothers. According to my observations daughters who were blessed with happy, wholesome relationships with their fathers are less vulnerable to male exploitation at a later date, and sons need an admirable male model to develop properly.

I visited a Day Care Center of Salvation Army the other day and felt right at home with the three to five year olds. I may go to help—Perhaps I shall become the story lady for I have always found children's literature fascinating.

Your monastery at West Park sent a beautiful introduction to you recently. May you continue your message.

Edna

August 5, 1982
West Park, New York
Dear Edna,

Your letter has been left unanswered too long, but I have been very busy getting the files of the Associates of Holy Cross in order. I have just taken over as the director for the East and Mid-west.

I am glad your Committee was able to agree on an Executive Director. I hope he was approved by the Board and that he was accepted. It does not surprise me that the lay Roman Catholic objected on narrow religious grounds whereas the priest did not. The teaching of laity has always been rigid—it is better now but it is still a matter of dogmatically-stated principles rather than an encouragement of thought. The clergy are somewhat better equipped.

Thomas Sole sounds like quite a person. He should go far. George would have been very proud of him and I know he appreciates your attending the wedding.

The news from Washington remains disquieting. I see the White House cowboy wants to transfer still more funds from social services to the armed forces. He is a most dangerous megalomaniac! And now the Senate has passed the balanced budget amendment. The result can only be less + less for public service + more and more for the armed forces. I am disgusted at the hordes of Democrats who voted for it, and proud of the Democrats + Republicans who opposed it. It is the purest jingoism. Please God the House may have more sense but I doubt it. I much fear the country is rapidly reaching the point from which there will be no recovery, no matter what happens in November.

The article in the spring newsletter was somewhat embarrassing, but one has to get used to that as one grows older.

The behavior of the Israelis is beyond all. I hope it will result in a solidification of the world against them.

I hope you are having a good summer and that, once the Executive Director is settled, your will be able to get away for a bit.

As ever,
Bonnie

August 26, 1982
Dear Bonnie,

You surely work hard—even more as the years go by. Your church is indeed fortunate to have you and it is most thoughtful of you to share your wisdom with another book.

Thank you for explaining why it has been easier for me to relate to the priest than the Catholic layperson. The Board of Directors of our Capitol Region Conference of Churches voted for our candidate—, who was ordained in the United Methodist Church in 1959 and is presently Executive Director of the Greater Bridgeport in Connecticut. The lady who spoke against him, cast the only negative vote, and one black Methodist minister in Hartford abstained. We had excellent attendance at the meeting, and the members seemed satisfied. One Congregational minister, who is quite discerning, mentioned as he passed by me, "As far as I am concerned, all the negative comments were on the positive side." I feel that we are very fortunate to have the new man, who comes aboard September 20th. He is very intelligent, honest, dynamic, sensitive, kind, and is willing to travel the extra mile. I have sent letters to all the candidates we rejected, and when I have written notes of appreciation to all the members of my committee, I shall have fulfilled my promise. The members were faithful and supportive. We all learned a great deal and grew to understand each other in the dedication to our cause. At least each one said exactly what he thought; I greatly appreciated the honesty.

I concur with all your political opinions. Surely Reagan is the most stupid president we have had since Coolidge, and our Congressmen are in a fog. How can anyone expect to win a nuclear war?

I have been busy doing whatever I can (telephoning, writing, delivering flyers) to help the candidacy of the lady, who is running for the State Senate in our district. She is a liberal and intelligent. We have a Democratic primary on the seventh of September.

Thus far, my car has been giving good service. Someday I hope I can give you a ride in it.

Even in my church, we have gained a certain conservative element with whom I frequently disagree.

I know I need to get away, but I have not yet decided where or when. My favorite sister-in-law, Florence, has been urging me to do just that for some time.

With my best wishes,

Edna

September 30, 1982
Dear Bonnie,

It is always good to hear from you; it helps. As usual, I agree with your political views. Somehow I am a bit optimistic about the outcome of the fall elections—perhaps that is because by nature I am ever hopeful. Basically most people seem to be concerned with the economic picture, and that is not good today. As one of our church members said recently, "The nuclear freeze is essential and realized by most, but if we do not solve the problems in the various trouble spots round the world—notably the Middle East—we are asking for a nuclear holocaust." The Israelis are too intelligent and crafty no to have known early about the slaughter in Lebanon. Begin and Sharon are not to be trusted. When will people realize that violence inevitably breeds violence? We do not choose to learn from the past—unfortunately.

I am glad that some of the American fathers are assuming responsibility for their Asian offspring.

We have had our first Board meeting with our new Capitol Region Conference of Churches Executive Director, and he shows great promise. There are those who feel sorry for the past Acting Executive Director and do not truly realize his shortcomings; our former head, who served some nine years, was too domineering. In all my life, I had never served on a board that was so apathetic. That feature has really improved over the last year and a half.

Mary and I found peace and great beauty among the hills and mountains of Vermont and New Hampshire. The color was glorious, the air exhilarating, and the walking rewarding. Our only reservation was for the first night in Manchester, Vermont at the Weathervane, an old favorite of mine. Since we did not start until late afternoon, we finished by driving in the dark, and I had not learned how to manipulate my high beam, but we made it. The first day I drove because we took my car, but after that we took turns, and Mary did a great deal of driving. (A guest at the Weathervane instructed us about the high beam—what a difference!). North Conway, N.H., another favorite of mine was a great disappointment for it is too busy and highly commercialized. When I go to the country, I like a truly rural atmosphere.

Since I received an invitation from your chairman and his wife, I decided to attend the Williams Reunion on the 8th. The scheduled classes interest me, but I think I shall substitute the Art museum for the Game on Saturday. If you come (You probably won't), I can give you a ride if you wish. Let us hope the weather will prove cooperative.

With all my best wishes,
Edna

September 2, 1982
West Park, New York
Dear Edna,

Your letter was awaiting me when I returned from Canada. It is good to hear from you and to learn that your candidate was accepted by the Board. You worked hard at his selection and I am confident that he will prove the man for the job.

Much as I hate to give Reagan credit for anything, I must admit his speech about Palestinian rights is the best any President has produced. Fortunately it will cost the Republicans Jewish vote which will be a help in November. But we must get out of Begin's pocket or the Arab world will fall completely into the hands of the USSR. Reagan, of course, will change his "mind" again on this as on everything else. But I hope it will be too late.

I do not share Judith Paterson's fears about the South. The new Republicanism is a problem, but it is merely a continuation of the southern Democrats who always voted Republican. I feel it is better for them to be so labeled. The Democratic Party has often seemed incapable of accomplishing its purposes when it is in "control," because many so labeled are crypto-Republicans. Thus at the moment the House, supposedly Democratic so far as the majority is concerned, has consistently acquiesced in most of Reagan's policies. I am greatly encouraged at the material coming from the Democratic National Committee. It recognizes the real difference between the two parties. I hope there may be at least a slight redress in November.

I do hope you take a vacation. You have worked hard and long over the new executive director. All the best.

As ever,
Bonnie

October 7, 1982
West Park, New York
Dear Edna,

Thank you for your card and letter. It is good that you had the trip to Vermont and New Hampshire. They are my favorite states in the East—and so for that matter, anywhere. For I much prefer the East to any other section of the country.

I consider it most important that the Democrats recapture Congress and some important governorships. But I find myself less hopeful that I was a few weeks ago. I gather there is considerable apathy, a feeling that no one can do anything about it anyway. I should be happier if the mood was "Throw the rascals out."

It is good that your new Executive Direct is off to a good start. You are quite right about the Acting Director. A person in that position should not be running for the permanent job. If he wanted to be considered, he should have resigned and become a candidate like everyone else. It is also fine that the Board is taking more responsibility. The paces you put them through in selecting the new Director contributed much to their awakening.

On the whole, I am more comfortable about the Lebanon + Near East situation. Begin has got himself in real trouble. The PLO, on the other hand, has behaved with dignity and advanced to the status of a viable diplomatic group. I wish we would recognize them. The assassination of the first president of Lebanon was sad, of course, but very fortunate. His brother is a more reasonable man and has a better chance of uniting the country. I must admit I am as angry at the Lebanese "Christians" as am at the Israelis.

I hope you have a good time at the Reunion. I shall be in Tennessee preaching at the ordination of one of our Brothers.

Love,
Bonnie

October 28, 1982
Dear Bonnie,

It is wonderful that you have an opportunity to travel about the country. Do you always go by air? I am glad that you prefer the East.

Let us hope that all our American voters will see the light Tuesday. For the most part, we have a strong liberal element in Connecticut, but one never knows. I have been working for Cynthia Matthews, a fine, caring woman, a Democrat from Wethersfield, who is running for our state senate. I have also contributed to the campaign for Toby Moffett, who is working very hard to be elected to the U.S. Senate. While Lowell Weicker, the Republican, has proved himself to be superior to most Republicans in the U.S. Senate, I feel Moffett is more liberal and dependable. The article by Harsch that I am enclosing I do not like, but I think you can evaluate it more incisively than I. Reagan's philosophy is so abhorrent to me that I cannot bring myself to vote for anyone who supports him. Our people do not understand government very well. Many individuals on my list to call informed me that they were not interested in the election. And so many Americans have sacrificed so much that we might have the privilege of the ballot.

I made the Williams Reunion, but arrived late. One of the old crowd kept smoking and talked too much. He did not stop even after I told him I was allergic to smoke. He is fast drinking and smoking himself into the grave. I could not understand why anyone urged him to drink more. Ted who sat at the same table had more sense. As usual, Jim and his wife were most gracious. Rhoda rode home to West Hartford with me. We enjoyed a walk around Litchfield en route. She has a beautiful home, and she showed me the pictures of her children and grandchildren who were precious.

Thus far, our CRCC is progressing under the leadership of the new Reverend who has a strong grasp on the situation. In the name of the CRCC the VP of the Finance Dept. presented me an orchid for my work on the Search Committee. I am not the orchid type, but it was very lovely. And I was fortunate in my committee who were most supportive.

The world is <u>still</u> <u>very</u> <u>beautiful</u> in its autumn tones during our most welcome Indian summer, and I remember Galsworthy.

May life hold only the best for you.

Edna

November 3, 1982
West Park, NY
Dear Edna,

Please forgive the paper. I picked up this pad in mistake for an unlined one and got home with it before I noticed it. I want to use it up.

Well, your columnist was right. The cowboy pulled it off in the Senate and I suspect that is all he needs. I do not see it as the endorsement he thinks it is, or pretends to think it. The races for the Senate were extremely close and the incumbent always has a slight edge. They won on that in almost every case. But the further difficulty in the areas where the Democrats had the best chance overall of unseating Republicans, was that the latter were almost all anti-Reagonites so far as a member of his party could be. And several of them were in important Senate positions where they could exert more influence than their opponents even if the Democrats had won control of the Senate. Weicker is a case in point and also the Republican from Vermont—chairman of the environment committee. So although there is no change in the number of party votes, I think Reagan may have more trouble with the new Senate. He certainly will with the House, although I just heard the television assert that conservative Democrats and Republicans could still form a Reagan majority. I doubt it, but we shall see. In this district we elected a Democrat to his fifth term, although it is a heavily Republican area. Our section of the county has just been put into his district, so I rejoice now to have a Representative who votes as I like to see him. We also elected a Democratic Assemblyman! Thank God Cuomo got the governorship. Lehrer was truly awful. Perhaps the most significant thing for the future is the election of Governors. They can be a great help in 1984.

I feel this ambiguous result may be all to the good. Had the Democrats got control of the Senate, the ball would then have been in their court. They could either refuse to do what the President wished and have their actions vetoed, or they could work out compromises that he would accept + thereby identify with his policy. The latter would leave them in a poor position for 1984. The former would not only paralyze the government, but would be to the Democrats' advantage only if it was obvious that they were advocating sound policies, which the President was frustrating. Now the Democrats at the moment have no leadership and no independent, still less worth-while, policy. So it is better to let Reagan continue his course, with such mitigations as may somewhat protect the poor and oppressed, until he crashes on the rocks and must take full responsibility for the shipwreck. It will be painful, but out of it may emerge some Democratic leadership and, please God, some new ideas. As I wrote you in a letter or two back, there was too much apathy this time. The Democrats did surprisingly well in spite of it, but Reagan was able to capitalize on it and plead for a bit more time. I think many voters felt that Reagan's policy had not completely failed and, since the Democrats offered nothing better, that they should give him a chance to see if the lower inflation rate, lower interest, and rising stock market might also eventually stimulate industry and lower unemployment. Maybe they are right—we shall see.

There is a good possibility I might be getting out of it. The Order is Founding a new house for our African members in Ghana, close to a new Anglican seminary, where our men can be prepared for the priesthood. The seminary needs faculty and the Superior asked if I would be willing to go. I said yes, and checked out whether the local bishop and the head of our house would welcome the kind of teaching I should want to give. Apparently the answer is yes, and today the Superior approved of my going out next fall. I am not making a final decision until I have seen my doctor for a check-up on the 16th. If he sees no obstacle and if my health stands up in Ghana itself, I may go out and stay for a considerable time. The economic situation there is extremely bad, but I gather one can adjust, and many people feel that the future both of the Church and of civilization lies in Africa. If I can make a small contribution to the former, it would be a most satisfying swansong.

I have not heard whether Cynthia Matthews won. Too bad about Moffett—he made a good showing. I note that in your electioneering you ran into the apathy I referred to above.

You certainly are a sport to keep going to the Williams reunions when you do not smoke or drink + when they are attended mostly by ardent Republicans. I am sorry about S—he always was a bounder. I am pleased that the new director of the CRCC is doing well, as you expected, and that they recognized your contribution to the process of finding him.

I hope all will continue to go well with you.

Love,
Bonnie

November 7, 1982
Dear Bonnie,

Your welcome and excellent letter arrived yesterday. It shook me up quite a bit; in fact, I could not sleep very well last night because I am deeply concerned for your welfare. (Please do not go to Ghana.) I cannot bear the thought of your being sent to that distant land that is beset by so many deep problems including poor hygiene. It seems suicidal to me. I cannot understand how your Superiors could ask you to take such great risks at this time just as I cannot comprehend how your doctor would let you go under all the circumstances. In seminary teaching you would be superb—they know that—but not in Ghana where the dangers are so many. You have numerous valuable gifts, and you have given them freely to your church and humanity all your life. You are far superior to your classmates that I have met at your Williams class reunions. You are needed in your own country where brilliant minds, lucid expression, sensitivity, and honesty are in such short supply.

I still hope to see you.

As always, your analyses of the various election evaluations and results are most penetrating and sound. It was a joy to read them.

Cynthia Matthews won, and I am grateful, but I hope Toby Moffett and Bill Curry who ran for U.S. House + for whom I worked remain in politics to run again in the near future; we need them. People do not realize how much they are needed at the polls. It is true there was still too much apathy. Some of my conversations with potential voters were most revealing. Most are not well informed.

I care about you and want only that which is best for you—whatever it is that you truly want.

Sincerely,
Edna

P.S. Your writing paper was fine.

November 20, 1982
West Park, New York
Dear Edna,

Sorry I caused you a sleepless night, I assure you, your fears are quite unwarranted. Africa is no longer the primitive place we so often imagine it. Even in Bolahun, which is very back country in Liberia, life is not too difficult. But I shall not be going there. Instead, the house and seminary are in Cape Coast. I have never been there, but I did visit Accra and Kumasi when I was in Ghana and they are thoroughly urban. So is Cape Coast, another principal city. We are building our priory now, so it should be quite modern.

I delayed answering you until I had seen my doctor for an annual check-up. He assures me there is no reason why I cannot go to Ghana. Actually, the diet will be far better for me than what I eat here. I shall have a hernia operation before I go, to get that out of the way. The doctor can anticipate no other problems that cannot be handled in Cape Coast. They have good doctors and a hospital.

As for usefulness, there can be no question but that the little I have to offer will be more useful there than here. Not only does the seminary need teachers, but I think I have something to offer, along the lines of my last book, that will bring some fresh air into the stuffy theological scene. Also my experience in the revision of our Prayer Book may be of use to them, since they are now embarking on the process of revision. Everybody is most flatteringly enthusiastic about my going, even some seminary professors, whom I should I expect to consider me under qualified.

I shall not be going until sometime in the summer. Meanwhile, I hope to write another book and to assemble a library for our house and the seminary. That should keep me happily busy. So please do not worry about me. If all goes well, I shall miss the personal contacts for a while, but we can keep in touch by letter. All the best.

As ever,
Bonnie

November 29, 1982
Dear Bonnie,

Your recent letter made it very clear that you want above all to take your swansong in Ghana. Since I want for you only that which will bring you true happiness, I wish you great joy and fulfillment in your new adventure and will dwell on only the positive elements. I promise not to play the part of mama bear with only one cub.

Surely both your mind and your soul will grow immeasurably in your quest to explore the new and to make for a better world. Your spirit will ever be young. There is no doubt that you have a great deal to give them, probably more than anyone else. Your last book was an inspiration and cannot help but bring "some fresh air into the stuffy local theological scene." To me it breathes new hope into your denomination. And your experience with the reunion of your Prayer Book will prove to be supremely helpful. Certainly, your understanding and compassion will touch the very fiber of each African being and bring them great comfort.

I am glad that your doctor gave you such a good report and hope that your operation does not cause you too much discomfort. When do you plan to have it?

Your new book as well as your preparation of a library should keep you "happily busy" during your period of waiting.

In your new world you will make many new friends—an experience which you always enjoy.

May you have a bright and satisfying future.

With all good wishes,
Edna

December 17, 1982
West Park, New York
Dear Edna,

You are very kind to take in your stride what I know seems to you a foolish venture. But I assure you that, if I can pull it off, it may well be of real value to the Church in Africa, or at least in Ghana. I think I have something to give them that they may not be likely to obtain from other sources. My contact with + integration of modern insights, not only in theology, but in other fields, are not often found in elderly persons who are willing to give up a potential career in this country (which, of course, I no longer have) to go to a foreign country to share it with them. And, as you say, I shall be richer for the experience.

I am writing from St. Luke's Hospital in New York, where I had a successful hernia operation yesterday morning. To be writing letters twenty-four hours later is an indication of how well I am recuperating. I was able to go to the toilet yesterday afternoon under my own steam, and I hope to take a walk down the corridor when I finish this letter. I am very fortunate in my recuperation powers.

The library is coming along well as far as duplicates I have been able to find go. I also have some hopes for cash grants that will enable me to purchase new books that would not come in duplicates.

My own next book seems to be taking shape in my mind very nicely. I am almost ready to begin writing. The stay in the hospital has also enabled me to get a few more books read. And as soon as I get out, I shall be able to take the time while I have to take things a little easy to finish up the rest.

May you have a blessed Christmastide.

Love,
Bonnie

December 25, 1982
Dear Bonnie,

Thank you for letting me know about your operation. Your letter arrived the twenty-second. Somehow I had a feeling that this event was taking place. It is wonderful that you are recuperating so quickly. The good life has its own rewards. From your account I inferred that you would be sent home a week after your operation at the latest. On the twentieth, I mailed you a Christmas package and trust it will reach you some time.

Do take all the necessary time to make a full recovery—Mama Bear.

The reasons you gave for wanting to go to Ghana are quite valid—you will indeed make a valuable contribution. I think I understand the urge and the opportunity involved. I am sure George would agree with you. [I never think of you as elderly.] Your outlook and youthful spirit will prevent your from growing old—and the years have given you a certain wisdom—Mama Bear hopes you will be prudent concerning health angles—etc.

Is your current diet short on fruit and vegetables?

Your new book will be a welcome addition.

Most Sincerely,
Edna

December 25, 1982
West Park, New York
Dear Edna,

How you do it I shall never know! My poor old alarm clock was just about to give up the ghost, when your splendid Christmas present arrived. I cannot tell you how much I appreciate it. It is already functioning gaily and silently at my bedside.

Once again, I hope you are enjoying Christmastide and that the New Year brings much joy.

Love,
Bonnie

P.S. Operation is almost a forgotten episode of the past.

January 8, 1983
West Park, New York
Dear Edna,

Your letter, I trust, crossed mine thanking you for the splendid present. It really is superb and just what I needed. Thank you also for your cards.

The recuperation from the operation went smoothly, I was out of the hospital the Monday after the operation on Thursday, but remained in New York to have the stitches out the following Thursday. Last week I went to New York again and had a check-up with the surgeon. All goes well. I did get the flu bug last Thursday afternoon and was rather miserable yesterday. But today it seems to have cleared up. I took plenty of rest and I suspect that was what I really needed.

My efforts to assemble a library for our house and the seminary in Ghana are meeting with success. Last week I found that my seminary has a large number of the books we need and I hope to get them. I am glad you understand so well why I feel impelled to go to Ghana. God has given me such exceptional health for my age I cannot but conclude that he has a use for it.

I hope 1983 is bringing you happiness and blessing and will continue to do so.

Love,
Bonnie

February 2, 1983
Dear Bonnie,

It is wonderful that your recovery has been so rapid, but I am sorry that you caught a virus. Did you not have a flu shot? Do take proper care of yourself.

It makes me very happy to know that my Christmas present was welcome; above all, I do not wish to give you that which you do not want—and I am never sure.

It must be fun to stock a library. Are you getting enough grants? At least, where you are going you will never be cold.

Last night I had a bit of an adventure. Since I promised to help the CRCC with legislation in Connecticut, I set off for the meeting at the Hartford Seminary Foundation. Unfortunately when I reached Hartford, I took a wrong turn and proceeded to drive around in all directions so that I was truly lost—and not in Hartford's best section. Finally, in desperation, I accosted a young Hispanic and his black friend to learn the correct route to Farmington Avenue. After giving me long and involved instructions, he decided it would be more prudent to drive ahead of me to show me the way. It was such a long, long way back but somehow I trusted them—and they kept the trust. I gave them some money for rescuing me—they were really very kind and helpful. I was only one hour late. I think I have a guardian angel and I know I have a poor sense of direction. This time I took the right turn on Farmington Avenue. I really get along very well with black people.

The other day I marched with some of my church members for two hours in front of our federal building in Hartford to protest US military aid to El Salvador. I helped make posters to carry and finally made my own by myself. Since I have never been able to do projects involving handiwork easily, it took me a long, long time to accomplish, but it looked all right eventually.

I thoroughly enjoyed the <u>Symposium (In Quest of Common Grounds)</u> chaired by Dr. Thomas Hoyt, Professor of Biblical Studies Hartford Seminary, a black man who was both intelligent and compassionate—very sensitive to people. There I met Nancy Carr, the member of our Search Committee who opposed our choice for director of CRCC. She told me that Mr. Floyd, our new leader, was doing a fine job and that I was a very ecumenical lady. We all worked together harmoniously in the Symposium.

How could Americans vote for such a stupid man as our president? Even when I was knee-high to a grasshopper I avoided the slow witted variety. He is not basically honest either. Which candidate on the other side do you believe holds the greatest promise?

I have been reading some books on Africa to broaden my horizons.

May all your prayers be answered.

Edna

February 12, 1983
West Park, New York
Dear Edna,

Thank you for your letter and the enclosures. The behavior of Nigeria was very cruel, and the African countries do turn a blind eye to offenses of their friends, just as USA does. But there is this much to be said. Ghana threw out the Nigerians a few years ago in the same way for the same reason. Two wrongs don't make a right, but it does make the second more understandable.

I shall not, of course, be doing anything heroic like the man in Kenya. Just living in a city and teaching in a seminary. Reagan's popularity is dangerous since we now elect our Presidents via TV. I fear from now on only people who come over the tube well will have a chance of election. They are likely to be movie actors, who function only at other people's direction. I am glad to note that the League of Women Voters in trying to do something about it. May they have success.

Yes, I had had a flu shot about 2 weeks before the attack. Probability that is what kept it so mild.

The library comes along well, and I am about to send out an appeal for more second hand books. So far no grants have come in, but I have to wait until the committee that awards them meet. I am hoping some will materialize in the next month.

I envy you the Symposium. It is too early to guess who will have the best chance against Reagan—or whoever runs. I think Mondale is the most intelligent with the best experience. Glenn seems a nice guy, but I am always wary of electing someone who is famous in an unrelated field—like generals. Astronauts come in the same category. Of the others, we shall have to wait and see if someone emerges. At the moment, I'm for Mondale.

Love,
Bonnie

March 10, 1983
Dear Bonnie,

It is always good to hear from you—and not just because you think so clearly.

I agree with your estimate of the way our people select a president. The success of a democracy is basically dependent upon caring, educated voters. How fortunate for us that the Spaniards did not prevail when our country was founded, for I fear we would be facing here all the problems in Latin America. We still do not assimilate our newcomers intelligently and those whose forefathers have lived here for some time too often lack compassion and commitment. It is no wonder that our schools have slipped. For the last 25 years, in my opinion, both the home and the schools have been too permissive. Children are truly much happier when they are faced with limits and work that is challenging. We still ignore the golden years from 2-5 when children are eager to learn. I agree that kindergarten should be open to four year olds.

I also believe that Mondale is our best prospect on the horizon.

Our new director of CRCC is continuing to prove to be a superb leader. At our last meeting of old and new Executive Board members in Windsor, he organized a program that provided excellent orientation and education. Fortunately, in spite of a dark night's heavy downpour, and splashing trucks on I-91, I managed to arrive in one piece. On the way home, my good Quaker friend, Elsa, drove ahead to show me the way through the back roads much better.

Our state has a dire need for its own income tax. Here we are second in the nation in personal income, but we don't spend on the needy. Hartford stands fourth in poverty amidst great affluence. Our CRCC has taken a stand for a state income tax and support for those on welfare, but there is much work to be done.

A professor friend from Eastern Connecticut University has just finished a week with me. She has found a pleasant niche in Newtown, PA, in a Quaker retirement village. She found New York City where she had lived too dangerous.

I am glad you library is progressing. Is there any way I can help?

I am enclosing a check for one more book of yours—God Who Dares To Be Man. I want to give it to an Episcopalian who is the husband of the chairman of our Unitarian Universalist Concerns Committee. She is an excellent leader and her husband is a fine man.

Please do take good care of yourself.

Edna

For once you must have seen enough snow. It is the most I have ever seen in Connecticut. I shoveled my front and back paths, but I managed to get two big boys to clear my driveway. The snow was very heavy. My 2-5 mile daily walks are a great help.

March 22, 1983
West Park, New York
Dear Edna,

Have you received Mondale's letter apropos of his announcement of his candidacy? It is, in my opinion, a thoughtful and convincing statement. If you have not seen it, you can get a copy (I presume), by writing The Mondale for President Committee, PO Box 5403, Washington, DC 20016. It is worth reading.

Congratulations once more on the selection of the CRCC director, which was due so much to your leadership. It is so gratifying when a choice like that turns out as well as was hoped.

Thank you for the check for my book. I believe it has been sent to you. There has been no increase in price.

I have finished the first draft of my new book's first two chapters. I hope to get work on the third and last this week. I have the research for it pretty well in hand. The Ghanaian library is coming along very well so far as gifts of books are concerned. But so far no grants have come in to buy the books we cannot hope to get as gifts—reference works and recent publications. However, Funds take their time about making grants, and still longer paying them, so one must be patient— about 50 boxes off to Ghana this week.

I did enjoy the big storm, despite its inconvenience to everyone. At the moment, it is snowing here again. I know March would go out like a lion after its lamblike first week. All the best.

Love,
Bonnie

April 19, 1983
Dear Bonnie,

Thank you for informing me about Mondale's letter. As yet, I have not seen a copy, but I will get one; I receive all kinds of mail, but that one missed me. Thus far, events look good for him.

I am glad that Washington won in Chicago and hope he will rise to the challenge. Friends who have lived in Chicago tell me that racism is bitter there and the political machine is corrupt. Chicago neighborhoods seem to be different from those in Philadelphia. My niece who is doing research at the Wharton School of the University of Pennsylvania keeps a big dog for protection in her apartment. Large cities surely have monumental problems.

Your book arrived the same day as your letter and has been given to my friends I have another place where your book is needed so I am enclosing another check. Your words answer many questions that continue to arise. Have you finished your new book? You write so easily and quickly.

Are you seeking only books on theology for your library in Ghana? When do you plan to leave for Africa?

There is one question I have always wanted to ask you. Why do Episcopalians all drink from the same cup during Holy Communion? I know that I am too germ conscious—I was brought up that way. There are so many diseases today, and I hear they present Africa's greatest dangers. I hope my question does not offend you—it is an honest question.

Of late, I have been somewhat inundated with various activities—church, RCAR, NARAL and Planned Parenthood. Our state legislature is faced with a dire need for tax reform including a state income tax, tightening of laws to keep drunken drivers off the roads, and defeating a move to legislate notification of parents prior to abortions. Nationally, Hatch is attempting to pass a constitutional amendment to ban abortions. In New Britain there is sharp controversy over the teaching of sex education in the public schools. Most homes are not equipped to handle this problem adequately, many churches do not assume this responsibility so that the poor children are left to muddle through, and society is left with unnecessary complications. To be sure, the most important factor is the teacher who must be emotionally stable, sensitive, and understanding, but above all must possess a spiritual point of view that shines through. Our young people are genuinely confused.

I suppose that if I did not have a cause to fight, I would be lost.

Spring with all its many beauties is soon to unfold.

May you enjoy its many pleasures and continue to be well and happy.

Edna

May 5, 1983
West Park, New York
Dear Edna,

Thank you for the letter and clippings. I fully share your political hopes. I fear Mayor Washington is in for a hard time. I hope he is up to it. I am glad my book arrived. I have put in your check and order for another. It should be reaching you by now.

To answer your questions: I have finished the new book and am in the process of typing the final copy now. I hope to get it off to a publisher for consideration, next week. The first installment of books was shipped over a month ago. I am somewhat worried about it because I am not sure letters necessary for handling it on its arrival ever reached the proper people. But there is nothing more I can do about it. I hope to leave for Africa toward the end of July.

The common cup at Communion is an important part of the symbolism—all sharing in one cup. The danger of infection I think is greatly exaggerated. The priest consumes what is left after everybody has received, and life insurance companies' rate clergy among the longest livers. Catholic-minded Episcopalians used to make a big fuss—dipping the wafer in the chalice instead of drinking from it. But when the Roman Catholics restored the cup to the laity, they said they could either "skip, sip, or dip." So now intinction is looked upon as entirely proper. Any who want may do so. Some of us use that method if we are down with a cold, etc. in order not to spread it. But I still think the chance of contagion is small.

Keep up the good work for all your cause and God bless you in it.

Love,
Bonnie

May 26, 1983
Dear Bonnie,

You must feel good about the completion of your new book. Do let me know when it is published. I am sure that you are looking forward to your new adventure and your friends—new and old are most fortunate to have you. Did your first installment of books finally arrive in Ghana?

Activities in Connecticut still abound. I drove some of our Unitarian Council members to Woodstock in northern Connecticut for a retreat where we could discuss our problems. The group included the various chairmen of our committees. Since each spoke his mind, the atmosphere was brisk and the confrontations sometimes heated. I fear I shall never be able to tolerate some forms of expressions with equanimity. Language needs to be beautiful. We must always remember that freedom must of necessity be allied with responsibility. However, we did reach some sane conclusions. When I reached home, I found I needed some new spark plugs. Machinery and I have never been on close terms.

Tuesday evening, our CRCC held its Spring Assembly. Since we decided to hold our assemblies in different churches, we met in the First Church of Christ-Congregational in West Hartford, a very beautiful edifice with plenty of spacious rooms to house our six workshops—Peace, Communication, Legislation, Elderly Hospital, and Schools. Our Executive Director organized them so that they were most productive. Since I was chairman of the committee on arrangements, I fashioned a dozen or more flower arrangements (I robbed my hemlock hedge and my rose azalea bushes) for the dining tables. I have always felt that a reuse of beauty is clarity allied to the spiritual. At the end, we held a worship service in the sanctuary. I believe people left with lighter hearts.

Last night the Hartford Chapter of the New Jewish Agenda and the Hartford Quakers held a Public Forum on the Palestinian and Jewish Question. I'm afraid the predictions of the article I enclosed on the problem in the Mid East will come to pass.

Next week I expect to march in the front of our State Capitol to protest the lack of concern for our people on welfare. All they want to give a family of 3 is 40 cents more a day and they are already below the poverty level. Most of these families are one parent arrangements with a woman as the parent.

I do hope I can see you before you take off for Africa—if you are not too busy. I would love to have you visit me in Connecticut or I could take you to the theater in New York or transport you to any destination you wish.

Edna

June 16, 1983
West Park, New York
Dear Edna,

Forgive me for being so slow in answering your good letter and the interesting enclosures. I have been away on a bit of a vacation. I go off next week on another installment of it.

I do hope we can get together before I leave for Africa, but I do not see how I can fit in a visit to you. I still have much to do on the library job; I have to get my own notes and papers in order; and I have to obtain my visa, get my shots, etc., etc. The best chance of a visit would be if you could drive over here, with a friend to keep you company. We might have a lunch together. We could put you up for the night if you wish. I expect to be back from my next trip on June 27th. After that I have only day trips to New York until I leave on July 28th. If we can settle on a day well in advance, I can arrange those trips to avoid being away when you come. I shall not get your letter until the 27th, so the visit had better be toward the middle of July.

Hoping to see you then.

Love,
Bonnie

The next letter is a copy of what Edna at first thought she wanted to send, but on her second thought she sent a different one a day later on June 26th.

June 25, 1983
Dear Bonnie,

Your last letter has left me in something of a quandary—to do or not to do. I have a friend who is willing to accompany me to West Park on Saturday, July 23rd, or I can find a friend to drive with me on some other day of your choosing. I can take you to lunch or dinner, put up at West Park until early the following morning or find another location for repose. However, with all your many tasks to complete, you might prefer to have me write you a letter of farewell and not come at all. Unless you find time to accomplish your many goals, you will find neither peace of mind nor peace of body—and time is short. Please be perfectly candid with me—consider yourself first—your needs and wishes. I am glad you had your much deserved vacation. You make the decision.

May peace be with you.

She noted: [not sent . . . changed]

June 26, 1983
Dear Bonnie,

I am very happy that you were able to take a much deserved vacation. I am sure you needed it.

If it is convenient for you, Dolores and I can drive over to West Park Saturday, July 23rd. I will take you to dinner or lunch or both—whatever—. We can stay overnight and leave early the following morning so that we shall be out of the way. I will pay for our lodging. Dolores is going on a safari to Kenya from the first of July until the fifteenth.

If this date is unsuitable, perhaps Mary will drive over with me on a day of your choosing.

Please arrange your schedule to your own needs and wishes.

May your new venture prove to be a joyous and fulfilling one.

Edna

July 1, 1983
West Park, New York
Dear Edna,

Saturday, July 23rd is just right for me. It is, in fact, one of the few days that would be. So I shall look forward to seeing you and Dolores.

Since that is my last weekend home and I do not know how much will remain to be done, I think it would be best if you could plan to arrive in the course of the afternoon, and we go out for the evening meal. If you wish, I shall reserve a table for the three of us at a good local restaurant. We shall be delighted to have you stay the night, and there is no reason why you have to rush off in the morning. It will be most interesting to hear of Dolores' safari.

I am writing this in bed, having come down with a cold yesterday. It seems to be getting better, but sitting in the doctor's office for an hour after the appointment I made, did not improve my illness or my temper. I heard there was an emergency, but even so, he took his time about it.

It will be so good to see you and we shall have much to share. I shall save it till then.

Love,
Bonnie

July 6, 1983
Dear Bonnie,

It is good that the 23rd is all right. We shall plan to arrive sometime in the afternoon, probably after the middle. Please do not let us interfere with your work plans for we understand. Will you please reserve a table at your favorite restaurant for us? If you have a friend you wish to invite, ask him. The whole treat is mine—for I very much want to do this. And we plan to stay overnight.

Please take care of your health. Good health is God given, but we are expected to prevent all the ills we possibly can. Forgive me for worrying about you.

We shall be delighted to see you and share your thoughts.

May the future hold all the hope and joy you envision.

Edna

July 28, 1983
Receipt of check of $100.00 to Holy Cross Monastery
Description: Fr. Spencer (C.F.)

July 28, 1983
West Park, New York
Dear Edna,

Thank you for your generous gift. I shall wait till I get to Ghana so as to see what I most need it for.

It has been wonderful to know you and I am most grateful for your visit here and Dolores accompanying you. I hope we shall all get together again in three years.

Meanwhile my love and prayers.

Bonnie

GENERAL LETTER
August 19, 1983
Cape Coast, Ghana

Greetings from Ghana!

Much as I would like to write you personally, I have decided to substitute a letter at regular intervals to all with whom I want to keep in touch. A correspondence in which one letter answers another is out of the question. It would take at least two months for the exchange of letter and reply. I have already been here three weeks and have yet to receive a single letter. So basically I shall be writing an account of affairs here and I would be saying much the same to all my friends. Hence a single letter distributed from West Park seems the best plan.

The trip out was uneventful, except that in Amsterdam I was sent to the wrong gate and found out I had to go the full length of the airport with barely time to catch my plane. But, thank God, I made it. I had no trouble with immigration or customs, was duly met by Br.

Vincent and Fr. Ralph Martin, spent the night with our good friend in Accra, Fr. Pain, and had a pleasant ride to Cape Coast the next day.

The big surprise is the weather. This is the "wet" season, though we have not had a real rain since I have been here. Day after day has been like the very best summer weather in West Park. The temperature is consistently around 78 and there is a nice breeze off the ocean. Food is as I expected. Usually rice, though sometimes kenki or cassava, as a base, with a soup to pour over it that, whatever its ingredients, is so peppery hot that it has no other taste. I have adjusted to it quite satisfactorily.

I have been kept busy cataloging the library. I found they already had a goodly number of books, some donated by the Bishop or from other local libraries, and some brought from Bolahun. The latter include many modern books on Africa which supplement the ones I am bringing, as also do many of the theological books. In fact the two libraries dovetail extraordinarily well. I first catalogued the ones I found here and am now working on my first shipment, of which 35 of 37 cartons got through. The papers I had mailed to get them through customs never arrived. So several cartons had to be opened which resulted in the loss. This time I brought the papers with me, so I hope we shall have better luck with the second shipment, which is now on the ocean.

We are living in temporary quarters, which for the rest of the Community are very crowded. But I am lucky. Since there was no way to squeeze me in, they got permission for me to live on the second floor of a guest house on the property which we have not been using. So I have a private room and bath. We shall soon be moving to a wing of St. Monica's School, where the Sisters who used to run it lived. Everyone (except me) will have more room, but I shall have the advantage of being where the library is at present, so will not be dependent on rides to get to and from work.

All in all I am adjusting happily and have kept in good health. The people are grand and most welcoming. The prospects for the Seminary are most exciting. I miss you, but that cannot be helped. Keep me in your prayers.

Love,
Bonnie

GENERAL LETTER
October 1, 1983
Ghana, West Africa
Greetings from Ghana.

It turns out that there is some confusion about getting our mail through P.O. Box 38, Cape Coast. As I have received four letters in two months, only two from USA, I am wondering if others have gone astray. Despite what I wrote in my last letter, I have answered personally each letter by now. If you have not received my reply, please repeat any important news when next you write. And please address letters to me: % The Rev. Canon David Pain, P.O. Box 4683, Accra, Ghana, West Africa.

The glorious news is that the second shipment of books for the Seminary library has reached me in Cape Coast. Not only have all 69 packages come through, but they have even found the two of the first shipment that were thought to have been lost. It is true that some of the boxes broke open in transit and a few books have been lost, but far less than the loss of whole cartons would have been. I have finished cataloging the library I found here and most of the first shipment.

The second big news is that we have moved into new "temporary" quarters. We expect to stay here until our new house is finished. At the rate the new building is progressing, that will be a long time. The problem is that materials are in short supply or not available at all. Thus the new building has been ready to have the floor laid ever since I arrived two months ago, but so far they have not been able to get the cement. I hear it is to be delivered next week. We shall see.

Our new temporary quarters have three main advantages. Since they formerly were a convent for the Sisters who ran the school in which they are located, there is a fine chapel for our Eucharists and Offices. In the old place these had to be celebrated in the narrow passage that served also as a sitting and dining room. Secondly, there is a bit more room for everyone. And third, it is in the middle of town, so that we can walk to most places where we need to go. In the past we all had to come in by car to work in the morning, be picked up an taken home for lunch, then back to work and home again afterwards.

Picking up people at various places made each trip 20 to 45 minutes. The only alternative was a three mile walk each way. Now I am not dependent on the car for my ordinary duties. The room where I am cataloging the books is just across the court from where we live. We are hoping to get the new temporary seminary building next week. When we do, the books will be moved there as soon as we have shelving for them. But that building is only a ten minute walk from here, so again I shall not need the car.

It may be of interest to you, as it was to me, to learn of the funeral customs here. At death the body is not embalmed, but is placed in refrigeration for about two weeks. Special facilities are provided for the purpose. The delay is needed to get ready for the funeral. Not only must the family be assembled by slow communication. But also the various churches have one funeral service a week, each main church taking a different day. So one can attend them all, as many do. At our Cathedral, the service is on Friday afternoon. There may be anywhere from one to five or more persons to be buried. The church is packed and the service is as elaborate as possible, with memorials of the departed, sermon, full choir, etc. Usually the night before the family holds a wake. The bodies are buried in the cemetery in order of death with no relation to other member of the same family. After the burial there is usually another gathering of a more joyous tone than the wake. On Saturday morning a second requiem is celebrated for those buried the day before. Perhaps you have gathered by now that people here love funerals. And the burial rites may not be the end of the matter. Often some months later a memorial service is held at the Cathedral after the Sunday Eucharist. It is sometimes announced by a poster with the person's photo and life story.

I keep well and happily busy. People are eager to learn. Even though the Seminary has yet to open, I already have some teaching assignments at the Cathedral. Next week I start visiting some secondary schools to celebrate the Eucharist for the Anglican students. Keep me in your prayers.

Love,
Bonnie

October 17, 1983
Dear Bonnie,

Your general letter from Ghana dated August 17th arrived here
October 13th from West Park. It was a great surprise. Since you did
not leave me your African address, I concluded that you no longer
cared to correspond with me. I wanted to write—but not if you
wished otherwise. Finally, I telephoned West Park to get your African
address. My visit to West Park bothered me. I sensed that you seemed
apprehensive where I was concerned and I did not understand for I
would never hurt you. Forgive me for inconveniencing you—I felt I
bored you. We should have dropped both of you at the Monastery
after dinner and then pushed on. Is it that West Park does not favor
women that come without escorts? Years ago, when Dolores and
I visited you, your prior looked at us so strangely as though we were
interlopers. We did not dare come again.

Your letter was most informative—I have long wondered how
your venture was faring. I am delighted that you are in good health and
that the weather is cooperating. I hope your new accommodations are
as favorable as your first. Does it really take two months for mail to
reach Africa?

From what I have read about Ghana, it seems to be rather unstable
economically.

October 24, 1983
(same letter)

Now your letter of October first has reached me from West Park
with your correct address. The material was fascinating. Teaching
carries its own intrinsic reward as you well know. I can feel your
enthusiasm leak from the page—wonderful. How do these students
differ from your former ones? Individuals are always a challenge.

In September I took a caravan tour through Norway, Sweden, and
Denmark. Fortunately the bus driver was most skillful for the highways
in Norway were rather intricate, but the scenery was heavenly. We were

guided by an excellent director who was an Icelandic native, and he had 42 tourists to oversee—far too many for comfort. One woman was emotionally disturbed (Some of us tried to help, and others avoided the unpleasant). One woman with a heart attack was taken in an ambulance to the hospital in Odeuse, Denmark where she later died. Fortunately, her daughter was with her, and the doctors were most helpful and compassionate.

In Stockholm, a beautiful, sparkling, clean city, we found a most impressive city hall. Hans Christian Andersen's Odeuse has always been a favorite of mine. Copenhagen with its exciting Tivoli Gardens and its refreshing harbor cruise was as fetching as ever. The Little Mermaid still guards the harbor and reminds us once again of her sad labor of love. I wanted to track down my great great grandfather in Copenhagen, but the Town Hall was closed—so my roots will have to wait a bit. The Danes are ever friendly and well organized.

I needed that trip—even though some of the bathtubs were so big I wasn't sure I would always make it.

The other night I had the good fortune to see Shaw's <u>Major Barbara</u> at the Yale Repertory Theater in New Haven. I always enjoy Shaw's humor, and it was well done.

Along with my duties in the Capitol Region Conference of Churches, I am campaigning for a worthy man who is running for reelection to the Newington Town Council. Myra and I traipse up and down the streets delivering fliers to all the voters. We have a new respect for our postmen who have to navigate all these treacherous stairs. More of our residents should attend the Council meetings to discover what goes on. They would be surprised.

I passed my annual physical check-up with flying colors the other day—thanks to my ancestors—so far so good.

I am distressed over Lebanon. We should have foreseen this disaster and have protected our men. Why does religion, which should redeem the world cause so much havoc and bitterness?

I have missed you.

With love,
Edna

November 16, 1983
Ghana, West Africa
Dear Edna,

Thank you for your letter. I had been wondering why I did not hear from you. I thought I had given you my Ghanaian address, so my failure to do so was an oversight. Neither I nor anyone else was apprehensive over your visit to West Park. I was concerned for your comfort and nothing more. The only thing I can think of that might have made my attitude seem strange was the proximity of my departure date which caused me to be preoccupied with last minute details. But I thoroughly enjoyed seeing you and Dolores, the dinner, and all other aspects of your visit. And I assure you we are quite accustomed to women guest coming "without escorts."

As you will note, I am answering your letter mailed on October 26th, just a little over two weeks later. Sending it through the Accra address speeds things up considerably. Foreign mail arrives in Accra and delivery then is rapid. But the service from Accra to Cape Coast is irregular and undependable. Canon Pain is a bank supervisor and sends messengers to the branch here at least twice a week. They bring the letters addressed through him.

Ghana is in an economically depressed state, partially as a result of previous governments running the country into bankruptcy and partially because of the drought and the consequent insufficiency of food. The present government is discouraging imports by an unfavorable rate of foreign exchange, so that the country will become more self-sufficient. But, at least as far as we are concerned, we have enough to eat. It is African food, but on the whole I like it. It is definitely filling and gives me plenty of energy.

It is difficult to answer your question as to whether there is anything I want. (Your generous gift before I left was most appreciated.) I do not know the kind of thing you have in mind. A pair of light weight slacks would be helpful. I did not bring enough of them and wear them much of the time. If you send anything in the way of food, it must be in tins and such as can sit in a hot warehouse for two weeks or so without spoiling. (Customs takes a long time.) All packages must be addressed to "The Christian Service Committee, P.O. Box 3262, Accra, Ghana, West Africa. Attention Fr. Spencer Anglican Diocese of Cape Coast." Only that group can get through customs for us without inordinate charges.

I do not know why it took so long for my first general epistle to be distributed. I am glad the second got out faster. I am answering each personal letter I get, but I do not necessarily repeat what is in the general letters. I plan to write a third general letter soon. They permit me to keep in touch with a larger group of friends.

Our quarters at St. Monica's school have advantages and disadvantages. On the plus side, we have more room and we are in the center of town. I can walk to the seminary in 15 minutes—twice a day gives me good exercise. It is on streets without sidewalks so one must be alert for cars which swerve all over the place to avoid potholes. But as there is very little petrol, there are few cars. The chief disadvantage is that our house is on the top of a hill. The water pressure in town is not sufficient to get up to the ground floor most of the time, almost never to the second floor where we live. So we have to get along with buckets. Also when the girls' school is in session the noise is incredible. I do not see how they learn anything because whenever I look into a classroom there seems to be a class of indifference. But that is not my worry. The girls leave about 2:30 and then peace reigns. I am mostly at the seminary in the mornings and so escape the worst of the racket.

The last I saw our new monastery—out in the country—the walls were about up. That was over a week ago. So things are coming along, but there is no telling how long it will take. The move there will be welcome as it will provide more room and plenty of water. But so long as the seminary remains where it is now, it will be over 3 miles from where we shall then be living, and we shall be dependent on cars for transportation. Incidentally, we have only 2/3rds of the space we are supposed to have for the seminary because one of the previous tenants in the building refuses to move out. The landlord has gone to court, but the last time that happened in a house we had hoped to rent, the court decided in favor of the tenants. The others are more hopeful this time, but I do not share their hope. One of the disadvantages is that we can shelve only part of the library I have already catalogued, and I have about 40 more cartons to unpack and catalogue.

I am glad you are keeping up your political interests. We get no news here, so I have only vaguely heard of the Lebanon crisis. I put in an application for an absentee ballot, but as I expected, it has never arrived. So I am afraid I shall not have the pleasure of voting against the lone/ham cowboy next year. I also rejoice that your health remains good. So does mine. I also have had a local check up and got a clean bill of health. The Scandinavian tour sounds grand. You are so wise to go off on trips like that regularly. I am still hoping to go to England next summer.

This should reach you in time to wish you a Blessed Christmas and a Happy New Year. My best to Dolores and any else I may know. The postcards are lovely.

Love,
Bonnie

December 13, 1983
Dear Bonnie,

A week ago I sent you a Christmas package air mail. I hope it reaches you intact. It contained two pairs of slacks (one tan and one gray), a date book, needles, thread, thimbles, tape measure, and a Christmas star. You did not give me your correct size, so I had to guess. If they are wrong, send me the size, and I will try again. If you need any other clothes, please send me your right size. I am a good shopper, and there will soon be some good sales. [Food]

Your letters both personal and general have been most interesting. You surely are working very hard. I can hear your girls babbling away; they must be having a very merry time. I knew you would enjoy the teaching. Eager students are a great boon.

A week ago the Capitol Region Conference of Churches held a Festival of choirs at my church to raise money to engage an Hispanic Chaplain to help the Hispanic inmates at the Hartford Correctional

Center; 30% of the people there are Hispanic, and they need one of their own. In our jails in Connecticut, we are truly breeding criminals not rehabilitating them.

The choirs came from different churches in the Hartford region—black, white, young and old—a good cross section. Then in our Fellowship Hall, we served refreshments. The people seemed happy to be there; they liked the architecture of our building, the festive air of the gathering and the warmth of spirit. Black students from Weaver High School did a dance that was most suitable. I strongly feel that people of different faiths need to work, sing, and pray together. This is the first time we have had this kind of celebration. My Quaker friend is a most enterprising member of the committee. I do like Quakers, they are so friendly and dependable.

Tonight I attended the annual meeting of Impact at the Hartford Seminary Foundation. Two of our state representatives—one of whom is a Williams man and another addressed us on "Political Power and the Struggle for Justice." They showed great vitality and faith. We selected the issues to pursue when the Legislature convenes in January. We chose Housing, Criminal Justice, Essential Human Services, Elderly and Income Maintenance, Public Education and Tax Reform. It was a good meeting. The Episcopalian Reverend is president of Connecticut Impact. For some reason, I find meetings stimulating. Playing cards and participating in gossip circles always bored me.

On a regular basis, I am attending the meetings of our Town Council and the Board of Education. More of our voters ought to go to find out what is going on.

The other night, I drove to Meriden to the Congregational Church where I attended a meeting of the CCAG (Connecticut Citizen Action Group). We managed to corral our Connecticut Commissioner of Environment so that we could put him on the spot regarding the disposal of hazardous wastes in this state. It was an exciting, well-organized meeting. Individuals from different parts of the state addressed the issues. They were intelligent and articulate.

Fortunately for me, the sons and friends of my good neighbors have grown up to be fine very young men who help me by caring for my lawn, planting my bulbs, and shoveling my snow. Thus far, we have not had enough to shovel.

I am deeply concerned about the foreign policy of this nation. If we have another four years of Reagan, we are risking a nuclear war. He has no understanding of the forces at work, and his kitchen cabinet is malevolent beyond belief. I have been busy calling our two senators— Weicker and Dodd as well as my U.S. Representative Barbara Kennelly to urge Congress to bring back our soldiers from Lebanon. We cannot solve this problem with weapons of war.

Edna

GENERAL LETTER
December 1983
Ghana, West Africa
Greetings from Ghana

This letter has been deliberately delayed so that your copy of it will not be mailed until after the Christmas rush. That prevents me from wishing you a blessed celebration of the feast and all the joy in the New Year, but you will know that I have you in my thoughts and prayers.

The first term of the Seminary has been successfully concluded. I enjoyed teaching very much. At first, as I expected, the men had some difficulty absorbing the lectures, but I think toward the end we were communicating better. Because of the activities during the final week, including a soccer game with St. Peter's Roman Catholic Seminary (they won 4-1), examinations were postponed to the beginning of next term. So I do not yet have them to indicate how much of my material was understood and will be remembered.

The library is coming along nicely. I think I shall have catalogued by the end of this vacation all the books that have arrived so far. I hope there will be another shipment sent in January. The problem at the moment is that we do not have room to make most of the library that is catalogued available for use. One of the "tenants," actually a squatter since no rent is being paid, has so far refused to move out of the house we are renting for the Seminary. That deprives us of the ground floor, where we hope eventually to put the library. Meanwhile, there is only one small room in which less than half of the books can be shelved.

Difficulties of one kind or another are so characteristic of Africa that one learns to adjust to them. At the moment the lack of rain has so reduced the water at the Nkrumah Dam that it cannot generate enough electricity. So it is rationed, that is, turned off for unpredictable and indeterminate periods. Since we are now in the dry season, this problem will probably be with us for a long time.

I have also been going to the non-Anglican secondary schools and colleges (corresponding very roughly to our high schools) to celebrate the Eucharist for the Anglican students about once a month. There are seven schools I am responsible for. This also has its frustrations. The students almost always turn up late, and sometimes not at all. But when they do, it is worth-while ministering to them.

The use of the Accra address given above have greatly speeded the arrival of letters. Mail arrives in Accra and the sending of it on to Cape Coast is slow and sometimes not dependable. From the Accra address it is brought by a bank messenger who comes a couple of times a week.

I trust the New Year will already be proving itself beneficial by the time you receive this, and I hope it will continue so.

Love,
Bonnie

January 23, 1984
Dear Bonnie,

It is a long time since I have heard from you—barring your general December letter. Did you not receive my Christmas letter and package? If not, I must trace the package. In it I included two pair of slacks—size 34. If they are the wrong size, give them to anyone you wish, and I will send you more—the size you tell me. And I promised to send you any other clothes you may need if you give me the size. Also I want to send you some food, but what do you prefer?

Are you all right? I worry about your problems with the water in Africa. On December 31st, I tried to reach you by telephone to wish you a happy birthday, but after a very long wait, I was informed that it was impossible because the cables were down. I have tried since but to no avail. Is the telephone number 042-2018 on your Philip Quaque Monastery stationery correct? I know you are five hours ahead of Connecticut time and I thought between six and nine o'clock at night (your time), might be the best time. If you do not wish me to try this, please tell me so.

You are working so hard and are so brave and understanding concerning all the trials and frustrations you face there. Back here our problems seem very small in comparison

Saturday, Dolores and I attended the Williams seminar in Hartford featuring Professor Al Goethars, Chairman of the Psychology Department, on "Presidential Campaigning and Presidential Character" and Professor Fred Stocking on "The Albert Memorial in London." We both preferred the first session which was stimulating and clever. While Professor Stocking was most fluent, we wished he had chosen another art object. This Connecticut Williams College Alumni Association event proved to be the most interesting of all their offerings to date. Professor Goethals listed five strengths a presidential candidate needed to win:

1. Forcefulness (must be a decisive leader)
2. Self-confidence—must feel good about himself, and be persuasive
3. Interpersonal sensitivity, warmth, a conscious sense of the needs of others, a quick sense of any change in the situation
4. Openness to information, acquisition of all the point before making a decision
5. Charisma, physical presence, ability to inspire, magnetism, eloquence.

He did, however, agree that character was most important. I am always troubled when people choose leaders who have charisma and not character. It seems to me that most people are so enamored of this charisma that they fail to perceive the true character of the individual; they are so easily fooled. I shall never forget my experience when I campaigned for Adlai Stevenson. One middle aged woman assured me she was a Democrat, but she intended to vote for Eisenhower because he had such a lovely smile. In this situation, there was nothing to do but fold my tent and move on.

At another time when I was campaigning for Chester Bowles for Governor, one woman told me she would not vote for him because his wife was so homely. I was astounded! When I subsequently saw Mrs. Bowles after she returned from India, I thought she was beautiful. Her face was serene and spiritual. I think the face of Mary in Michelangelo's Pieta in Rome is the most beautiful face I have ever seen. As voters in this country, our people are truly illiterate too often. Our schools have failed in teaching the meaning of good Government. I think we show a lack of understanding when we expect all these third world countries to become democratic overnight. It requires so much good education. Surely democracy should be our goal for both fascism and communism court similar evils. As a people we need to care more about the welfare of others. You do.

January has been the month of the deep freeze, but the snow has been truly beautiful—I always think of you when it bounces down. I am sure all this snow is healthful.

[this next section is crossed out] "I still keep busy with all my political activities, but I wish all the people would become more interested and literate; it is a rather lonely vigil."

You mentioned the possibility of being in England this summer. Mary and I have signed up for "British Journeys" from May 17th to June 3rd. It is sponsored by a California company located at Walnut Creek. At least on this trip we get to stay three nights each time we stop over. We start and finish in London after touring Devon, Cornwall, Cotswolds, Lake District, Edinburgh, and the Scottish Highlands. Mary and I—since we are two people think it would be safe for us to stay over a little longer to see some things on our own. If you are there in June, we would love to see you and take you to dinner. Just name the time and place.

Edna

February 6, 1984
Accra, Ghana, West Africa
c/o The Rev. Canon David Pain
Dear Edna,

Thank you for your letter. I am writing this now, although I have not yet received your package. It may well be in Accra. I received a slip for a registered package that had to be signed for. I sent the slip with one of the Brethren who was taking our mail to Accra. He handed in the slip, but your letter had arrived and the clerk gave him that for the slip. I still think that the slip was for your package, in which case I have neither the package nor the slip. When we go to Accra next, I am sending your envelope and a note pointing out the possible mistake and asking the Post Office to check for the package. I do hope I can get it, for I should much appreciate having the contents which you so generously have sent me. I am writing now so that you will know the situation. I do not want to wait until we have tried again, because I do not know how long after that it will be until another letter can be mailed. As soon as I get the package, I shall write again. You might send out a tracer, but I do not think that will accomplish much.

I think what fooled the Post Office was the "Express Special Delivery" stamp on the letter. Your previous letter had such a stamp and came through without having to be signed for. But I think this time the clerk thought it was the reason for the package slip. Unless the stamp does some great good in USA it would be better not to use it. Over here it simply causes confusion. If they succeed in delivery, that is as special as they get. Incidentally, the only size I know is that my waist is normally a 34. At the moment it is down to 32, but I hope to put on some weight. However, if I get your slacks, I shall not need more clothes. Also, if you ever send another package, I shall tell you how to best handle it. Preferably by sending to West Park to be brought out the next time someone comes. The other possibility is to send it to The Christian Service Committee, PO Box 3262, Accra, Ghana—For Rev. Bonnell Spencer. Philip Quaque Monastery, Box 38, Cape Coast. They are better than anyone else at handling packages.

The Festival of Choirs must have been a splendid affair, and it is always good to hear of churches cooperating in a good cause. And thank God, for your diligence in attending meetings where an interested citizen can both have influence and gain information to arouse concern elsewhere. I share your worry about the cowboy' foreign policy. I hope your senators can do something, but I doubt it. One blessing here is that I know nothing about the day to day happenings and so can put the whole mess out of mind.

The big news about me is that the authorities here are so eager that I shall be in full health and vigor for the next year's teaching that they want me to spend the summer in England. The idea is that getting out of Africa for a spell will help. I doubt that, since I am well and happy here. But I did want to get to England to do some research, to see about books for the library (Blackwell's and Parker's at Oxford are the best second hand bookstores in the world for religious books), and to see some friends. I had not planned to spend as long as 2 1/2 months, which is what the authorities want. I have agreed to 1 1/2. Vacations bore me, but I think I have enough to keep occupied for that long—and it may still be that I shall stay the full time they desire. Anyway, it will be a pleasant change as well as a chance to get some work done. I shall let you know my address there in good time before I leave on June 15th (as is now being planned).

The clippings you sent are most interesting. The bombing in the Arab area is most difficult because of the Moslem fanaticism. As they demonstrated in the 7th century, when they really got started they are almost unstoppable. The one hopeful aspect at present is the divisiveness between the Arabs. If they ever could get together on a belligerent religious program we should be in serious trouble.

I shall keep working and hoping on the problem of the package. All the best.

Love,
Bonnie

PS. I share your love of the Frick museum. Thanks for the card.

outside of envelope: "N.B.: Package has arrived! Many thanks"

February 16, 1984
Accra, Ghana, West Africa
c/o The Rev. Canon David Pain
Dear Edna,

Although I have not actually seen your box, I am reasonably sure it is here. I had forgotten I told you to address it to The Christian Service Committee. They have a long, light package for me, which sounds like yours. By the time the people who went to Accra in search of it had tracked it down, the person who had the key to where it was stored had gone home from work. It will be picked up on the next trip, which should be soon, because much of what they hoped to accomplish yesterday was not done. This letter should be mailed on that trip, so I still will not have actually seen your lovely gifts. The size is just right. Please accept this letter as my inadequate attempt to express my gratitude.

I have answered every letter of yours as soon as I received it. I know there have been two, and I think a third. If you have not had an answer to each letter you wrote, then one of yours or mine must have gone astray. I enjoy your letters and their enclosures greatly.

As I wrote in the letter mailed yesterday, I am to spend most of the summer in England. Unfortunately, our times do not accord well. I cannot fly up until June 15th. On arrival I shall need to go to Willen Priory, Miton Keynes, Bucks, MK15 9AA. Tel (0908) 663749, which will be my headquarters, to settle in. So I could not get to London before Sunday, June 17th. That would make it a long time for you to stay over. It would be good to see you, but I hardly expect you to wait that long.

Incidentally, we have no telephone here. Even if one does, it rarely works. So people here take it for granted that no contact by phone is possible. If it is essential for us to get in touch with the US, it can sometimes be arranged at great difficulty and expense by going to Accra. Since I have been here we have had to resort to that only once. It was good of you to attempt to phone me, but quite impossible of accomplishment.

Thank you for your offer to send food. It is better to send that than money, because western food is hard to get here and extremely expensive. Any food that is sent must be such as will not spoil in a long journey and perhaps as much as a month in a hot warehouse—customs takes its time. For myself I should especially appreciate a jar of instant coffee and a tin of Ovaltine. Cookies of the not too sweet type are appreciated here as are jams, jellies, marmalade, peanut butter (unsweetened—it is used for sauce), canned meat, fish, and the like. I am putting down what occurs to me—do not attempt to include all articles or restrict yourself to them if you think of something else. In the way of clothing, I shall be well taken care of if your package reaches me safely. One item that would be welcome is a pair of sneakers or other light shoes, size 8 1/2. I tell you all this because you have asked. We get enough to eat, but treats are always welcome. Please, if you send anything, address it through, The Christian Service Committee, PO Box 3262, Accra, Ghana, West Africa. For me—Philip Quoque Priory, Cape Coast.

I am feeling fine, working no harder than I fully enjoy, and hardships and frustrations are minimal. Mostly they give something to talk about.

I am glad you got to the Williams affair. The lecture on Presidential campaigning was given (in 3 lectures actually) to the Old Guard Reunion last spring which I attended. As you did, I found them interesting and discouraging. I fear we are to be governed henceforth by TV actors. A competent actor can project forcefulness, self-confidence, interpersonal sensitivity and openness, whether he had them or not, and charisma is his stock-in-trade. For example, the average American would attribute all the first four to our Cowboy, and he has none of them. But he is not an actor for nothing. You are quite right about the unreadiness of developing countries for democracy. Corrupt politicians can manipulate the voters even more easily than they can in USA, and there is not a core of informed and intelligent people to criticize them.

I hope you will forgive me if I do not write again when I have received your package, unless something goes wrong. I shall wait until you have been able to answer this and my letter mailed yesterday, and send my thanks in advance. All the best.

Love,
Bonnie

March 12, 1984
Dear Bonnie,

Both your February letters were gratefully received after my three week stay lacking two days in the Hartford Hospital. Only twice before in my life and then only about three days each time was I so confined. On the 25th of January Mary and I drove to Hartford to find an attachment for her sewing machine. She parked on Sherman Street and we walked about a mile to the store—to no avail. Then we walked back to the car and almost reached it when I stumbled over an upheaval in the sidewalk and landed in a snow bank. I was taken to the hospital in an ambulance and then operated on for a fractured right hip. The doctor pinned me with a Yale Nail and finished after midnight. It was quite an experience. My therapist is most encouraging. My x-rays have all been fine. Now I get about with a walker; next it will be a stick with prongs, then a cane and then—three cheers! Dr. Burnett says it will take six months to heal completely so Mary and I have changed our trip through England to September 2nd. We can fly earlier so that we can see you if you are planning to be in England the latter part of August—that is if you want to see us. Just where are you being stationed? I am so glad your people truly appreciate what you are doing in Africa and want you to have a sojourn in England. You have earned it!

I will try to send you all the food and shoes you need this week. You told me shoes 8 1/2, but you did not mention the width so I shall have to guess. I am delighted the slacks were the right size and you received them. The day I mailed the packages, I will write you so that you can be on the lookout. Thank you for telling me about the foolishness of special delivery stamps in Africa—sorry.

With my walker, I did get out to vote for the Democratic Town Committee and I made a trip to doctor's office. As soon as our new snow disappears, I shall venture forth again.

I am rereading The Palliser Trollope Novels of Anthony Trollope. And I have ample time to think.

I am distressed about the rise of Gary Hart as a candidate for the US presidency. Instinctively, I neither like him nor trust him. He reminds me of a Democratic Reagan. He does not seem genuine to me. As a student at Yale Law School he was not brilliant. I am writing our Senator Christopher Dodd to chastise him for supporting Gary Hart. I do believe that Dodd is doing this so that he can have an opportunity to be chosen for VP, but he is not ready for this. Gary Hart's emphasis on youth and new ideas is ridiculous. He doesn't understand the meaning of history and maturity any more than Reagan does. Mondale is a far better choice—character, sensitivity, background and understanding. The people in this country are swayed by such inconsequential matters. If they cannot think any better than this, our country is doomed. Our movies, our TV, our modern literature and our art all show how far we have sunk. Surely, our president is the worst of all. The antics of many of our students, especially those in public institutions of higher learning make me cringe. But we do have some fine ones mixed in!

Edna

March 1, 1984
Accra, Ghana, West Africa
c/o The Rev. Canon David Pain

Greetings from Philip Quaque Monastery!

The big news is that the squatters have finally evacuated the first floor apartment of the building we are renting for the Seminary. That has made it possible to shelve the whole library already catalogued, and thereby to make it available for use. This comes at the end of term, and it will take time to get the books arranged in the right order.

So the full benefit will not be realized until after vacation. But it is a milestone.

Had I written this letter a month ago, I would have enthused over the progress on our new monastery. The builders wanted to get the walls of the whole plant up before putting on the roof. As a result, the guest reception room, the chapel and sacristy, and the common room-library were enclosed and we can see what the whole will look like. It is most impressive and will be thoroughly functional. The supervisor of the work was there when I visited it and gave the impression that the roofing was to begin right away.

That was over a month ago and nothing has been done since. The cause seems to have been the inability to produce the iron rods needed for the structure. That has been the history of the project all along. Shortages of essential materials have delayed for months each new stage of buildings. We hear that the rods have now been procured, so perhaps we shall have another spurt forward. But no doubt when it comes time to install the plumbing or wiring further delays will occur.

Speaking of the latter, electricity is now rationed. There is not enough water at the Nkruma Dam to generate all that is needed. For the past month the current has been turned on from 9 am to 2 pm and from 6 to 9 pm. That has been fairly easy to adjust to, be we hear there may have to be further cutbacks. Even now, there is not enough power to pump the water into the heart of the city with sufficient force to get it up to us on the top of a hill. We have to ship in most of it in barrels. But one adjusts. The most distressing aspect of the shortage to Ghanaians is that the refrigeration plants have closed down and bodies cannot be saved for the big weekly funerals.

For myself I can only report that I remain healthy and happy. I am enjoying the teaching more and more. It has been decided that I am to spend most of the summer in England. The powers-that-be think I shall profit from getting out of Africa for a while, though as I keep insisting I am feeling fine here. But I welcome the opportunity to do some research, to look for books for our library, to make a long retreat, and to visit friends and associates. I shall make my headquarters at Willen Priory, Milton Keynes, Bucks, MK15 9AA, telephone (0908) 663749. I plan to fly up on June 15th and will stay possibly until August 31. If you are in England, do try to get in touch.

Father Superior is visiting us and it is a joy to have him here. I am sending this letter back with him to be duplicated and mailed to you.

Love,
Bonnie

March 1984
Accra, Ghana, West Africa
c/o The Rev. Canon David Pain
Dear Edna;

If you have received my last two letters you know that your Christmas package arrived safely. The two letters probably arrived together. I had intended one to be mailed on the trip before, but I asked the person handling it to write on the outside if he received the package. As the package was not at the post office, he did not receive it there, and so did not mail the letter at all. I assumed that he had; hence my second letter. But the important thing is that I have received the package and I am delighted with the contents. The trousers are just what I wanted. They are (as always with me) a bit long, but someone here will take them up. Also the belts can be adjusted to fit my slimmer waist until such time as I get my weight back. (One of the reasons for the trip to England this summer is to fatten me up. We shall see. When I was in England 1931-1933 I lost weight down to about what I am now.)

Although I had said I would not write again until you had a chance to answer my last two, I am taking advantage of our Superior's visitation to have this one mailed to you in the States. So please look on this as a non-letter. IF you have already answered the previous two, do not reply to this until I have responded to yours. Correspondence can get too complicated when letters are continually crossing each other. But I do want you to know how much I appreciate you gifts— all of them—and your lovely card. The star will decorate our house next Christmas.

I forget whether I told you we have at last got full possession of the house for the seminary and the library is almost shelved. It is a joy to have the books coming available. The term is about to end, but everything should be shipshape when the men return. I hope the winter is not being too hard on you.

Love,
Bonnie

GENERAL LETTER
March 1984
Accra, Ghana, West Africa
c/o The Rev. Canon David Pain

Greetings from Philip Quaque Monastery!

The second term of St. Nicholas Theological School, Cape Coast, has just ended. It went very well. The twenty-two men who are being prepared for the priesthood in the Anglican Church come from all six dioceses in Ghana. At present they are in their first or second year. Next year we hope to have all three classes that will complete the full course.

We have a small faculty, so each of us has to teach several courses. I am handling church history, liturgics, and the prophets. Next year I hope to add a course in apologetics. The students are eager and responsive, and a joy to teach.

All the library that has reached us so far has been catalogued and is on the shelves. The books are either gifts from friends or purchased with grants received for the purpose. We are hoping to continue getting books; in fact, a shipment is on its way out at present. A good library is essential to a seminary and already ours is quite adequate. But we intend to keep aiming at no less than the best.

Africa deserves that. The church here is very much alive. One difference that one notices on arrival is that, unlike in American and England, people go to church. On Sunday morning at our sizable cathedral there are three services. The first two are well attended, and the third has a wall-to-wall congregation. Gradually the people are learning to get over their stiff and former Anglicanism. Native hymns, drums, dancing are being introduced.

It is essential that Christianity be Africanized. For too long it has been associated with an alien culture. If it is legitimate for Anglo-Saxons to portray Christ with blond hair and blue eyes, it is equally appropriate here to present him as African. Actually, a first century Galilean, with a swarthy complexion, black hair and dark eyes, was more like the latter than the former. Now that the clergy of the Anglican Church in Ghana are all natives (there are only four white priests, three of us at the Seminary) the time is ripe to integrate Christianity into the indigenous culture.

The African membership of the Order of the Holy Cross is also growing. We have now two life professed Ghanaians and two under annual vows. The novitiate is here at Philip Quaque Monastery and has three members. It is a great privilege to have a part in developing the Church and the Order in Africa.

This summer I am to be in England, doing some study in preparation for my work here next year. If you should be going there this summer, do get in touch. My headquarters will be Willen Priory, Milton Keynes, Bucks, MK15 9AA, telephone (0908) 663749 from June 15 to August 31.

I hope all is well with you.

As ever,
Bonnie Spencer

April 4, 1984
Accra, Ghana, West Africa
c/o The Rev. Canon David Pain
Dear Edna,

The news of your accident and all the consequent discomfort distresses me, but it is good to know that you have come through so well and are taking it so patiently. I hope you are working through all your aids in walking on schedule, but when you get to the cane, I advise you to stick to it. I use a cane every time I go walking. I find it a safeguard against falling when I contact an irregularity in the road, of which there are many here.

As for your trip to England, you have now postponed it beyond my stay there. I have to return to Ghana on August 31. I should be delighted to see you earlier that week if you can arrange to be there. It looks now as if August will be a busy month for me, but I can spend a day or two with you just before my flight home, and that will be a real pleasure to climax my visit.

As always, I enjoy your enclosures. The news about Gary Hart comes as a surprise. I was getting the impression that Mondale was a shoe-in. I fully share your opinion of him. I believe he would make a great president. The only difficulty is that he does not have a chance of being elected. He's too intelligent and honest, like Stevenson and Humphreys. That kind never get elected; they do not have enough charisma. So although Gary Hart may be, as you say, a less worthy candidate, I think he had a far better chance of defeating the cowboy, and that is the most important thing at the moment. In fact, if he gets the nomination on a wave of enthusiasm that sweeps him past Mondale, I think the Democrats may go into the election with sufficient vigor to carry it off. If Mondale succeeds in getting nominated by merely having accumulated enough delegates, I am afraid many people will just not be interested. Incidentally I should like to have voted for him in the New York primary (the only real opportunity there was Glenn) but my ballot reached me too late to be returned in time to be counted. I fear the same will be true of the election ballot, so I shall have to sit this one out.

If, when this reaches you, you have not sent the shoes, my size is 8 1/2 B. I did not think the width made a difference in the kind of shoes I had in mind. However, if you have not sent the package by the time you get this, you might put off mailing it until August. Packages in particular take forever in transit, since customs feels it must sit on them for a couple of weeks or more to show its importance. Therefore a package sent now would probably not reach me until after I have left for England June 15th.

We have just had a good thunderstorm—this is the rainy season—which has cooled things off beautifully. For the past month the weather has been oppressively humid, even though not much hotter than usual and with cool breezes to relieve the heat. But the humidity kept one in almost perpetual sweat, which in turn produced prickly heat. So the change is welcome.

The candidates for the next class at the Seminary are taking their entrance exams today. It sounds as if we shall have the full number. That will mean that next fall the Seminary will have all three year classes which is the full complement. I hope to have courses for the men in each year, two for the new comers and one each of the other two. This coming term I shall have seven lectures a week because I am having to catch up the second year men with what they did not get last year.

It is too bad that the American electorate is so moronic. But that is how it is. Only a person who makes a strong positive impression on TV has a chance. Unfortunately the Democrats are up against an experienced actor. As long as he sticks to the script provided for him by the best public relations firm in the country, and skillful speech writers, he is hard to beat. He can do this all the better because he had not enough intelligence to have any ideas of his own that might get in the way. So I do hope the Democrats can put up a candidate who can give him real competition and possibly even defeat him.

Keep up the good work and get well as fast as you can. But don't try to rush it. Slow but sure is the best progress.

Love,
Bonnie

April 20, 1984
Dear Bonnie,

It was good to receive your letter this week. Two weeks ago I sent your light shoes—soft gray leather trimmed with white—Bass shoes—8 1/2 medium. My brother and his wife took my walker and me to Lord & Taylor where I found them. I insured them—air mail. More than three weeks ago Mary took me with my walker to two grocery stores where I parade up and down the aisles looking for products. I sent you some 21 pounds of food—canned tuna, salmon, corned beef, peanut butter, cookies, coffee, Ovaltine, tea (and some orange marmalade from Mary). The post office refused to insure food so heaven only knows when you will receive it.

Mary and I plan to leave for London via British Airways Monday, August 27th and will arrive Tuesday, the 28th. We are going to stay at the Park Lane in London. I have always enjoyed that hotel and hope it is still good. Can you give us the 29th and 30th? You can show us the sights, and I will pay the expenses. You wrote me your location but where is it? Perhaps you can give me some advice on the rest of our stay in London before we embark on our tour. Since Country Inn Tours of Walnut Creek, California did not have enough guests sign for the September 2nd "British Journey," they have booked us for September 9th. I thought we might do Kent, Oxford and Cambridge before the tour.

My therapist thinks my progress in healing has been splendid. I can now take steps without my walker so I expect Thursday when I see my doctor that he will give me the cane with the prongs on the bottom. When I reach the stage of a regular cane, I think I will follow your good advice. My six months will be up in July. I think I have really been very fortunate. I have been able to attend some of my Capitol Region Conference of Churches meetings, walker and all. I have walked around our circle outside. I get my meals, do the dishes, and wash my clothes, etc. I try to be as independent as I can.

Somehow I think Mondale will make it. The Christian Science Monitor and the Wall Street Journal carried articles relating to the story of Hart's escapades when he was a senior in high school. He and his pal stole the final chemistry exam the night before. Since they were only C students, the teachers wondered how they could get most of the 50 questions right. He found out how they did it and graded them both C. I would have flunked them! He could not have been very bright if he had to cheat, and he was old enough to know better. I began to teach when I was seventeen. We do not need any more tricky

Dickies for president. The Yuppies are too selfish to care about those who are less fortunate. Hart's ideas are not so new, and I think he lacks depth. I fail to see how he can be called handsome; he does not have a good face.

Your new monastery sounds most impressing, and I am happy that you have found so much joy in working with your students. There is no more fulfilling occupation.

I did a telephone opinion survey for the Democrats and found it both interesting and revealing. One man told me that he had not voted in 20 years and he was not planning to vote this year. Our people do not appreciate their democracy and they know so little about it.

Keep well and happy.

[on envelope: "My Reply April 20 not received]

GENERAL LETTER
May 1984
Accra, Ghana, West Africa
c/o The Rev. Canon David Pain

Greetings from Philip Quaque Monastery!

This is the rainy season. That does not mean that it is raining all the time. We have many sunny days; others that are cloudy or partly cloudy. Every now and then there is a downpour. It usually does not last long but it is plentiful. I gather we are getting more rain than in the recent years. It is hope that the drought cycle is ending.

The storms are usually accompanied by thunder and lightning. Last week the local power station was struck and its transformer burnt out. For what they say will be at least a month the electricity is not rationed but off altogether. After 6 pm there is not much to do but go to bed. Machinery that depends on electricity cannot operate. But despite the amenities that are usually available, the people here live close enough to a more primitive way of life that they can revert to it when necessary.

The plans for my summer in England are shaping up. I am registered for a week's course at Oxford and for a ten-day retreat with the Community of the Love of God there. I have a couple of appointments to visit with friends and I hope to set up more after I get to England, so that I can see as many of our Associates there as possible. My headquarters and address, in case you have misplaced it, is Willen Priory, Milton Keynes, Bucks, MK15 9AA, England.

The Seminary is rapidly approaching the end of the academic year. On the whole, I think my teaching has gone as well as could be expected. Communication has been difficult because, among other things, I have tried to crowd too much material into a lecture. I shall know how to simplify them for next year.

Last Sunday the American ambassador visited Cape Coast and invited all US citizens to meet him at the Franciscan Priory. About twenty of us turned up. All were engaged in religions or educational work, most in fact both. The other churches represented, as far as I could discover them, were Roman Catholic, Mormons, and the Bible Institute. The ambassador led a discussion on embassy policy and inquired whether we knew of any difficulties that Americans were experiencing. No problems in relations to the Ghanaian government were raised, which is very encouraging. I was impressed by the ambassador and his wife and believe they are doing a good job as our representatives.

My trip to England prevents me from attending the centennial celebration at the Cathedral of St. John the Divine, New York, on June 2nd. I hope, if you are near enough, you will be able to attend. I wish you a pleasant and restful summer. When I write again next fall, I shall be recounting my English Experience.

As ever,
Bonnie

The following letter is a repeat of her April 20th letter, which was not received in Ghana since Br. Spencer had left for England. This July letter is also written after her phone call to Bonnie in England sometime in June.

July 1, 1984
Dear Bonnie,

It was good to hear your voice, but you seemed so far away, of course you were. I'm so glad you have gained weight. Did your doctor tell you that your loss was due to your African diet? I hope he had good news for you.

I am sorry that neither my packages nor my letter got through to you. I kept expecting to hear from you. In March I sent you 21 pounds of food (canned tuna, salmon, corned beef, as well as peanut butter, Ovaltine, tea, coffee, cookies, etc. Mary sent you orange marmalade. The post office refused to insure the food. Mary took me with my walker to two grocery stores where I paraded up and down the aisles looking for desirable items. I hope the one who finally got them was in dire need.

On April 6th, I mailed you light shoes—soft gray leather trimmed with white—Bass shoes—8 1/2 medium. My brother and his wife took my walker and me to Lord & Taylor where I found them. They are insured.

Mary and I plan to leave for London August 27th and will arrive Tuesday the 28th. We are going to stay at the Park Lane in London. I have always enjoyed that hotel and hope it is still good. I am delighted that you can meet us the 29th at the Park Lane. I have reserved a room for you at the Park Lane for the 29th and 30th so that you can make your plane on the 31st. You will be my guest. Do tell us what you want most to do when you come. Is there a play you would enjoy? The English theater is always superior. We can take you wherever you want to go.

Since Country Inn Tours of Walnut Creek, California did not have enough guests sign for September 2nd for "British Journey," they have booked us for September 9th. I thought we might do Kent (Canterbury Cathedral, and Dover), Oxford, Cambridge, York and Norwich before the tour. We will make London our headquarters. Do you think it would be fun for us to use the trains as a means for transportation? Mary has never been to England before.

In summer 1937 I came to London with a Boston University (my alma mater) group to study at the University of London. When it was over, four of us toured the cathedrals on our trek to Liverpool for our ship home. I loved Wells; we stayed at the vicar's close.

I have continued to improve since my accident—thank goodness. I am basically healthy. I progressed from my walker to a regular cane. I can walk a mile at a time outdoors. In the house I can manage without a cane. I take therapy twice a week at the Jefferson House in town. Next week I hope to be able to drive my car and it will be wonderful to be independent once more.

You wrote me your location, but where is it? I am so glad you have the opportunity to live in England this summer.

I hope Mondale does not select Gary Hart for his V.P. Whom do you prefer?

We both look forward to greeting you on August 29th.

Note on separate page:
Last letter April 17
Mine April 20
2 pkg. food, shoes (April 6)
Park Lane August 27, 28 29 & 30?

Note on envelope:
My answer July 1 after telephone call to England

July 23, 1984
Willen Priory
Milton Keynes, Bucks, England
Dear Edna,

Thank you for your letter. I am looking forward eagerly to being with you at the Park Lane Hotel. You are most gracious to arrange this. I shall probably telephone you on the evening of the 28th to make sure you have arrived safely. I expect to get to London on a train due at about 10am and shall proceed at once to the Park Lane. I am glad to learn you are recovering so well from your accident. I am happy to leave it to you to decide what we should do. I know nothing about what plays are on, so if you want to include one, I leave the choice entirely up to you. My only suggestion is that, if we go, it be on the night of August 29, because I shall have to be up early on the 31st to make my plane, so would prefer to get to bed earlier on the 30th. But visiting with you is the main thing, and a theater party is not essential. Your mention of going to Kent leads me to wonder if you would like to run down to Canterbury for a one-day trip. Again, this is not necessary, but it might be a possibility for the 30th. The train would be best as they have one-day roundtrips.

I have written Ghana about your packages. My hope is that they are at the Christian Service Committee. They never informed us about your Christmas package until we asked for it. I suspect they have done the same thing with the last two. I have told the Brethren to inquire about town.

I have just seen the doctor for the third time. He gave me a thorough check and al the tests and everything came out normal. I have already gained about 20 pounds since I have been here—which is about half of what I had lost. The doctor thinks it is simply a dietary deficiency and I hope to see a dietitian in order to find out what supplement I can take to overcome it. The doctor is thoroughly happy over my physical condition, as am I. I never felt better.

I know you rejoice that Hart did not get the VP. We can discuss the choice (which does seem to have helped) and the prospects when we get together. I am trying very hard to convince myself that there is a chance. I shall certainly keep praying for it. I cannot vote because absentee ballots reach us too late for the election.

All the best. See you August 29th.

Love,
Bonnie

August 11, 1984
Dear Bonnie,

The report on your health is superb, but it worries me to think that you lost 40 pounds in Africa. It must have been the diet as well as the climate—and you never complained! I promise to feed you well in London. Please order all your favorite food.

I hold the confirmation of the reservation that I made for you at the Park Lane. We shall be in the lobby to greet you when you arrive after 10 on the 29th. It will be so good to see you. Do call me on the evening of the 28th as you suggested. We expect to arrive in London (Heathrow) at 6:40 am on the 28th and shall go straight to our hotel. Fortunately for me, I sleep easily on planes, but Mary does not. We now have all our necessary documents. We shall try to get tickets for a good play on the 29th. Your suggestion of a train trip to Canterbury on the 30th is fine with us. While you are with us, we want very much to embark on ventures that are most pleasing to you—so just tell us what you most wish to do.

My personal physician, dentist, and opthamologist have all given me a clean bill of health. On the 17th, I shall get my last check-up from my surgeon. Usually I walk one or two miles every day, not including my shopping expeditions and household chores. One day I walked four miles. I feel far stronger.

I now drive my car—although I am presently braking with my left foot. (Mary has always done that). It is delightful to be on my own. And now I am able to enjoy the luxury of a warm sit down tub bath every day. I hope I don't get lost in some of those big tubs in Britain. Around the house, I navigate without my cane, but outside I generally use it. In all, I have been most fortunate, and I am ever grateful to my ancestors. I rejoice that I have never indulged in alcohol or tobacco.

The political scene has grown quite exciting. Every evening I watched the Democratic Convention. I thought Mondale did very well. Jackson is a fine speaker, but I have some questions about him. Thank goodness—Gary Hart lost. As VP I don't believe he would have been loyal to Mondale. I think Ferraro will be an asset; I am relieved that she is pro-choice on abortion. The prelates up our way are not reconciled to this position—unfortunately. I still believe that it was providential that the leaders who founded our country were Protestant. I shudder to think what the dominance of the Spanish at that time in history would now be in the same dilemma as Latin America. Ireland has not recognized true religious freedom as yet. In my books, there is no one church. All my ancestors have been Protestant ever since there were any, but I have good friends of all faiths.

We shall be happy to see you on the 29th at Park Lane—remember you will be my guest.

Edna

September 2, 1984
Accra, Ghana, West Africa
c/o The Rev. Canon David Pain
Dear Edna,

How can I thank you enough for the wonderful two days in London? The hotel was, as you predicted, most comfortable and homelike. The meals were superb. It was good to see the National Gallery and Hyde Park again, and Canterbury was a great joy. Then on top of that was your most generous gift, including the much appreciated taxi ride to Heathrow. The whole was a perfect end to my stay in England. The flight to Accra was uneventful, except meeting some interesting people, including one of the Catholic bishops—a Ghanaian. I was met by the sub prior and the senior novice and drove at once to Cape Coast arriving about 10:30 pm.

When I got here I found the shoes you sent. They are perfect and could not be a better fit. Again my gratitude is more than I can express. If there was anything else in the package with the shoes, it was purloined. There is no sign of the other package—nor of your letter. We have had so much trouble with the Christian Service Committee, that I suggest, if you send anything else, you address it to me:

Anglican Diocese of Cape Coast
c/o The National Catholic Service Center
PO Box 0257 OSU
Accra, Ghana, West Africa

I think they will be more reliable.

This should reach you just about the time you get home. I hope your whole trip came up to your expectations and that it did not tire you unduly. Please give my best to Mary. It was a pleasure to be with her also.

Although I have been here only three days, I am fully settled in. This morning, I got to the Seminary and have things organized for cataloging the new books on hand and getting the shelving reorganized before term starts. I must say that, much as I enjoyed England, it is good to be back home.

I hope your optimism regarding the election is justified. I regret not being able even to vote—but I shall pray. I do feel the present administration is deplorable.

May God bless all your endeavors.

Love,
Bonnie

October 5, 1984
Dear Bonnie,

How thoughtful of you to send a letter that awaited me when I arrived home from England. Whenever I return from a journey, I am hit by an empty house, and your letter helped. My brother Clifford met Mary and me in New Haven where the CT Limousine had deposited us. My brother Charles had filled my refrigerator with the necessary articles of food. My good neighbor had cared for my house, plants, papers, and mail during my absence.

It was a joy to have you with us in London, but the time seemed so short. I missed you—I wish you could have been with us on our whole journey. We covered Devon, Cornwall, the Cotswolds, the Lake District, and Edinburgh. We spent too short a time in Wells— my favorite. In cathedrals, I like to spend time enough to let the atmosphere seep into my veins. Coventry cannot be compared to the old cathedrals for they are far superior. All of Britain seemed so neat, and fondly cared for. I am especially taken with the Salisbury Cathedral. Years ago I stayed overnight at the Vicar's Close in Wells—I have many fond memories there.

Somehow I managed to walk (too slowly) up and down all kinds of stairs. I fear that I slowed Mary's progress. By Christmas I expect to be back to normal. I can now walk a little faster than I did. Unfortunately, I picked up some kind of flu virus in Edinburgh—probably from some other tourists in our group; they were not careful about covering their mouths. I was in bed for one full day, but managed to carry on the rest of the journey and reach home. Mary now has it, but she has been in bed for a week. Don't catch it if it comes your way for it is most enervating.

On the 9th, I shall try sending you another food package—not so large as the last one so that it may get through. I will try the new address you gave me. What kind of clothing or what other articles do you wish me to send? Things take so long to reach you that I need to send your Christmas package soon. I do suspect that someone stole the letter of April 20th I mailed in the post office. I do hope this one reaches you

I am so relieved that you took a taxi to the airport; I could not bear to think of you lugging all that heavy baggage any other way. Thank you for letting me have a tiny stake in Africa where you are giving your all. How is your weight holding up? Do take better care of yourself.-even though you have grown a beard—it startled me—but perhaps you need it in Africa

As Ever,
Edna May

GENERAL LETTER
October 1984
Accra, Ghana, West Africa
c/o The Rev. Canon David Pain

Greetings from Ghana to '31!
Dave Vipond's request for class notes on what we are doing at 75 reached me too late for a reply before his deadline. Anyhow, I am not 75 until December. But this letter will give you some idea what I am up

to. It is most stimulating and I must admit I feel as young as ever. On the other hand, my grey beard is an advantage in Africa, where age is accorded greater respect. All in all, I am having a ball.

St. Nicholas Theological College, Cape Coast, has opened for its third year. For the first time, therefore, we have all three classes. I now teach four courses: Church History and Liturgics for the first year men, a group that has made a very favorable impression on me in its first sessions; the Prophets to the second year me; and a new course called Proclamation for the seniors. Technically, it should be called Apologetics, but I dislike that title because it sounds so defensive. Its purpose is to relate contemporary theology and practice to African culture and to the parishes where they will be ministering. It is a discussion course in which the students' contribution is more important than mine. It is already off to a good start.

Philip Quaque Monastery is also prospering. We now have five professed members, three of whom are Ghanaians; and five in the novitiate—four Ghanaians and one Liberian. The Rector of St. Nicholas Theological College is also living with us. That makes us rather crowded and prevents us from admitting any more aspirants so long as we have to remain in our temporary quarters. We have a monastery in the country which is about two-thirds built. Unfortunately, we have not been able to do any more work on it since last winter because the Centenary Fund has not yet produced for us the $50,000 needed to complete it.

My summer in England was very helpful. I regained much of the weight I had lost and recharged my batteries both intellectual and spiritual. Now it is good to be back in Ghana and at work.

I am sorry I missed the fall reunion. I hope it was a success. I am still looking forward to our 55th.

As ever,
Bonnie

P.S. If you were one of those who sent me a note from the reunion last spring, I thank you. The remembrance meant much to me.

ANOTHER GENERAL LETTER
postmarked October 30, 1984
c/o The Rev. Canon David Pain
Accra, Ghana, West Africa

Greetings from Ghana!

My summer in England was a great success. I regained about 25 pounds and no longer look like an inmate of a concentration camp. The Society of the Sacred Mission in both its Milton Keynes and Lancaster houses was a gracious host. I got around much of England and Wales visiting Associates, and was able to see the 18th century Scottish Communion Offices in the National Library in Edinburgh. I have been wanting to see those for years. I had an excellent course of study for a week in Oxford, including lectures on Whitehead and Heidegger by our Associate, Dr. Macquarrie, with whom I stayed. Also at Oxford I made a ten-day retreat at the Convent of the Sisters of the Love of God. Finally, in various places I assembled a large number of books for our library here. They have yet to arrive from England.

Here in Ghana St. Nicholas Theological College has now opened for its third year. We therefore have all grades for the first time. I am teaching Church History and Liturgics to the first year men; a course on the prophets and wisdom literature for the second year; and a course called Proclamation to the seniors. That course is designed to relate modern theology and practice to the parishes in which they will be ministering. As the latter are biblically fundamentalist and doctrinally firmly wedded to turn-of-the-century Anglo-Catholicism, the gap that must be bridged is enormous. But Ghana is beginning to live in the 20th century and, if the Anglican Church is going to hold its intelligent members, it must come to terms with contemporary thought. The course is conducted as a discussion to which the men will be contributing more than I do. They seem already to have grasped the purpose and importance of what we are attempting and are responding well.

Philip Quaque Monastery is also prospering. We now have 5 Professed OHC (3 are Ghanaians) and 5 in the novitiate (4 Ghanaians and 1 Liberian). Fr. Ralph Martin, SSM still lives with us. Sr. Jean and

Sr. Rosina (when she arrives) live nearby and join us for Office and meals. So our choir has 13 members—probably the largest in OHC! Also our 11 residents crowd our living quarters. Meanwhile, our new monastery out in the country stands 2/3rds finished, with no work having been done on it since last winter. Unfortunately, the Centenary Fund has not yet produced for us the $50,000 needed to finish it.

Otherwise all goes well and happily. I am feeling fine and seem to be holding my weight this time. I deeply appreciate the opportunity to teach and I am enjoying it immensely. Please keep us all in your prayers. All best wishes.

As ever,
Bonnie

November 5, 1984
c/o The Rev. Canon David Pain
Accra, Ghana, West Africa
Dear Edna,

Because of your letter of last spring which never reached me, I am getting concerned that I have not heard from you since we parted in England. Did you get my letter which I wrote on my return here? In it I told you that the shoes have reached me, but nothing else. They fit perfectly and are just what I wanted. Thank you again for them, for the glorious time in London and for your most generous parting gift.

Probably your letter is en route, but I want to get this off with someone who is going to Accra on Wednesday. I have received a slip from the Post Office in Accra that says a registered package is awaiting me. I shall give him authority to sign for it and I hope he can get it. My guess is that it may be from you. If so, it at least is in Ghana. But if it is from you, I am the more surprised that a letter telling me of it has not arrived. Today I received a letter post marked in New York October 19th. * that is the date on the package slip. Also <u>Time</u>, mailed about then, has arrived.

I had planned to delay this until after the news of the election. Voice of America should be announcing the results by Wednesday. We have heard that Mondale made a good impression in the first debate and that there seemed to be a slim chance of his getting somewhere. One of us listened to the second debate and again felt that Mondale showed Reagan up as very stupid. The Voice of America was going to give the reaction of the country a couple of days later. Again someone tuned in and just as it was to start ran to get me. When we got back we heard only the final sentence, "It was the most significant event of the campaign." Significant for whom? Since then we have not had a word. So whether, contrary to my expectations, there is any hope for Mondale, I do not know. Yesterday my absentee ballot arrived—much too late to cast, of course. So all I can do is pray. For the good of the country and the world I hope that phony cowboy is defeated.

Word of Indira Ghandi's assassination has reached us and of the attempt on Margaret. It is getting dangerous to be a ruler these days.

All continues to go well here. I am enjoying my classes more than ever. We are past the midpoint of the term. My health remains good and I seem to be holding on to my weight.

We shall have some temporary changes here beginning next month. Since last winter we have not been able to do any work on our monastery which is about 2/3rds built. It is imperative that we get the funds. So our Prior, Fr. Swayne, is going to America to get the funds. He is resigning his position at the Cathedral. The Bishop calls it a sabbatical, I gather, but Fr. Swayne hopes not to take the work up again. Although the income has been essential in the past, we think we can make it up in other ways, and the job has tied down the only person who could be getting around the country. In any case, Father needs a good rest. He has in fact been sick for the past week with malaria and something else. While he is gone Br. Leonard will be in charge as sub-prior and beginning next summer as prior. He is a Ghanaian. Ever since I got back from England he has been handling the day to day running of the house and is doing a fine job. The novice master is also a Ghanaian so leadership is passing into their hands, as it should. I am very happy about it and get along splendidly with them.

Two of the Sisters of the Order of St. Helena are with us. Sr. Jean teaches in the seminary and is a great backer-up to me. Sr. Rosina, a Ghanaian, is teaching in the church schools, the head religion instructor. It is a joy to have them and they are making a splendid addition to our life and work. Unfortunately, they are here only till Easter and their community says that it cannot find a house at present. But we are hoping that their success will change that decision before long.

I hope you had a glorious time in England and that all is going well since your return.

Love,
Bonnie

[in envelope with letter from Bonnie dated 11/5/84 is the following package list from Edna]

Contents

Cafe Amaretto	8oz	$2.49
Brim Decaf Coffee	8oz	$5.99
Ovaltine	9oz	$1.89
Peanut Butter	18oz	$1.79
Orange Marmalade	16oz	$3.39
Salmon	15.5oz	$3.59
Corned Beef	12oz	$1.49
Tuna Fish	6.5oz	$1.19
Hormel Turkey	6.5oz	$0.99
Swanson Chicken	5oz	$0.99
2 Butter Shortbread Fingers	14.2oz	$0.38
1 Pep. F. Brussels Cookies	5oz	$1.29
1 "" Lemon Nut ""	5oz	$1.09
1 Lipton Tomato Soup	3oz	$0.85
1 Tuna Fish	6.5oz	$1.39
1 Mandarin Orange Segments	11oz	$0.75
		$32.55

November 10, 1984
c/o The Rev. Canon David Pain
Accra, Ghana, West Africa
Dear Edna,

What the Post Office notice had designated a "Registered Package" turned out to be your letter. By registering it you assured its reaching me, but the need to sign for it delayed its reception until someone was going to Accra. Fortunately, someone was, shortly after I got the notice, so I had to wait only a few days for it. But sometimes it is two or three weeks between trips to Accra on a weekday, especially in term time when we all have classes. The Post Office is not open on Saturdays. If you have received the letter I wrote and had mailed at the time your letter was picked up, you know that I was eagerly awaiting it and so I am relieved and delighted to receive it. I rejoice that the trip was such a success and the homecoming accomplished without difficulty. I agree with you about the old cathedrals, though I found Coventry interesting except the horrible tapestry that make our Lord look like a bumble bee. Wells is also one of my favorites. It is interesting, however, that its best feature (in my opinion)—the crossed arch, was erected in the 19th century because the chancel arch was collapsing. It is rare that a necessary bit of repair work turns out to be so appropriate, especially if it was done in the Victorian era.

I am writing this letter now in case anyone goes to Accra in the next few days. If not, I shall hold it until Fr. Swayne leaves early in December. By mail from here it can hardly reach you much before then, and I shall feel safer if it is mailed in USA. In either case, it certainly will not reach you before you will have sent the Christmas package, if you try to get it here before the end of the year. So your request for suggestions no longer applies. You own selections are better than anything I would ask anyway. However, for future reference, a very light white cap (visor and net top) would be useful. A black 34" belt (one inch wide) is another item hard to get here. Handkerchiefs and a light, short-sleeved, blouse type shirt would be welcome. I am in no immediate need for any of these. I list them only because you have asked me to do so.

I am sorry my beard startled you. I thought everyone knew I had one by last summer. It is a nuisance to shave every morning without running water and often without a light. Furthermore, the beard makes me look a bit older, which is an advantage in Africa. But I admit my chief reason for growing it is because I like it.

Alas, I gather the cowboy was reelected by a land-slide. (I have not yet seen the details.) As you know, I expected this all along. After what I heard of the debates, As I indicated in my last letter, I entertained a bit of hope, based mostly on my continued ignorance of how the country was reacting. But I should have known better. I was hoping that the issues might make a difference. I forgot that the American electorate NEVER votes on issues, only on charisma, the phonier the better. If a person with decent policies has the charisma—like FDR, Truman, Kennedy, Johnson (and Carter by a whisker over Ford), the country is in luck. But Stevensons, Humphreys and Mondales have no chance, no matter how sound and necessary their policy is. I noticed that <u>Time</u> some weeks ago published a poll in which half the questions were on personality and half on essential policy. The personality was 60-70% pro-Reagan, and the policy was pro-Mondale by the same percentage. But, as usual, that made no difference. If my health holds up and I am still wanted, I shall probably stay in Africa for another term. I don't want to live in USA while Reagan is in the White House. The real tragedy, however, is that the "moral majority" will now take over the government, including the Supreme Court, and we are condemned for a generation to government by bigots. Abortion, of course, will be made illegal and capitol punishment restored. Civil and human rights, expect for the wealthy whites, will become a good memory. Eventually, of course, the whole Hollywood extravaganza will collapse, but I doubt if we shall live to see it.

I am sorry you and Mary had the flu. So far I have escaped and my weight is holding up. Please give Mary my regards. Take care of yourself and don't try too much too soon. Thank you again for everything.

Love,
Bonnie

I shall be on the lookout for the food package.

December 7, 1984
c/o Rev. David Pain
Accra, Ghana, West Africa
Dear Edna,

Your letter of November 21 has reached me. I am uncertain which letter of mine you had received the day before. I wrote you on November 5, but it seems unlikely that the letter could have reached you so soon. In that letter I told you that a notice of a "registered package" had reached me but I had not been able to collect it. It turned out to be your registered letter. When I got that I answered but kept the letter to be mailed by Fr. Swayne when he went to New York on December 2 (arriving the 3rd). I trust that by now you have received it. So your last two letters have come through all right. Despite that one letter which went astray last spring, I think most of my mail has come through.

But not the food package. Since that is easily identifiable, I fear someone in the Post Office sees no reasons why it should go to me instead of him, and accordingly appropriates it. We would have greatly enjoyed the contents you list, but I can only conclude someone else has enjoyed them for us. The upshot of this is that I am convinced that food packages will not be delivered, so I suggest that you stop sending them. Much as we would like the goodies, we get sufficient food—I seem even to be gaining weight this time, and I hate to see you waste the money and effort. I hope that your Christmas package arrives, as it should since it is insured. I do not know whether you addressed it to the Catholic Service Center or to me c/o Canon Pain. I have told the Catholic Center to be on the lookout for it, and I am sure the slip for it will be sent on if it comes to Canon Pain's box, as the slip for your registered letter was.

I am also grateful for the subscription to The Christian Science Monitor, and I do hope it comes through. But I am afraid it is not likely to make it. My brother gave me a subscription to Time. The first two copies reached me in mid-October, and not a single one since. Apparently magazines and newspapers, like food packages, are appropriated en route. (We have had this trouble with magazines before.). It is all very frustrating, when people are trying to be helpful to us in ways that we greatly appreciate. We shall see what happens to the <u>Monitor</u>, and I hope for the best till it proves otherwise.

December 13, 1984

I stopped this letter at the above point because I had heard that there were two packages waiting for us in Accra, and I thought I should see if one of them was from you. We now have the packages and neither was. So what I wrote above is still correct.

I have now given my exams and have corrected three of them. The men have not done too badly. In the review sessions I told them just what I would expect and I allowed them to bring notes and books to class. They seem to find it very hard to keep things in their heads for exam purposes. My main objective is to see if they understood certain points I have made and if they can demonstrate that from notes, it is all right with me. This year they seem to have understood more than last. Perhaps in part it is because I am teaching better. My material is more digested and I am more aware of their limitations.

What a coincidence that the Provost of the Cathedral in Accra should turn up next door to you. I probably have met him, but so far as I know, only in a group. I rarely get to Accra and have almost no contact with the clergy there.

Thank you for the clippings. Reagan is determined to do nothing for the poor. His clientele is the rich. I wish I could agree with Keven Phillip's analysis of realignment, but I see no hopes of it, unless there is a total economic collapse into depression. I fear the present situation is more like the pre-World War I Republican era followed right after the war by the 1920's It also, be it noted, was terminated by a major depression. Republican policy produces great riches for the portions of the population that is noticeable, but has no solid foundation in general well-being. It is an inflated bubble that eventually bursts. But what I think the greatest danger at present is that the "American way of life" as the Reaganites conceive it, is losing favor throughout the world, especially the third world. As more and more turn against it, the Reaganites will become more determined to defend it at any cost.

The obsession over increasing armaments is a clear indication of this. Also the intensification of economic exploitation and the upholding of totalitarian fascist regimes in South America, etc. that live off the exploitation of their own countries.

On that pleasant note, I wish you a blessed Christmas and New Year.

Love,
Bonnie

December 18, 1984
Dear Father Swayne,

It is very good of you to carry my Christmas package to Bonnell Spencer in Ghana. I have encountered great difficulty in reaching him with both packages and letters; some never arrive. I have sent to you at West Park a traveling case filled with clothing, a handy kit, Ammens medicated powder, soap, Velamints, a tin of coffee, and cookies via the United Parcel Service. I carried it to their station in Newington on December 17th and insured it for $200. In this letter I am enclosing a key that you may need to unlock the case if you are questioned at Customs. I am also enclosing a check for forty dollars that I hope will ease your path a little (taxis, etc.) on your way to Ghana. With this letter I have included a letter to Bonnie (with an additional key). Will you please give him this note?

If perchance the travel package does not arrive, will you please let me know? If you have any questions, feel free to call me collect—203-666-9452.

Thank you once again for your consideration. I am sorry to burden you.

May you have a safe and pleasant journey back to Ghana.

Sincerely,
Edna May Sole

December 21, 1984
West Park, New York
Dear Mrs. Sole,

Your letter and the package for Bonnie Spencer has arrived and I will be happy to carry it to him. Many thanks for the check for $40.00 which I greatly appreciate. I return to Ghana January 11th, so the package will reach Bonnell soon.

Have a Merry Christmas.

Fr. Christian Swayne

December 19, 1984
c/o Rev. David Pain
Accra, Ghana, West Africa
Dear Edna,

Miracle of miracles! The food package has arrived. As I had given up all hope for it, I did not keep you list of contents. I think most everything arrived, although it had been opened, of course. Somehow I seem to remember you mentioned Ovaltine, and if so, that has gone. But there has arrived: instant (Brim) coffee, Cafe Amaretto, tomato soup, corned beef, chicken, turkey, tuna, salmon, orange segments, marmalade, peanut butter, shortbread fingers, and lemon nut crunch. It was beautifully packaged and everything seems in good shape, though I have not opened anything yet. (Perhaps the crunch is a bit crunched!). The timing is perfect, for they will be a great addition to our Christmas cheer. You are very good to us and all you do is greatly appreciated. Thank you.

The arrival of the food raises my hopes that the Christmas package will get here in the next month or so. The Catholic Service Center seems better than the Protestant one, but that judgment may be unfair. I did not know about the food packages last spring and so never told them to be on the lookout for it. When I told them about the other package they did find the shoes. This time I have been hounding the Catholics about the two packages for a month. Whether that has made the difference I do not know. It may have been that the Protestants got the other package and, as we did not ask for it, never delivered it; or perhaps because they did not ask for it, they never received it. In any case, it is most important that we know of what is enroute, so that we can be asking for it. Your missing letter was the real problem last spring.

As it is now so close to the holidays and many are away until then, I shall keep most of the goodies until we start celebrating. So if you feel a warm glow from Africa during Christmastide, you will know it is our appreciation wafting across the ocean.

December 20, 1984

I changed my mind and decided to celebrate the arrival of the box by opening the Lemon Nut Crunch and to my surprise and delight the cookies were not crunched at all. So the packing was perfect. Also today we could not find any fish in the market, so we had the can of tuna in our "soup." The "soup" is what goes over the rice, cassava, yams, kenki, gory, or whatever the solid base consists of. The combination is really quite good, and the tuna was a real treat.

I do not remember whether I have told you that I hope to go to England again this summer. There were some Associates whom I did not get to see last year, and others whom I want to see again. I also plan to attend a Gaudy at Exeter, my Oxford College, which is holding one for oversees graduates for the first time. As you will remember from Dorothy Sayer's <u>Gaudy Night</u>, it is a reunion. Classes do not mean much at Oxford, so Gaudies are usually for graduates within a span of years. But that will not apply this time.

I also want to look for more books, though where we shall shelve them is a problem. We have already filled a big room and the hall. Those I bought or collected last summer have mostly arrived. I have given them all their call numbers but have a few more cards to type for the files. I should be finished with this lot tomorrow. There is another package for us waiting in Accra which will be picked up tomorrow. I hope it will contain the few remaining books unaccounted for.

I am finishing this letter so that it can go to Accra tomorrow. Even so, it will not reach you in time to wish you a blessed Christmas, but with luck it should not be too long after the New Year to wish you prosperity. I hope your hip has finally healed by now. I was amazed at the amount of walking you did when I was with you, and how well you accomplished it. I often think back on those days together with great joy.

Please give Mary my regards. Don't work too hard. There is much need for you, so you must conserve your strength so that it will be available down the years. All the best.

Love,
Bonnie

Part Two:
December 22, 1984

The mail was forgotten on the trip to Accra yesterday and so did not get to the Post Office. I have therefore reopened this. Mail that had come for us to Accra was picked up and it contained the first number of the <u>Christian Science Monitor</u>, which I have read with great interest and profit. I am most grateful to you for sending it to me, and I hope that it will keep coming despite our unhappy experience with <u>Time</u>. Anyhow, you have done your best and we shall appreciate the copies that reach us.

I hope this time the mail will go to Accra tomorrow so I hasten to close again

With love,
Bonnie

We shall keep asking whether the Christmas package has arrived.

PART FOUR

1985

January 13, 1985
c/o The Rev. Canon David Pain
Accra, Ghana, West Africa
Letter 1.

Dear Edna,

Your Christmas presents have safely arrived. Thank you! Thank you! Thank you! In one of my recent letters I considered suggesting that you send the box to West Park for Fr. Swayne to bring, but I did not because I thought you would have mailed it before my letter got to you. It is splendid that you learned of his visit in time to send it through him. In order to get the items into his luggage he had to open the box and pack them separately. I think he has now given them all to me, and what an array they are. Forgive me if I do not mention each item separately. The shirts are superb. I have tried one on and it fits perfectly. I shall save them for dressy affairs. I much appreciate the handkerchiefs which have rescued me from being in short supply. The cap is just what I wanted and the right size. How did you know that the Jets are my favorite New York team? The belt also is just what I need. We wear one now with our habits instead of the cincture. (I prefer the latter but the Order decided otherwise and one must conform.) The sewing, et al. kit will be most useful, providing many items I lacked and much need. It will be convenient for taking to England as well. The various threads and accessories give me now a wide range for any necessary repairs. (I am not much good at sewing, but at the moment some Sisters are visiting us and one of them has volunteered to do some for me.) The goodies are most welcome. As I write, I am holding back on the first lot you sent me until the Christmas treats and banquets are over. With these additions we shall have something for special occasions through the winter. The medical things are also welcome. And the postcards are beautiful and remind me, in most instances, of places I have been. So a week after Epiphany I am celebrating Christmas in a big way.

Also I am happy to report that the <u>Christian Science Monitor</u> is still coming. Two copies arrived and then nothing for a considerable time. I was afraid the same pattern was developing as with Time magazine—two issues and then no more. But the next two copies of the Monitor arrived within a couple of days of each other. The Christmas mail, plus I think a short Post Office strike, help up delivery. I gather that a newspaper is less attractive to the sticky fingers of Post Office clerks than a glossy American magazine. I hope that is so, for we are all enjoying the Monitor greatly.

As I write this I am having a cup of Brim. Most of the rest of the family have gone to the Cathedral. I celebrated here early and that is enough for me. The Cathedral service is interesting because there is some native music and dancing as part of the Eucharist, but it goes on interminably, as does everything else around here, so I go only when I have to preach. There is a group from California visiting us for two weeks. Tourists cannot usually come because the official exchange into cedis makes foreign currencies almost valueless. We are able to arrange for this group to come because they have paid for their expenses in dollars to our American account and we are using cedis we have earned here to pay for what they need in Ghana.

The others are off getting water which has not reached our house on the top of a hill for a couple of days. This is the chief reason why we are impatient, from the point of view of comfort, to get into our new monastery. Fr. Swayne reports that he has collected enough for the work on it to begin again, so perhaps it will be completed before long. Of course, the main reason we are eager for it is because we do not have room for any more novices and other vocations are waiting to come. Training novices, after all, is the principal work of the house.

I am enjoying the vacation from the seminary and using it to revise my lectures. I now know better how much I can cover in one and perhaps also how to get it over. So a good many lectures I used last year have to be revised. That, of course, is what good teachers do anyway. To give the same material unchanged year after year is deadly dull. I am also doing much reading and incorporating that material along with what I learned last summer in England.

I have begun writing to people there to plan this summer's trip. I hope it will be possible to visit an Associate in Dingwall (near Inverness) both to see him and that part of Scotland. He was away when I wanted to see him last year and when he returned it was too late for me to arrange the trip. Also the reunion for overseas alumni at Exeter College, Oxford, is still on and I hear over 200 have signed up for it, so it should be quite an affair. I doubt if any contemporaries whom I know will be present, though perhaps one or two might show up. But as you are aware, I am a great believer in reunions and I am eager to encourage the college on this, its first venture of the kind. England is slowly learning from America. Concern for the alumni pays big dividends as Williams has discovered to its great benefit. Had you heard, by the way, that 1931's 50th anniversary gift of $2,100,600 was surpassed by 1934—$2,500,000! I thought our record would last longer.

The weather is behaving splendidly. We had a heavy thunderstorm last Friday which will greatly benefit the crops. It was unusual for this, the dry season. Apparently, the years of drought are ending at least for Ghana. The result is that more food is available. Ghana is trying to become self-sufficient in that area, a commendable goal.

Once more I hope 1985 is being good to you. And thank you again and again for all your lovely presents.

Love,
Bonnie

Letter 2
January 14, 1985

In my usual haste to get things done, once more I have to do them twice. Fr. Swayne has had so many things to do since he arrived, especially because of the California visitors, that he has been able to do his unpacking only at odd moments. So he found and gave to me the presents before he came across your letter, which he had among his innumerable papers. He had just told me of your most generous gift to help him with the expenses of getting you presents here. You will be getting tired of me saying thank you, but it is my only way of expressing my deep felt gratitude.

As I have already told you, Fr. Swayne had to unpack your traveling case. The problem was that only a limited number of articles are allowed on the plane. He already had the maximum number without your case. However, scattering the presents through his luggage has not lost any. All those listed in your letter are present and accounted for.

I have already expressed my delight in the presents, but your letter leads me to make a further comment on two of them. I forgot I had specified short sleeved shirts. The real reason was because my arms are shorter than most and consequently sleeves are usually too long. That is not true of the shirts you sent. They are exactly the right length and they give me two more formal shirts, which I actually needed more than short-sleeved ones. Last night I went to a party with the Californian tourists and I wore one of your shirts, which was greatly admired by the Brethren. It also, as you predicted, turned out to be delightfully cool—much better than my short sleeved ones for that matter.

The hat, as I have already said, is just right. Everybody here wears American football, baseball, or what-have-you hats and T-shirts. There is no need to find and send a white one. Again, all the Brethren are very envious of the one I have.

I have not yet discussed the possibility of another term in Ghana with the officials. I am still inclined to it, but they may think me too old to continue teaching. In any case, my taking another term would be considered only if my health remains good. Furthermore, I will have a sufficient vacation between them. I have planned all along to leave after the second term of 1986, since I have things in May that I want to do in America. If I return, it will not be until near the end of September. SO I shall have time for a good rest and opportunity to see my friends. But all is still undecided and probably will be until the last minute. All African decisions have to be made that way because there are so many contingencies.

As usual I find myself in full agreement with you in regard to American politics. Although I am perhaps more pessimistic about immediate prospects, I certainly want everyone to work as hard as possible to improve the situation. Pressure on our elected officials, especially in the legislatures, state and national, is vital, and I rejoice that you are in a position to exert some effectively. Even more important is to improve the electorate. Only informal citizen can vote intelligently and it is necessary to compete against massive misinformation given them by TV. But those who work persistently will achieve much.

Improved school administration is assuredly the key to rescuing public education. I was delighted to learn that Williams gave a doctorate to Feoretta McKenzie for her work as superintendent of the Washington, DC schools. Also the Olmsted prizes to secondary school teachers, nominated by the senior class, is a splendid idea. I certainly am grateful and proud of my association with Williams.

The thing I fear most from the moral majority is that they will get federal legislation enacted making abortion illegal. That would be a great hardship on the poor. The members of the moral majority will have the money to get one properly performed illegally when they want it. Legislation of this kind is like prohibition, the most serious possible violation of the separation of church and state. And it can lead only to the increase of gangsterism, which got its start through Prohibition. But people will never learn.

I guess that concludes all I have to say in epistle 2. Keep up the good work and take care of yourself.

Love,
Bonnie

P.S. The Velamints are delicious.

A GENERAL LETTER

February 1985
c/o The Rev. Canon David Pain
Accra, Ghana, West Africa

Greetings from Ghana!

Since I have by now settled into a routine here, it is difficult to find things to write about. I fear you will begin to consider my letters to be just more of the same. But let me at least report on the first term at St. Nicholas Theological College that ended before Christmas.

The new men in the first year class have turned out to be a fine group. They are younger than their predecessors. The first two years brought to the seminary mostly men who had been catechists for years, who at last had the opportunity to prepare for the priesthood. This year's neophytes have come to us in the normal course of their education. I found them easier to teach, partly no doubt because I am getting better at communicating, and I was encouraged by the examinations they wrote. I had them for church history twice a week and liturgics once.

With the second year men I had only one course, on the prophets. They also did well on their exams. My biggest joy was the new course for seniors. This is the first time we have had a third year class. I call the course "Proclamation." In it I am trying to relate contemporary insights, both religious and secular, to the Gospel on the one hand and to the parishes to which they will be going on the other. They wrote a term paper and I was pleased that they seemed to have grasped at least the main points I had been emphasizing. Some of them reproduced the details as well. We were able to meet only once a week because I also had to finish the liturgics course with them. So we dealt just with rather theoretical preliminaries. This term we have two weekly sessions and I hope through their contributions to the discussion to relate the theology to African concepts and to the situation in the parishes.

Another project is the preparation of revision suggestions for the West African Book of Common Prayer. Our bishop has formed a diocesan committee for that purpose. Sister Jean of the Order of St. Helena is with us. She has a masters from Notre Dame in liturgics and is teaching in the seminary. She and I are acting as advisors to the committee. It is a joy to be able to make available to them my experience on the Liturgics Commission when we were revising the Prayer Book of the Episcopal Church. The committee has given provisional approval of the first draft of the eucharistic liturgy.

We are hoping that the funds which are coming in, thanks to Fr. Swayne's visit to USA to solicit them, will enable us to complete our monastery soon. It will be wonderful to have our own house out in the country with more room and comforts than we have now. We have aspirants who want to enter the novitiate when we have a place for them to live.

My health remains good and I seem this time to be gaining weight instead of losing it. I plan to visit England once more this summer. If you are to be there, let me know. We may be able to get together somewhere. May you be richly blessed in 1985. Please pray for me

With love,
Bonnie

February 23, 1985
c/o The Rev. Canon David Pain
Accra, Ghana, West Africa
Dear Edna,

The Superior of the Order is visiting us and I intended to write you a letter to be taken to USA and mailed there, even though I did not think you would have had time to get an answer to me of my last. But your reply arrived yesterday. I am most grateful for it.

Like you I had given up hope of the food package when it arrived. Everything in it was in first-rate condition, glass jars included. I do not think you need to have any concern about them. However, it takes so long for packages to arrive and I plan to leave for England in June, therefore, I suggest that you do not send another one until late spring or early summer, which might come through to us in the fall when I return. We are still eating the one you sent because I held it back while we had all the Christmas goodies and when a tourist group from California was with us. Since then we have finished off the peanut brittle (much enjoyed) also some of the cans of fish and meat. Brim is almost gone as well as one of the special coffees. I am afraid I selfishly keep them for myself, and a friend when I want to entertain. I am even more selfish about the Velamints. The marmalade is being held back because recently there has been a shortage of bread.

The clothing is excellent and I particularly like the shirts. The Jets cap has made a big hit.

Plans for England are developing. Tentative dates are June 25-September 20, a little longer than last year. The Oxford reunion registration has been sent in. One possibility is a visit to the vicinity of Inverness, a part of Scotland I have always wanted to see.

Reagan is, as we have agreed all along, a disaster, but he is what the people, especially young people, want. America top nation at whatever cost to the rest of the world: The Hartford Courant editorial on the budget is right on target, but I shall be greatly surprised if anything can stop Reagan. The Monitor article last week on the disintegration of the Democrats is all too true, and will continue as long as Tip O'Neil is Speaker. I doubt that the Democrats can get into executive power nationally for another ten years, and the Supreme Court is already lost for the next twenty. And they may never get into power, because before then the Republicans may have set up a fascist state. The America uber allies crowd are going to be under increasing pressure from the Third World, which will be forced to turn to the second if America insists on exploiting and oppressing them. The setting up and defense of dictatorship among them will ultimately demand one in USA as well. The anti-Soviet myth bas been carefully propagated by the Pentagon ever since World War II in order to keep itself in full operation. I have heard that FDR's original plan for the Pentagon building was that after the war it would become a military hospital. Never before have we maintained a huge military establishment in peace time. So the Defense Department has kept us at war ever since 1945. Now the military-industrial complex is completely beyond the control of any federal government and of course the present crowd are putting the country more and more at its mercy. Truly the distances from where we are now to a military dictatorship is getting perilously short. It is later than anyone seems to realize.

I am glad your leg keeps improving but do keep using your cane. I never go out here without one. Not only are the roads full of potholes, etc., but also I do not have as good a sense of balance as I used to. There is nothing shameful at our age in carrying a cane and it is a sound precaution.

Today we have a major event, the life profession in the Order of Brother Boniface, one of our native Ghanaians. The service will be at the Cathedral and a huge party is planned here afterwards. They have chairs for 200-300 people set up in the courtyard. We have several houseguests for the weekend. So far things have gone with minimal confusion, thanks to the work the Ghanaian brethren have put in all the past week. Ghanaians love parties with endless speeches, singing and dancing, with food and drink distinctly subsidiary, though feeding such a crowd is a major chore. However, they feel it is worth it and events that run on for three or four hours are considered normal and pleasant (I get bored to death!).

The Monitor has sent me a questionnaire on the arrival of the paper. So far it has been regular and has arrived usually shortly after the date printed on it. The issues they want information about are those in March, so I do not know whether the good record will keep up till then. But we all enjoy it immensely and are most grateful to you for it. It really is important to keep abreast of things, even if selfishly one enjoys not being constantly reminded of the general distress and deterioration. So I read it from cover to cover with great appreciation before I let anyone else get ahold of it, because it often disappears after I put it down.

Give my best to Mary. I hope you have a blessed and happy Easter.

Love,
Bonnie

March 25, 1985
Dear Bonnie,

Both your last general and personal letter were greatly appreciated. Ghana is indeed fortunate to have a man of your ability, background and dedication; and teaching has its own rewards.

As always, I share your liberal political outlook. I agree that Reagan is a disaster, and our people are too often stupid and uncaring. Our educational system has failed, but as long as I can. I am fighting the establishment.

I had to fight to get born and so I have battled ever since; it just comes naturally. When I was knee high to a grasshopper my mother used to look at me thoroughly perplexed and ask, "Why, when there are two ways to accomplish a goal, do you always choose the more difficult route?" It must have been the challenge it afforded!

In a small way, I am trying to help. I volunteer for office work at the headquarters of our Connecticut National Abortion Rights Action League, and I support the Planned Parenthood in Connecticut. We have far more teen-age pregnancies in this country than Britain, France, Sweden and the Netherlands. Most of our criminals were once unwanted, unloved babies. So many countries are unable to feed their large populations. Sex education needs to be taught in all the schools—but by the right teachers, wholesome, well-adjusted individuals.

I belong to State and National Impact that does its best to sponsor enlightened, sensible legislation. I recently attended an all-day legislative conference at our Lutheran Church in Hartford. I joined the workshops on Peace and Economic Justice as well as Education. It was a day well spent.

I have attended hearings at our state legislature in Hartford. I became quite excited about the one concerning a Constitutional Convention for a Balanced Federal Budget. It lasted nine hours, but I was present only seven hours, for I had parked my car in a garage and had to leave early because the garage closed at 10:30pm. I signed against the bill and planned to speak—but there were too many before me. I have been known to remain until midnight in the past. My niece scolded me for being out so late at night alone in Hartford. But I made it! I was aghast that our Constitution State, would consider agreeing to call a constitutional convention. Former Governor DuPont of Delaware would appear to speak for it. Our two US Senators—Dodd and Weicker—opposed it, so have the leaders of both parties in our state legislature; but a young "cocky" freshman state senator is hoping to climb the Republican ladder quickly and so he is pro-Reagan and for the Convention.

Too many voters do not remember their history—the Constitutional Convention of 1787, James Madison, and Thomas Jefferson. Then we sent three good men—Oliver Ellsworth, William Johnson, and Roger Sherman, but I do not believe we would be apt to send that caliber today. Many of the states that have signed the resolution for a convention—32—did not hold hearings and some had no committee reports. Today a constitutional convention could abolish our Bill of Rights. No one could limit the items for discussion. The only way we can balance our budget is to elect the right president and the right people for Congress. However, our state does show more discretion than some states in the selection of those we send to Washington. Unfortunately, U.S. Rep. Rowland, a Republican, replaced Ratchford, a Democrat, in our last election. Convention opponents included economists, lawyers, and professors of political science.

In April and May (twice) some of my Unitarian friends and I will be responsible for helping the Coordinator from Family Relations Court introduce persons with repeated offenses related to alcohol to Alcoholics Anonymous. We furnish all the refreshments at the Salvation Army. Various churches in the Hartford area sponsor this mission at different times. Since I am a teetotaler, it seems quite fitting that I should do this.

Soon I am planning to become a Literacy Volunteer in Greater Hartford—to teach English as a Second Language to adults and older teenagers. Thank you for your sound advice about the use of a cane outdoors. I usually do, but once in a while, I forget. My leg continues to gain in strength. I am so happy that you enjoy The Christian Science Monitor. I am renewing your subscription. Since you also like Velamints, I am going to try sending you some by mail in a strong envelope—maybe two at a time.

It is good that you are going to have a change of scene this summer—one in Britain.

I have not reached a firm decision yet, but I may be in England sometime this summer. I should love to see you—if it is convenient. What is the best time? If you wish, I could have my agent reserve a room for you at the Park Lane again—for days or a week. I could have her order a Brit Rail pass for you for a week if you wish. We could take day trips by rail. I will take care of the expenses—for the good of the order.

I am sure that you will have a blessed and happy Easter.

A GENERAL LETTER
April 1985
c/o The Rev. Canon David Pain
Accra, Ghana, West Africa

Greetings from Ghana!

We are able to continue the building of our monastery. Thanks to the generosity of our friends we have the funds at least to start the work once more. It has taken a long time to get going. We found it necessary to terminate the contract with the man who had been building it and set up new arrangements. That has occupied us for the past two months, but now we have control over the progress of the work. We have collected most of the material needed and, unless the few items that are still lacking prove harder to get than we anticipate, we should be able to complete the monastery in a few months.

One important factor in making this fresh start possible was the contribution many of you made to the project. It was most generous of you and much appreciated by us. As far as I have been informed as to who contributed, I have written personal letters of thanks. If you gave and have not received one, it is because either I was not informed or my letter has gone astray. In that case please let this assure you that your support is appreciated.

My health remains excellent and the teaching at the theological college has been even more rewarding this year than last. We are soon to graduate our first senior class and we believe they will make good and much needed priests in the Anglican Church here.

This summer I hope to be in England again, from June 25 to September 20. My headquarters once again will be Willen Priory, Milton Keynes, Bucks, MK15 91AA, telephone (0908) 663-749. I expect to be traveling around a good deal, including a return visit to Wales and a stay in the Scottish highlands around Inverness with some time in Yorkshire en route. Otherwise I shall be near enough to London to see people there. So if you are able to get to England this summer, please let me know. Perhaps we could get together.

One year from this month I expect to be returning to USA. Much as I love it here, I am looking forward to a time at home again. And of course I have arranged it so as to coincide with our 55th. I hope to see you there.

Meanwhile take care and enjoy yourself.

As ever,
Bonnie

April 17, 1985
c/o The Rev. Canon David Pain
Accra, Ghana, West Africa
Dear Edna,

Your letter and the April 5 issue of <u>The Christian Science Monitor</u> arrived in the same mail and both have been read with pleasure. I am most grateful to you for renewing the subscription.

It is incredible the amount of work you do, and I am sure the results in the long run will be significant. Most politics operate on the basis of opportunism—what seems for the moment advantageous. But people with principles who persevere in promoting them eventually see them put into effect or succeeding generations see them. Principles and truth have a staying power that mere policy does not. I am particularly happy over your work with abortion rights and Planned Parenthood. I was interested to read what a photographic fake the picture <u>The Silent Scream</u> is. That puts it in the same class as Reagan, a phony artificially created by the media. But sooner or later reality will assert itself. The modern farm crisis in the American mid-west reminds me of the 1920's when a similar farm crisis in time of prosperity precipitated the Great Depression. I hope we can come to our senses before that, but I fear we may not. The 1929 crash was caused by over indebtedness in the private sector. The next will be the same in the international area.

I am getting perspective on the political situation I should like to discuss with you. I believe there is a major shift—in population, politics, economics, and culture—from east to west both in USA and Canada. And I believe the future of both countries will be largely dominated by the west. If so, the only hope for the Democrats is to build up strongly in those area. I see some hopeful signs that they at least realize it and are trying to meet the challenge. Incidentally, I share your concern over a constitutional convention. The Bill of Rights will be in real jeopardy. After all Justice Renquist, before he was appointed, said publicly that he had dedicated his life to getting rid of it. Abortion rights are sure to be rendered unconstitutional. Even without a convention they may be by amendment to the present Constitution.

It would be grand if you decide to visit England this year. I also should love to see you. At the moment my plans there are uncertain. In February I wrote four letters about possible visits and have heard from none of them. I suspect my letters went astray. I have just written them again. I am hoping in early August to visit Dingwall near Inverness. If it works out, I will probably spend the last half of July visiting in Yorkshire en route. Earlier in July, after my reunion at Oxford, I shall probably visit Wales again. I am making my long retreat in Sussex September 1-12. If all this works out, probably the best time for me to visit with you would be just before I return to Ghana on September 20th. I could go back to Milton Keynes for the weekend after my retreat and then proceed to London, packed and ready to leave. If I do all the traveling I plan, I think I should prefer spending a few days quietly in London, seeing things there. So let me know if you decide to go to England. But the time I hear from you, I should know more about my own plans. I leave here, incidentally, June 24th, and my headquarters in England will be as last year; Willen Priory, Milton Keynes, Bucks, MK15 9AA (0908) 663-749.

All the best. Don't work too hard and take care of yourself. You are very valuable.

Love,
Bonnie

May 22, 1985

Dear Bonnie,

In all probability you have not received the Velamints I sent you—two sets enclosed in different large envelopes—one with a short note and the other with a card. I suspected that anything with edible contents would be eagerly pilfered.

I did enjoy both your last letters (personal and general).

While I have not finalized my plans for a visit to Britain, I have almost decided to travel in September. IT will be convenient for me— if it is for you to stay in London at the Park Lane from September 13th through the 21st. You will be welcome as my guest any time during that period. Just let me know when you wish to arrive; stay as long as you wish—the longer the better. I will have my agent make a reservation for you. It will be good to see you and talk with you. You decide what to do and see in London.

I appreciate your liberal outlook in politics and economics; it is a great comfort. If Reagan does not carry us into some kind of conflagration, it will be a miracle. When I converse with many individuals I understand how Reagan was elected. They neither read nor understand what is going on.

Recently our Social Concern Committee of the CRCC met with a Russian—Dr. Vladimir S. Shinkarenko from the Institute of General Pathology at a luncheon held in my church. He was rational and most informative. We must converse with these Russians. The mayors of Hartford and New Britain insult them. Americans seem to think that any country can become a democracy overnight. After 200 years, we have not done so well ourselves—considering all the advantages we enjoyed in the beginning.

Presently I am tutoring a young Polish man, a veterinarian's assistant in Poland. He works in a factory here and does not like it—I don't blame him. Since he has a young wife who speaks both Polish and English, I have her come with him. In that way, we can progress at a much faster pace. I bought a blackboard, and he is making a stand for it. Both he and his wife are intelligent and eager to learn. It is fun to teach. They are going to have their first baby, so I have lent them some books about rearing children. Love is the most important ingredient.

I asked for two students so that I could work with them together. The Literacy Volunteers Department assigned a Jamaican to me, but he would never be able to work with my Polish student as a team. I plan to meet with him to determine his needs and then decide whether I have time to tutor him separately. I teach here in my home.

As part of my duty to the Social Concerns Committee of the CRCC I picketed the front of our nursing homes in Hartford to help the employees gain recognition for their union, an organization they sorely need. Tuesday just before the strike the management for Hillside manor gave in. Thank goodness.

Right now I am most concerned about the operation of State University system. Two of our universities, Central (where I taught) and Eastern have fine presidents, but the other two are not so fortunate, especially Southern where it seems like the Mafia is in control. I am trying to figure how I can best help. Before I retired, I was chairman of the Advisors Committee to the Board of Trustees for the four institutions—then colleges, now universities. I think they paid too high a political price for the university label. It is truly amazing how many pay too much for their whistles. In all probability I shall have to seek the help of the Hartford Courant, which is the oldest and best newspaper in the state.

I look forward to our meeting. Keep well and happy.

May 1, 1985
c/o The Rev. Canon David Pain
Accra, Ghana, West Africa
Dear Edna,

Thank you for the Velamints, and the card and clippings that accompanied them. Your card makes me uncertain whether I have missed one of your letters. I received one in the middle of April which I answered at once, though it was not mailed until the 24th. In your letter you said you were considering a visit to England this September and raised the possibility of another time together in London. I replied that the days prior to my return here on September 20 would be best for me, since I could again leave from the hotel to the airport. I also said that, after much travel throughout the summer, should prefer to stay quietly in London during our time together.

I am most grateful for the Velamints, which came through in good condition. But if you have not yet mailed another batch, please do not do so. Parcels coming through the Post Office have to go through customs and the duty charged on the Velamints was more than you paid for them in the first place. Food and other packages sent through the Catholic of Protestant service centers get in duty free for the most part, but we have no such arrangement for letters. I do enjoy the Velamints, but actually consume them rather slowly. In fact, I still have an unopened package of the first batch!

I am glad Connecticut dropped the endorsement of a Constitutional Convention. My guess is that there is little chance of one being held. It really would take a huge effort to assemble one, as well as an expense which the present government is not likely to be willing to spend on a non-military venture.

We should not be surprised at the success of the government's brainwashing. After all the Communist countries and the Fascists have been doing that for a long time, and in this, as in all other important matters, we imitate them. The trouble with you and me is that we conceive of democracy as a government in which the people express and achieve their will through elected representatives. This was not, of course, what the founding fathers had in mind. They set up an oligarchy in which only land-owners had a vote. Women, workers, not to mention slaves, were disenfranchised. We have corrected that, but we are now a manipulated democracy.

So is Ghana. We have elections, but there is only one party and so one set of candidates. But they are most insistent that it is a democracy. In USA we are more subtle. The party with the most money can hire the best Public Relations company and control the communications media. Naturally, it is the least educated and intelligent who are taken in—but our education system itself is so brainwashed that even college graduates are for the most part incapable of independent thinking. After all, examinations are usually multiple choice. It takes no intelligence to answer them, and the choice demanded is the party-line slogan. I could never pass one because for almost half of the questions I should consider all four "answers" wrong.* The only hopeful sign is that there are newspapers, as illustrated by the clippings you have sent, that expose the falsehood of the official propaganda. But at the moment, with the "Democrats" in Congress as eager as the Republicans to toady to the cowboy, I see little hope of curtailing his antics.

I hope you decide for England and we can get together there.

Love,
Bonnie

*I have a terrible time with written drivers' license tests!

May 31, 1985
as from Milton Keynes, Bucks UK
Dear Edna,

The packages of Velamints have safely arrived and are much appreciated. They will keep me supplied for a long time.

On April 17th I answered the last letter I have received from you, in which you said you might be going to England again this summer and suggested that I might stay with you there. I replied that I should be delighted and that the days just before my flight back to Ghana on September 20th, would be most convenient for me. I also said I should rather spend them in London than to travel around. Since at this time last year I failed to get one of your letters, I am beginning to wonder if mine or your reply may have gone astray. I shall send this with Father Swayne when he goes to USA on June 12th, and shall keep it open until then. So if you receive this letter you will know that I have still not heard from you at that date. In that case, a note to me at Willen Priory will be welcome.

We are getting ready now for final examinations and our first graduation exercises. In view of the pressure of that period I am writing this letter as far in advance of its mailing. But I shall change it if I receive a letter from you.

As ever,
Bonnie

June 10, 1985

Still no letter received from you and by now I think we shall not receive any mail before this has to go. My guess is that because Canon Pain is on vacation there has been a hitch in getting the mail to us from Accra, since we have received none for the past ten days. But a letter from you to me at Willen Priory will repair the damage. If your letter does come before I shall leave on June 24, I shall not answer it from here but will wait till I get to Milton Keynes when I can reply to it and the one which will be awaiting me there at the same time. A letter from here via air mail would not get to you any sooner.

Love,
Bonnie

June 18, 1985
Milton Keynes, Bucks UK
Dear Edna,

Apparently you have not received one or two of my letters. I wrote you after each package of Velamints arrived, answering your letter in the first. They came through safely but were slow in arriving because the Post Office had to send us a notice that they had been received. Then we had to wait until someone was going to Accra with time to locate them and pay the custom's duty. During term time we were rarely able to get to Accra on a weekday when the Post Office was open because all our drivers were in school. But I received them and answered them. They are most appreciated.

By now you should have received the letter I asked Father Swayne to mail you in USA. If so, you probably have sufficient information about my acceptance of your invitation to keep you from telephoning on July 1st. I certainly have no objection to your calling me, but I shall not be at the Priory on that date. I hope to be at a reunion at my Oxford College. But I am writing this now, not waiting as I expected until I get to the Priory and have received your letter there, because I want to mail it at the airport as soon as I get to England, in the hope that it will reach you before July 1st.

I cannot be absolutely definite about my schedule in September, but it looks now as if I can join you in London on Monday the 16th. After I finish my long retreat I have to go to Milton Keynes to do my final packing, since, as last year, I should like to go directly from the hotel to the airport. That saves someone at Willen Priory from having to drive me there early in the morning.

If we have our time together, we shall have plenty of opportunity to commiserate over the state of the nation and the world. From the latest <u>Monitors</u> that have arrived, I gather that opposition to the cowboy is developing in Congress. I earnestly hope it continues. There seems to me a good chance that it will, since apparently a substantial minority of Republicans are disaffected with his policy. Much as I hate to admit it, I fear what hopes there are depend on the Republicans. The Democrats are in such desperate disarray that I doubt whether they recapture the presidency before 2000.

I am delighted, as always, to learn of your work on so many fronts. You make me feel ashamed that I do nothing but bemoan the situation. But of course here in Ghana, there is nothing I can do politically. I do encourage the clergy to stiffen their backs against the bishops, who, though they are all Ghanaians, have taken over from imperialist colonial bishops who ran their dioceses as unchallengable autocrats. Having known no other model, the native bishops assume that is their prerogative. But things are changing.

I do hope we get together in London. Meanwhile, take care.

Love,
Bonnie

July 5, 1985
Milton Keynes, Bucks UK
Dear Edna,

Since I mailed a letter to you on arrival in England, which was in answer to the first of the two I have recently received from you, I decided to wait until now to answer the second. I think I have received all of yours and I hope you have eventually received all of mine. If so, you know that I am delighted to accept your invitation to the Park Lane and I am hoping to join you there on Monday, September 16. It looks as though my other appointments are working out so that I shall have time to pack up for my return to Ghana by that date so that I can spend the last days with you before I go.

I have just come from the reunion for overseas alumni the Exeter College held for the first time. The Rector, Lord Crowther-Hart, has been influenced by Williams College, where he got an honorary degree, to use some of its techniques to encourage financial support. His college is embarking on a fund drive to enlarge its buildings and increase its endowment. So the college put on a four-day affair like Williams does each year for its Old Guard. The association between Exeter and Williams has been close since 1929 when the first Moody scholar went there. I followed him in 1931 and it soon became an established custom that those scholars always go to Exeter. There were four of us at the reunion. Now Williams is setting up a house in Oxford where its undergraduates can go for their junior year. Exeter is doing what it can to integrate them into the Oxford community. Also a fund is being raised to enable an Exeter man to attend Williams. I am very happy about this growing relationship. The person who was originally supposed to head up the Oxford house has now become president of Williams, so we can count on the administration there to continue to support the project.

I find that our smiling cowboy is not held in much repute here, which is not surprising. Margaret's popularity also seems to be waning. But I do not expect that there will be a change for the better in either country for some years to come. The opposition is too hopelessly disorganized.

My itinerary for the summer seems to be working out as I hoped. I shall be reporting more on it as it develops. I hope you have a good summer. I am sure it will be, as always, a busy and useful one.

Love,
Bonnie

August 1, 1985
Dear Bonnie,

It will be wonderful to see you at the Park Lane on September the sixteenth. My agent has reserved a room for you from September 16-20 as you desired. It has taken ne all this time to plan my itinerary. I fly Pan American at 9 pm from Kennedy on the sixth of September and shall reach the Park Lane on the seventh. On the eighth I shall embark on a Trafalgar seven day tour of Devon and Cornwall including Oxford, Bath, Tintagel, Lands End, Plymouth, Exeter, Salisbury, Winchester, and Windsor. This means that I can visit the Wells Cathedral once again. On the 14th I shall return to the Park Lane to be ready for you on the 16th. I hope you will find the accommodations comfortable and restful. If it is not too inconvenient, perhaps you could call me at the Park Lane Sunday night, the 15th.

On the 20th, I plan to take a three day Thames Tours to Chester, Snowdonia, and Caernarfon. The 22nd, 23rd, and 24th I shall try the Clifton Fords in London so that I shall be ready to fly home the 25th. That will enable me to help with the arrangement for the Capitol Region Conference of Churches Awards Banquet on the thirtieth of September. I am responsible for the flowers. We are honoring your Bishop Walmsley along with five others. The keynote speaker is to be The Rev. Dr. Arie Brouver, Ex Director National Council of Churches.

I am so happy that you are having an opportunity to travel around Britain to visit your friends. Your account of your Oxford sojourn was most promising. You were indeed lucky to have had that Oxford experience during your student days—and you richly deserved it.

The choice of the new president for Williams seems auspicious.

We are not so fortunate in Connecticut with our public universities. The new president at Southern is a mere politician, inept, dissolute, utterly unfit. The mafia is in control and I am getting ready for the fray. Fortunately, at Central our president is a man of integrity and ability—and he has a very fine wife.

My Polish pupil and his wife continue to provide me with a rewarding experience; after my two-hour stint, I am not tired.

I heartily agree with your estimate of both Reagan and Thatcher. Our democracies have fallen and I fear education has not fulfilled its obligations. A democracy cannot function without an informed and caring electorate.

All the best,
Edna

August 10, 1985
Milton Keynes, Bucks UK
Dear Edna,

You letter was awaiting me when I returned yesterday from Scotland. I am delighted that your trip to England has been arranged and I look forward eagerly to being with you at the Park Lane September 16-19 (I leave early on the morning of the 20th). I shall telephone you on the 15th (evening) to let you know when to expect me the next day. If you need to get in touch with me meanwhile you can write or telephone here. I shall be away August 29-September 12, but a message could be left for me.

You itineraries sound excellent. I followed much the same path on my first trip around England, when a friend of mine at Oxford and I hired a car and drove through Devon, Cornwall and the midlands. My second trip took in north Wales. This summer I have gotten to Wales again. The weather was not as good as last year—cold and some rain. But we got to Hay-on-Wye, a village full of second-hand bookstores. They were somewhat disappointing, but I found one book I particularly wanted and some others that will be useful. I had a good time in Cambridge with an associate, seeing another in London en route, and another in Cambridge, both being Americans visiting here. The climax of the trip was in Scotland where I stayed with another associate, who is an excellent cook. He fed me so heartily that I gained 10 pounds and now weigh about 125. Everyone remarks how much better I look this year, although my health in general remains about the same. The weather in Scotland again was cold, but we had only occasional brief showers, and the cloud effects greatly enhanced the beauty of the landscape. He took me on drives every day to different parts of the dioceses of Moray, Ross, and Caithness, of which he is the dean.

Now I plan to stay here at Milton Keynes for most of the rest of this month. Then I go to Sussex for a visit and to make a ten-day retreat at a monastery there. So I should be refreshed in body and soul when we get together on September 16th. I hope you have a good summer till then, especially on your Trafalgar tour.

Love,
Bonnie

September 25, 1985
Ghana, West Africa
Dear Edna,

How can I ever thank you for your overwhelmingly generous hospitality at the Park Lane and your gift as well? I can only assure you that I appreciate all of it, but especially the opportunity to be with you and talk about our common interests.

I hope you recovered from your sore throat and enjoyed the tour of north Wales and the trip home. I developed a bit of fever the last evening we were together, but it broke in the middle of the night and I was fine in the morning. In the end I took a taxi direct to the airport. When I tried to get one at the backdoor, they refused to take me to anywhere other than the airport. Finally, the doorman took my bags to the Piccadilly door and called a cab there. I told him to take me to the Airbus. He asked, "Why not the airport?" I said it costs too much. He said, "Would 12 pounds be all right?" That sounded enough better than 21 pounds, which it cost last year, so I agreed. Actually, with the tip it came to 16 pounds, but after the rather bad night, I guess it was worth it. However, since I had allowed time to get to the Airbus and for the hour's trip to Heathrow, I arrived via the taxi before 7 o'clock, which gave me two hours to visit before scheduled departure and another half-hour before we actually took off. But I had myself a huge orange juice freshly squeezed, which helped keep the cold from developing. The rest of the trip was pleasant. Although we were a half-hour late leaving Amsterdam, we made up time and were only 15 minutes late at Accra. Getting through immigration was a chore, but I made it and was met and driven home that evening.

Unfortunately, there does not seem to have been as much accomplished on the new monastery as I had hoped. There was a delay getting the timbers for the roof, so they are just starting on that. Such is Africa. But the climate is delightful after England. Before I arrived there was some rain, but since I have been here, it has been cloudy with no precipitation. The breezes make it delightfully cool. I am busy cataloguing the books that came to the library over the summer, and looking forward eagerly to the beginning of lectures next Tuesday.

The household here is what I expected. Vincent Shamo left for England just after I arrived, so I had a chance to see him. Boniface Adam is on vacation, visiting his family. He is still hoping to get a visa to go to West Park for a year. The other, including the three novices and the three postulants who came in July, are still with us and seem to be doing well. We are very fortunate in our African members, which is another reason why I am glad to be here. And several of last spring's graduates have dropped in and made a point of greeting me. You and I are fortunate at our age to be wanted and appreciated.

I hope your many activities are prospering. Just remember to keep from getting too busy. You still have much to accomplish. Thank you again for the glorious finale of my vacation.

Love,
Bonnie

P.S. I forgot to mention the back door taxis rig their meters to overcharge tourists.

October 15, 1985
Dear Bonnie,

Your good letter was most welcome for I have been concerned about your welfare. I sincerely hoped to make your brief sojourn in London both beautiful and restful, but I felt I failed. I'm sorry I caught a cold and then gave it to you—that was my fear. And then I cannot walk fast as yet—although I will get there. Thank you for accompanying me to see the doctor even though you were reluctant to undertake the venture. You did not need to worry for I told the MD who you were and he regarded you as the Good Father who was trying to shepherd his flock. It is a pity you had to miss the Thames expedition to Kew Gardens. I am sure you were happy to escape to Africa. Even so, I did enjoy being with you and miss your guidance 'round London when I returned after my Wales Tour.

On the Wales project, I came down with a bad cough—something rare with me—but I managed to carry on regardless. In fact, one man looked at me, smiled and called me indomitable. Wales was beautiful, and the people were most cordial and helpful. We had only one rainy day—at the tumbled down castle. The terrain was varied indeed. I had no idea that it was so rugged.

When I returned to London, I stayed at the Clifton Ford on Necheck Street. My agent wanted me to try a different hotel. The room was comfortable and pleasant, the food was excellent, and the surroundings were attractive.

You will be amused to learn that on my last day I had to rise at five to make the Trafalgar Bus to the airport. Fortunately, I had brought my own alarm clock for they forgot to call me, get my baggage, and engage a cab. I managed by myself though. I almost missed my plane, though because I became engrossed in the Duty Free Section. When I realized 20 minutes before Pan Am left for America. I dashed—baggage and all. Of course my point of entrance was the most distant of all, but I encountered the British Airways carrier with only the guide, who saw my predicament and carried me through—just in time. Sometimes luck is on my side.

It has taken me nearly a month with American medicine to recover from my cough.

I'm beginning to think you have a point about tours. I caught a germ or a virus last year too. So did Mary.

Did you see the comments about you in the last Williams Alumni Review? If not, I will cut the blurb and send it to you—most complimentary.

I am delighted that you took the cab straight to the airport—you needed that as well as your orange juice. I do hope the cold did not flare again.

I know that you are wanted and appreciated by many. I never think of you as old. I thought you looked fine—you have a beautiful head of hair, and I like your ties and your spirit. Your students are indeed fortunate.

I have acquired another woman to counsel—a divorcee with two teen-age sons who are living with the father. I am trying to get her to forget her ex-husband, who does not want her. She is also under the care of a psychiatrist and wants to come live with me. She says it is most peaceful in my house, but I cannot have that for my house is not big enough for two women. I will try to help her though. Friday I go to school with her to talk to the school psychiatrist for her sons. Do pray for me.

Thank you for the information about the rigged meters at Park Lane. Of all things!

Sincerely,
Edna

Another General Letter
November 1985
Ghana, West Africa

Greetings from Ghana to Class of '31:

After a pleasant summer in the United Kingdom, I got back to Cape Coast on September 20th. On my return I was disappointed to learn that work on the new monastery's roof, which was supposed to have started just after I left, still had not begun. We had been unable to get the lumber we needed delivered. Now we have it and the aluminum sheeting, so the construction of the roof is progressing.

Since work on the interior has had to await the completion of the roof, it is impossible to predict when the building will be ready for us. You may be sure we shall move in as soon as we can, even if we have to camp out with what furniture we have until we have the wherewithal to equip it properly. We are impatient to get into our own home in a country area, surrounded by a farm to provide our food, rather than coping with the disadvantages of an upstairs wing of a girls' school in the heart of the city. We are fortunate to have this place to live while the monastery is being built, but enough is enough.

The Theological College is off to an excellent start this year. I seem to be communicating better with the students. Perhaps this is because I can understand their remarks more clearly. English is a second language for them, and their Afro-British accent has been difficult for me. Also after two years teaching I have been able to improve the organization of my lectures, simplifying them and concentrating on the main points. But in addition, all the faculty are remarking that this year the students seem more responsive and eager to learn. That makes teaching more fun for all of us.

I am particularly happy about my course for seniors in which I try to relate the Gospel to the insights of contemporary knowledge. It is important that their preaching shall be relevant in the twenty-first century and not merely reflect the religious concepts of the nineteenth. They already seem to be grasping what I am aiming at and recognizing its importance.

I have now decided, if my health holds up to return to Ghana in September, 1986 for a few more years' teaching. As long as the Lord keeps me fit for the job (such as I am) I might as well be useful. But I plan to return to USA next April. I want to have as long at home as possible and to be in good time to get ready for our 55th. So I hope to see you in June. Meanwhile all the best.

As ever,
Bonnie

November 16, 1985
Ghana, West Africa
Dear Edna,

Thank you for your letter, which I am delighted to receive. I was beginning to fear that my September letter had not reached you. I did not want you to think that I had not written to thank you for all you had done for me. I assure you that letter expressed my sentiments as well as I could. So I am distressed to learn that you feel you failed to make my stay in London both beautiful and restful. I certainly considered those adjectives exactly appropriate. I am extremely sorry if my attitude and response did not so indicate. I cannot imagine why they did not, for that is how I felt. I was sorry, of course, that you began to come down with a cold the last day. But I was glad to accompany you to the doctor's and I enjoyed the walk back through Green Park. You walked fast enough to suit me. As for the trip to Kew Gardens, I merely thought it would be pleasant to sit on the boat and chat, so I was not unduly disappointed that we could not go. It was being with you that I most enjoyed. It is good to converse with someone who has the same interests and discusses them intelligently.

You did not give me a cold. In fact, I may have given it to you. Before I came to London, I had a "non-cold," a feeling that I might be coming down one and then didn't. So I may have been distributing the germs. The last evening I seem to have had a fever, although I did not know it and it certainly did not prevent my enjoying our last dinner together. I discovered the fever only when it broke in a good sweat. The next morning I was fine and never saw a sign of it or the "cold" again. I am sorry to learn of your persistent cough and trust you are feeling cured of it.

When I last wrote I had not yet discovered how much better teaching would be this year than the last two. And I have found out why. The senior class last year had training as catechists and some of them had been promised ordination to the priesthood after serving a couple of years in a parish. Instead, they were sent to seminary for three years. They needed it, but they did not think so and bitterly resented it. They conveyed their attitude to the whole college. With them gone this year, the whole atmosphere has changed. The students are eager to learn, responsive, and clearly enjoying the courses. Needless to say, so am I. I am particularly happy about the proclamation course. The men seem already to have learned more than the seniors did all last year. I have not yet had a paper from them, so that may be a disappointment when I get it, but even so it will not destroy the pleasure the discussions themselves have been.

I have not yet seen the remarks about me in the Williams Alumni Review. It reaches me about three months late. They have been very good in running notices about me in nearly every issue. Also about 30 of my classmates contributed to our new monastery bere—over $1,500. I am looking forward eagerly to seeing them at our 55th reunion in June. I shall leave here shortly after Easter. I have things I want to do in April and May so I am not staying for the last term this year. I can make up my main courses next year if I get back in September as I hope.

I am glad that you are counseling with the woman and her children. I am sure you will be a great help to them. You are wise not to have her live with you. You can be of more use to her if you are more detached. Counseling and living together are two quite different things.

I shall be looking forward to seeing you in USA sometime next summer. Plans are not definite enough yet for me to suggest dates. I must first arrange things that involve a long trip. The rest of the time I shall be in the New York area so it will be easy to arrange for us to get together.

All the best.

Love,
Bonnie

P.S. Fr. Bonifice Adamorte will be mailing this in USA.

December 5, 1985

Dear Bonnie,

Your letter arrived the day before Thanksgiving—providential timing—for I was more or less housebound with the shingles. I had three invitations for Thanksgiving, but I dared not accept any one lest I give my virus away to some unsuspecting mortal; it is the same virus that causes chicken pox. I think it started when the dentist worked on my mouth to recap a front tooth which I broke. Neither my regular physician nor my surgeon warned me that I should take an antibiotic before dentistry because I have a Yale nail in my right femur. It affected my throat, right ear and head. However, I am most grateful it did not reach my eyes for that would have been a true disaster. (When this infection hits an eye, the patient must seek the help of an ophthamologist immediately.) I had one lined up in case of need. Fortunately, after a month, I have nearly recovered. The ear specialist was surprised I healed so quickly. I was most careful not to get near anyone, and I let no one in my house.

Thank you for your letter of reassurance. I had no wish to distress you. I am delighted that you are well and enjoying your new year.

Are you still receiving your **Christian Science Monitor?** I renewed your subscription Dec. 9. I will send your Christmas present if I can find one as well as a food package; may they arrive safely.

Christmas card, check enclosed.

Thank you for your advice about counseling and living arrangements—I quite agree with you.

It is good that you will have an opportunity to come to America this coming summer. If you like, you may stay here as long as you wish. I drive and can drop you wherever you wish to go provided you do not ask me to drive through New York City. I can prepare your favorite dishes if you will tell me what they are. I am a strong believer in good nutrition.

This fall I engaged some men to clean up the grounds and prune the shrubs. A college boy next door planted about nine dozen bulbs (tulips and daffodils). After enjoying all those beautiful flowers in

England, I am determined to produce some colorful flowers this spring and summer.

I hope next week that I can indulge in my various activities again. I plan to continue my tutoring of Peter, my Polish pupil. In November he and his wife had a new baby girl—From what Angie tells me over the phone, he is a devoted father—I knew he would be. It is a good marriage—I can tell. I always recommend the state to all my friends.

I do not know how I can stand three more years of Reagan. It is unbelievable how stupid he is—and the people do not see it. I keep calling our CT Senators to recommend certain courses of action. Those IRA terrorists from Ireland should not be allowed political asylum here. Our people do not recognize true charisma when they see it; moreover they overrate it.

Sincerely,
Edna

Food Package: Bonnie, December 13, 1985

$23.40 postage

1.1 lb	Walker's Shortbread	7.95
5 oz.	Choc. Chip Cookies	1.09
5.25 oz.	Brussels Cookies	1.45
9.75 oz.	Three Cracker Assort.	1.79
2.25 oz	Cookie Sampler	0.79
4 oz.	Maxwell House Coffee 3	0.19
4 oz.	Folgers Crystals	3.19
15 oz.	Sunmaid Raisins	1.09
8 oz.	Dried Apricots	2.79
3 oz.	Lipton Tomato Soup	0.95
1.5 oz	Chicken Noodle Soup Lipton	0.95
9.6 oz	Carnation Dry Milk	1.69
12 oz.	Skippy Peanut Butter	1.35

12 oz.	Libby Corned Beef	1.79
19 oz.	Campbell's Chunky Soup	1.29
13 oz.	(2) Star-Kist Tuna	1.98
7.75 oz.	Red Salmon Steak	2.29
14.5 oz.	Whole Tomatoes Del Monte	0.79
8.5 oz.	Sweet Peas " "	0.43
8.5 oz.	Lima Beans " "	0.59
8.5 oz.	Sliced Carrots " "	0.41
	Total:	37.84

A General Letter
December 1985 (Form Letter)
Ghana, West Africa

Greetings from Ghana!

It was my intention to get this off in time for it to reach you by Christmas, but I have left it too late. At least you will know that I am thinking of you and hope you enjoy much happiness at Christmastide and throughout the New Year.

I have decided to ask my friends to address any letters to me that they may care to write to Philip Quaque Monastery, P.O. Box 761, Cape Coast, Ghana, West Africa. Canon Pain is returning to England permanently next month. Although we shall keep his box in Accra for our use, we shall not have the courier service. So we shall be able to pick up our mail only infrequently. On the other hand, last month two letters reached me from USA through Cape Coast in 20 days. I think that will now be the better route.

But letters should not be sent to me in Africa after March 1st. Right after Easter I expect to go on furlough. My headquarters will be Holy Cross Monastery, West Park, NY 12493. I shall be traveling around the country a good bit. Whether there would be a chance to see you I do not know, but you might let me know where I could find you during the summer. The chances that we can get together are slim, but I should not want to discover afterwards that I had been in your vicinity and not made contact with you.

I plan to return to Ghana in September. My health remains good, I am enjoying the teaching more than ever, and I am still needed to cover the courses I give. This year, in fact, I have found the students more responsive than previously. I guess we are communicating better with each other. It is also fine to have last year's graduates dropping in on us as priests. It makes us feel that we are really accomplishing something.

We are beginning to get hopeful about the new monastery. The roof is well along in the process of being erected and already we are able to work on the interior of some of the rooms. It may be possible to begin moving in sometime after the new year. It will be a blessing to get away from the noise and confusion of the girls' day school where we now live. Fortunately, as I write, Christmas vacation is soon to begin and, if we move in January, we shall be gone before school reopens.

Once more, all the best for 1986. I hope it may be possible to see you. Keep us in your prayers.

As ever,
Bonnie

PART FIVE

1986 - 1991

January 19, 1986
Ghana, West Africa
Dear Edna,

Thank you for your letters and the check. You are so good to me. I am going to send your check to USA with Fr. Superior at the end of this month so that he can put it into my custody account and I shall be able to spend it during my vacation. There is really nothing I want to buy here, and it will add greatly to my enjoyment while at home.

Both your letters arrived in the same mail. Things were badly held up in Accra by the Christmas rush (and Post Office vacation December 23-January 3!). I am now asking my friends to use the above address. Canon Pain is leaving for England. We shall keep the box in Accra for our use, but we shall not have courier service. Mail through our box in Cape Coast is coming quite rapidly.

The package has not yet come, of course. I suspect it will be some while before it arrives. We shall be on the lookout for it. I assure you it will be appreciated. As for clothes and the like, I suggest we wait till I get to USA. There is nothing I particularly need at the moment. I shall be getting in touch with you soon after I get home. I hope to leave here on April 2. (I am counting the days.)

Just this morning I received the two remaining December issues of the Christian Science Monitor and the first of January. They are a great joy to us. There is no need to change their address to Cape Coast, and the attempt to do so might lead to confusion. Computers, in my experience, are not very adaptable. I am so sorry to learn of your attack of shingles, but it is good that your eyes escaped and the rest of the trouble is over. I had it once, but only on my back and chest, which was annoying but not serious.

My plans for the furlough are not yet fully worked out. I shall probably be fully occupied in April and May with doctor's check-ups, etc . . . and other appointments. I should like to spend a while in Toronto visiting our house there. Then in June to mid-August I shall be in the West and South. I may be able to visit you in my first two months home, but if not, I shall certainly plan for August— September. The furlough seemed a long time when I first arranged it, but now fitting everything in is not so easy. I shall get in touch with you when I get home and have things more in perspective.

We had the dedication of our new monastery yesterday. It was a grand occasion with a big crowd of friends present. We still will not be able to move in for a while, however. The louvers for the windows, the plumbing, and the electricity have yet to be installed. When the domestic part of the house is occupiable, we shall move in, but the finishing of the chapel and common room will take much longer.

Unfortunately Planned Parenthood does not seem to have much influence here, unless their program is to encourage ten children to a family! The place is teeming with babies and children—of parents of all ages. If Cape Coast is any indication at least 50% of the population of Ghana must be under 20. And they all seem to be healthy and thriving. Many thanks and all best wishes.

Love,
Bonnie

This will be mailed in USA by a returning friend.

January 30, 1986
Dear Bonnie,

I am presently in something of a quandary. Except for your general letter of December of '85, I have not heard from you since November 27th. I wrote in response on December 5th and mailed my letter on the 7th. I mailed you a Christmas card with a check for one hundred dollars enclosed. It was a cashier's check that I obtained from my bank—The Connecticut National—because I thought it was safer. On the 13th, I mailed you a food package, which you probably have not received yet. I sent in care of the National Catholic Service Center. On January 22nd, I mailed a late birthday package to you at the Philip Quaque Monastery at Cape Coast. In all probability, you have as yet received this last parcel. I do not know whether my letter, Christmas card, or anything else has reached you or whether you prefer not to write, or are ill, or too busy.

I offered you hospitality at my house for any period you wished when you come to America. Only you know best what you want to do; it is your holiday.

Mary wants me to accompany her sister and sister-in-law on a Scandinavian trip (Sweden, Norway, and Denmark), for two weeks beginning June 28th. I have not yet decided what to do as yet.

I have acquired another Polish pupil—a young woman who is employed as a Unit Aid at the Hartford Hospital. She has been in this country for five years and has taught herself English. In evaluating her needs, I found her greatest concern involved English grammar, which I am presently endeavoring to teach her. She must view the framework as a whole and understand how each part fits. She is intelligent, logical, sensitive, and quickly responsive. She has a good marriage and a three year old son. She is the wife of my other pupil—Peter's brother-in-law. I thoroughly enjoy both my Polish pupils and rejoice that they have happy marriages and good offspring.

I am still quite involved with activities of the Capitol Region Conference of Churches.

I trust that you are now located in your new monastery and rejoice that your health remains good and that you enjoy your teaching more than ever.

I miss your letters, but if you choose not to write, I will understand.

Edna

March 15, 1986
Ghana via West Park, New York
Dear Edna,

Your birthday presents have finally arrived and are greatly appreciated. The tie is lovely. You have excellent taste. I needed a good tie because my best one was the club tie of The Players, of which I am no longer a member, as I gave it to the Superior, who is. Yours will take its place. The handkerchiefs are again most useful. Somehow they disappear over here rapidly. I am writing with one of the pens and I shall use the pocket diary to keep track of appointments and happenings when I am in USA.

The <u>Monitor</u> keeps coming and is a joy to us all. I am writing this at once because I cannot delay longer in expressing my thanks even though I shall not mail the letter until I get to New York on April 3rd. It will reach you more quickly and safely that way.

I shall be busy from now to my departure. The Bishop of New Hampshire sent his library to the theological college and I am frantically trying to check and catalogue several hundred books before I leave. And I still have my lectures to give and term papers and exams to correct. I must also pack, both what I shall take and what I shall leave. It does not look as if we shall be in the new monastery before I go, so things have to be ready to be moved after my departure.

I trust I shall be able to see you while I am home. I expect to do much traveling but have not been able to work out my itinerary in detail, since I have asked people to respond to my suggested dates to West Park. If they have, I can arrange things then and I shall get in touch to see when we can get together. Meanwhile, much love and thanks.

Bonnie

April 22, 1986
Dear Bonnie,

It was both a surprise and a joy to hear from you that Sunday morning. You sounded chipper. If I seemed far away I had just awakened but I soon came to. That was really the best time to reach me, for I am in and out like a dog at a farm.

How did you ever accomplish your many tasks before embarking for America? I know you think quickly and work fast—but that was a real mountain you had to unearth.

It must be most gratifying to meet with your many friends. Does your native country seem different to you after your long absence?

In my books, President Reagan moved most unwisely in bombing Lybia; but then that stupid man invariably acts first and then thinks afterward—perhaps. I agree with the position our Senator Weicker took. Somehow we have to solve the Arab problem, but ammunition is not the answer. I am worried about our democracy because too many voters are ignorant, self-seeking, and uncaring.

I am enjoying my two Polish students who are intelligent, worthy, and hard working. In fact, I have agreed to take two more Polish students—a man and his wife, who are on different levels of learning. Thus, I teach all of them separately—two hours a week for each. I even let them bring their babies if they wish. Krystyna, who already has a three year old son, is happily pregnant. I am always happy when the right people have children. Somehow I seem to get along very well with the Polish people. I admire their industry, ideals, and cleanliness.

Twice I have visited our CT Legislature to attend hearings on bills to provide sex education in our schools. Our young are in dire need of guidance in this area, but not every teacher is equipped to provide this kind of direction. When I left and reached the area outside the capitol, I met Senator Gunther, who unexpectedly remembered me. He agreed with me about the importance of the teacher in this field, but he also emphasized that neither are all doctors the best leaders in their sphere. Teachers must possess the right state of feeling to guide the young here.

I remember the time long ago when I discovered a sixth grade boy harboring a pornographic magazine. I confiscated it but said nothing. As soon as possible, I took the whole class to the art museum for a lesson in nudes. I told them that we were all born without a stitch on and that if there was something wrong with that, God would have found another way to get us born. Years later when he had grown to manhood, I met him in a store. I did not recognize him, but he knew me, came over to my side, and asked, "Do you remember what you did to me?" I answered, "Yes." So he did remember.

Unless the adults show deeper understanding and consideration, we shall continue to have more teenage pregnancies.

Wisdom is truly in short supply.

Monday, I mailed my acceptance of the invitation to the 55th Reunion of the Class of 1931 at Williams. Rhoda and I are planning to go together; I am driving. I enjoyed her the last time. As CT Yankees say, "She is all wool and a yard wide."

My invitation to you still stands—whether it is spring or fall or both. Please do that which you most want to do. I know you have many friends, and heaven only knows when you will get another furlough.

Edna

May 2, 1986
West Park, New York
Dear Edna,

Your good letter was awaiting me on my return from Canada. I was visiting our new priory there. It is grand to be back in USA and able to see the Brethren here. My schedule is rapidly filling up and it looks like one delightful time after another. But as you know, I like to keep busy.

I am so happy to learn that you are to be at our 55th reunion. That gives me the chance to see you before I leave for the West. I have wanted to do that, but did not see how it could be fitted in. I am sure you will enjoy the reunion. Apparently, a goodly number of us are planning to be there.

I want also to begin planning for my visit in September. I have to preach in a parish in your neighborhood on Sunday, September 14th, and want to visit with the priests (husband and wife!) that weekend. I could come to you either before (Sept. 10-12) or after (14-16). Would either of those dates suit you, and if both, which would you prefer? We can settle the details when we get together at the reunion, but I should like to arrange my schedule as soon as possible.

The bombing in Lybia was a disgrace. At last our cowboy got the war he has wanted. The atomic disaster in the USSR is frightening. I have not been following the TV or newspapers closely, but I have seen nothing of the cowboy offering assistance. If he has not, it is a great chance missed. But of course he prefers anti-Communist hostility to Christian charity. Fortunately, he goes out of office in two years, unless he declares himself president for life, which he well might! (He could possibly get away with it, the way people worship him.) Whoever succeeds him, even another Republican as is most likely, is bound to be an improvement. It would really take some doing to be worse. Oh well, possibly we shall survive.

Keep up the good work. I am looking forward eagerly to seeing you.

Love,
Bonnie

May 9, 1986
Dear Bonnie,

It is most gratifying to know that you are having such a delightful time. Do continue. Your possible visit here (Sept. 10-12) or after (14-16) would be find. Choose both if you wish. If you prefer only one, perhaps the one (14-16) would be preferable. On the twelfth I have a meeting (about 2 hours) of the Social Concerns Committee of the Capitol Region Conference of Churches. That noon I could take you along or leave you to your own devices unless you know some enchanting spot where you would enjoy being deposited. Arrange your schedule to your own advantage.

It will be good to see you at the reunion in June and in Newington in September. At Williams you can give me the necessary details. It has been a long time.

We agree completely concerning the many deficiencies of our foolish president. If he does not succeed in precipitating a nuclear war, I shall be surprised. The stupidity of our electorate is beyond belief.

As ever,
Edna

May 13, 1986
West Park, New York
Dear Edna,

If the only difficulty with putting the visit on September 10-12 is the noon meeting on the 12th, I should prefer that to the later date. Sometime that day I shall have to transfer to my friends at the Good Shepherd (155 Wyllys St.), so I shall need to get into Hartford. If it would be all right for me to attend the Social Concerns Committee, that might be fun. Or if it was better for you and my friends, perhaps you could deliver me to them before the meeting. Again, the details can be worked out at the Reunion, or even after I get to Newington. But I thought it well to establish the dates at this time.

See you in Williamstown.

Love,
Bonnie

May 29, 1986
Dear Bonnie,

Lest there be some confusion I thought it prudent to verify your Newington dates. I shall be delighted to see you September 10-12 and will pick you up wherever it is most convenient for you. And I will transport you to your friends sometime after dinner on the evening of the 12th if that suits you. I shall enjoy taking you to the Social Concerns Committee of the Capitol Region Conference of Churches. The Reverend Robert Felman, a Lutheran minister, is chairman and a fine leader. He recently lost a daughter of twenty-four, who was to have been married in a month. Our Committee unanimously endorsed the Harare Declaration and sent it to our Board of Directors, who in turn have sent it back to us for clarification. The Reverend Roger Floyd, a Methodist minister, is our Executive Director—a man who is liberal, honest, compassionate, energetic and courageous. He has worked diligently to help the black people realize their potential. He knows how to build bridges.

I know the Hartford church where you are going to preach. At one time, a former minister of that church was president of the CRCC. He and his wife were most unusual and well loved.

Your picture in the summer issue of <u>Holy Cross</u> was excellent—your best. Your friend looked most genial. I thoroughly enjoyed that issue.

As Ever,
Edna

September 17, 1986
West Park, New York
Dear Edna,

Thank you for the glorious time you gave me and for the presents you bought me. They will be a great help because they are precisely what I need. I both enjoyed and was much edified by the committee meeting. It clearly knows what it is doing and doing it well. Please tell Mary how grateful I am for the luncheon she gave us. But best of all was the chance to be and talk with you. (Why does a pen always give out in the middle of a letter?)

Thank you also for bringing the magazine and picture. I was most distressed by your fall. I hope there have been no ill effects from it. I shall hope to write you again after I get to Ghana.

Much love,
Bonnie

October 2, 1986
Cape Coast, Ghana
Dear Edna,

Yesterday when I was checking through the books that had arrived for the seminary library, I discovered your box of food which had arrived during the summer but which was apparently assumed to be books. We were delighted to get all the food you sent. It is still in good condition. Some of the cookie packages got a bit crushed, but I sampled one and it tasted fine. I am most grateful for the package. The delay in finding it has been all to the good, as far as I am concerned, for I shall be in on the eating of it, instead of it being consumed before I got back.

Speaking of food, I find myself delighted to get back to African meals. I enjoyed all those I had in USA, especially those I had with you, but somehow I find the simpler African food easier to digest. And the climate since I have been here has been just grand. I have had two days of lectures so far, and I find the men more responsive than ever. All goes very happily.

Since I have been back (over a week now) I have not seen a copy of the Christian Science Monitor. They say that they arrived during the summer, but even the back copies have disappeared, which probably means they came a long way back. So I think it might be well for you to change the address to Cape Coast now. My guess is that the process of getting mail to us from Accra is deteriorating more and more as time goes by.

The new monastery is grand. I found my room almost finished and a few extra shelves in the wardrobe completed the essentials. All my things are put away except I lack a bookcase for my books. That will come soon. The workmen are busy putting up the ceiling and lights in the chapel so that we can use that. At present we are using the reception room for the purpose. The individual rooms have windows at each end and the steady breezes have been so strong since I arrived that I am beginning to think I live in a wind tunnel. But after the hot, humid weather I had during much of the summer in USA, I am enjoying the change too much to close the louvers and cut it off.

I hope all goes well with you. No doubt, I shall soon be hearing from you, but I want to let you know about the package and thank you for it, so I am not waiting for your letter before writing. I shall write again when it comes.

Love,
Bonnie

October 17, 1986
Dear Bonnie,

It was good to receive your two letters; they are the first since May. I have missed them.

Your visit was delightful but quite short. The house seemed rather lonely after you left. I liked your friend, Dr. Brewer. My fall was quite unexpected, but it left no ill effects because I landed on my posterior, which is well padded. After my last x-ray, my surgeon said my hip was completely healed, and when I asked him if I had osteoporosis, he looked at me with some disdain and replied, "You have the bones of a 40 year old woman!" I hope he is right.

It was a joy to see you at the Williams Reunion, but I was puzzled. At the dinners Friday and Saturday evenings I felt that you deliberately avoided me; you did not even speak to me until I bade you good-bye when I was ready to leave that Friday evening. Thus, I took the hint and proceeded to keep to myself thereafter. I have never had any wish to interfere with your friendship with others—that is against my principles.

I gave Mary your message, and she was pleased. She has been a good friend of mine for some 37 years.

I am happy for you that all goes well for all at Cape Coast. I am sure they appreciate you. This past summer in Connecticut has been the worst I have known as far as the weather is concerned.

Please forgive me for having my house painted during your visit. You must have felt that you were living at Grand Central Station with all the commotion. I had made arrangements to have the work done in the early spring, but he did not get round to the task until September unfortunately. Somehow all my life the unexpected seems to befall me. Thus, I have learned to cope with fate as best I can. During my teaching career, my fellow teachers often remarked, "Things always seem to happen wherever you are." At least, I am never bored.

In all, I have had six Polish students to tutor; I just acquired two more—husband and wife. They all have happy fulfilling marriages including delightful children. In addition, they are intelligent, industrious and live according to a fine value system. I am always glad to see them. Teaching has always given me release. And in my youth, during my high school years, I thought I wanted to study law—I loved debating so much. En route, I began teaching at seventeen and became so engrossed I never gave it up except to study myself. The search for truth is indeed exciting. You possess a very youthful spirit. Never lose it for it is precious.

I called Boston about the <u>Christian Science Monitor</u> and changed the address to Cape Coast. I renewed your subscription in the early part of June. If you do not receive it now, please let me know for I shall continue it. I am surprised that you finally received the food package. What a long trip! What do you most desire?

Our mendacious President still continues on his mad journey. I cannot bear to listen to him on television. Star Wars is indeed a most costly nightmare. And our voters neither read nor think. I am worried about my country. Our people have lost their way. Material things are not our most precious possessions. We seem to have lost our spiritual bearings. I have enclosed a superb article by Barbara Tuchman—an analysis of our problems today.

Keep happy and well.

As ever,
Edna

November 5, 1986
Cape Coast, Ghana
Dear Edna,

Thank you for your letter, which has safely reached me, and for the article interviewing Barbara Tuchman. I have read <u>A Distant Mirror</u> and used it in my lecture on the fourteenth century. Her analysis of the current crisis is penetratingly correct.

I am much relieved that your fall produced no ill effects. I was genuinely worried, but as you seemed to be uninjured, I did not want to bother you by fussing about it.

I am sorry I gave you the impression of avoiding you at the reunion. It was not my intention to do so. I was trying to visit with as many classmates as possible and, if I seemed to ignore you, that was its cause, and not anything deliberate on my part. I greatly enjoyed and appreciated our dinner together on Sunday. As for our visit, the painting of your house was no problem to me. Things like that have to be done when you can get the workmen, and it did not bother me in any way. I was sorry my stay had to be so short, but it was difficult for me to fit in what I wanted to do. The necessity of a small operation and post-operational visits (which were necessary only for the doctor's peace of mind) crowded my last month home unduly.

I appreciate your renewal of the <u>Christian Science Monitor</u> and the change of its address. It has not yet started in arriving through Cape Coast, but those changes always take a long time. The people who forward things from Accra are hopeless. I think I wrote you that they sent six weeks' issues in one package, several weeks late in October. Since then I have received none. Presumably they are saving them up again. They seem to have no conception that one wants it week by week. So I look forward to its coming through Cape Coast. I have no idea when the food package arrived. It may have come soon after I left in April. The people here thought it was books for the library and therefore took it to the seminary to await my return. However, the food was still fresh and we have enjoyed it greatly. But I really think the whole process of getting packages here causes undue trouble and expense. I was most grateful for the clothes you bought me and at the moment I am well supplied with everything I need along that line.

By now you know how our election has come out. It will be a long time before I hear, if ever. I am eager to know who has control of the Senate and of the House. Being, unlike you, a pessimist, I fear the worst. Everyone I talk with shares our contempt of Reagan, but alas the American electorate idolizes him. It is disastrously sad. I should not be surprised if he and the CIA had their hands in the murder of the president of Mozambique. Reagan will do anything to support South Africa.

I trust you keep well and busy, but are not overdoing.

Love,
Bonnie

A GENERAL LETTER
November 1986
Cape Coast, Ghana

Greetings from Ghana!

The new monastery fulfills our fondest hopes. The building itself is now complete. Our individual rooms are comfortably furnished with adequate closet space. The kitchen, pantry, and refectory are in operation. The chapel is outstandingly beautiful, especially the paneled ceiling. What remains to be done is the furnishing. The shelves for the library are now in process, so that I can get it catalogued and arranged. We hope next to make the altar, stalls, and pews for the chapel.

When Orlando and I arrived, we were given the last two rooms. The full house was still preventing us from receiving new postulants. But now we have started our work in Kumasi. Orlando, Thomas, and Charles are resident there and Christian commutes back and forth, so that he can take the Sunday Eucharists at the parish for which we are responsible, and continue teaching in the seminary there.

That gives us room for recruits. We hope for some in January. In fact, two who live in Cape Coast are spending the weekends with us while they continue their jobs in town. We are happy about our novices who are committed and persevering.

The rainy season, which usually ends in September or October, is still with us. That means that our garden is flourishing. One of our sows has just produced a litter of piglets. The rabbits are fine, but so far as I know, have no offspring. We have two dogs and two cats, a normal menagerie. The dogs are a bit of a nuisance at times. They have strong objections to others of their kind on the place and express their disapproval by loud barking while keeping as far away as possible.

My classes at the seminary are more fun than ever this year. It was glorious to be home for my sabbatical, to visit all our houses, and to see so many old friends. But I must admit I am glad to be back in

Ghana. My health remains good and I enjoy the climate, the food, and the teaching. What more can one ask?

May God richly bless you. Please keep us in your prayers.

Love,
Bonnie

January 17, 1987
Dear Bonnie,

My last personal letter from you came the 18th of November. I enjoyed it and answered it on the 26th, but perhaps it never reached you for I stuffed the envelope with news clippings. Possibly someone thinking it was money appropriated it. In December I received your typed general letter filled with encouraging information about your new monastery. It must indeed be very beautiful and comfortable. Your students are most fortunate to have you as their mentor.

On December first, I sent you a food package in care of the National Catholic Service Center as you instructed. You will enjoy a bit of humor in the story of its pilgrimage en route to the post office. Somehow I managed to get it into my car and out at the post office. Then first one person and then another assisted me in the journey to the post office desk. Unfortunately I discovered that my bundle was one ounce over the permissible 22 pounds. Fortunately for me, one of the post office men, who has always been especially kind to me, opened the package, eliminated a light article and then proceeded to put the package back together again. He did compliment me on the efficiency I had shown in the original packing. Was I not lucky? It holds plenty of cookies and coffee besides other kinds of food.

On the 18th of December I mailed your Christmas package in care of the National Catholic Service Center. I presume you have received neither parcel as yet. I tried.

Are you still receiving The Christian Science Monitor? You should be, for I called the Boston headquarters about it.

I still follow my program of daily activities—it keeps me out of mischief. When I was a wee one, I was delighted to get to school when I had something worthwhile to do. The authorities should have permitted me to enter a year earlier, but I outwitted them and skipped a grade later.

Currently, I am attempting to induce the Social Concerns Committee of the CRCC (the one you visited) to work toward the adoption of a program by the state to provide free nursery schools for the little ones from the age of three to five. We shall never be able to raise the level of the minorities in any other way. So many of them have very little at home to stimulate their imaginations. If we supplied the best facilities and the finest teachers, we could bring about great changes in one generation. The very young want to learn. Of course, I would mix the "have-nots" with "those that have". They both have "much to learn from each other".

I continue to enjoy my four Polish students who are progressing. [Note: The following, in quotations, is crossed out] "Our new minister, John Luoka, who possesses a Finnish background, and is a product of Harvard Divinity is only 30 years old, but he has the maturity of a 60 year old. He has a wife and a baby daughter to whom he is devoted. January has proved mild with one beautiful snow storm. However, we are due for a good storm this weekend."

Unless our citizens improve their morals and use their heads to better advantage, our democracy will fail. The Iran scandal proves the duplicity and ignorance of Reagan. When he appeared on television to prove himself concerning the publicity, his eyes and general demeanor were exactly what I say mirrored in the faces of boys who tried to deceive me during my teaching career. I sincerely hope the Democrats in Congress will be equal to the present challenge. I am continually appalled by those who lack the courage to stand against evil. [Note: The following, in quotations, is crossed out] "I still attend all the meetings of the Board of Trustees for the four state universities. I have passed out to some of the leaders pertinent articles in the <u>Christian Science Monitor</u>."

I checked with the father of the boy I helped years ago, the one whose wedding I attended this past August. He is now head coach of basketball at Harvard. I liked his wife and they are very happy. He had a God given gift of understanding people-even as a young boy.

[Recently, I enjoyed a dinner visit with two of my Polish pupils at their homes. I met their two young sons (five and six year olds) and many of their friends. Fortunately for me, they picked me up and delivered me safely home afterwards during one of our worst snow and ice storms. My Polish pupils possess fine living values including warm family ties.]

Soon I shall mail you a letter filled with clippings including one that Anne sent me. She wanted me to mail one to you. The article by Schlesinger about Reagan is the best I have seen. I did not see the newspaper obituary about Harvey. Anne telephoned me the news. I talked to her over the phone and I have invited her to lunch when the weather permits. Bonnie, I am sorry that you have lost a friend, and I will try to help Anne recover from the loss of her husband.

It seems eons since you were here. There are always so many things I want to discuss with you, but I never seem to get there.

As Ever,
Edna

January 30, 1987
Cape Coast, Ghana, West Africa
Dear Edna,

It is a surprise to me that I have not received an answer to my letter of November 6, especially as your reply would be a Christmas letter. As I have learned that a letter was mailed to me in October from another of my regular correspondents and has never reached me, my guess is that you also have written and the letter gone astray. Therefore I am writing to inform you that, as of this date, I have not heard from you, lest you think I have failed to answer a letter.

In my last letter I think I said the <u>Monitor</u> had not yet started to come via our Cape Coast box. It began to arrive the week after I wrote and has come regularly ever since. It is a great joy and help to us, not only keeping us abreast of what is going on, but also presenting the news in a reasonable manner.

Have you heard of Hob's death? Stew mentioned it on his Christmas letter, but gave no details except that it was sudden and unexpected. It must have been a great shock to poor Ann. I never thought Hob would predecease her, since her health has not been good for the past two years. But somehow it often seems that the sicklier one outlives the healthier. Needless to say, Hob's death is a tremendous loss to me. He and you are my closest ties with Williams, which makes me the more eager to hear from you again.

Things here continue to go well. The monastery is now nearly finished. The chapel is fully furnished and the sacristy is in the final stages. The library books are all catalogued and shelved, except those that should be arriving soon (they are already in Accra.) The common room furniture is also built, but the room is still having to be used to store building material, so it is not yet fully in order.

The seminary also has a new room for its library and the books have been moved into it. It gives more space and therefore makes the books more easily accessible, but already it is almost full and probably will be when its books in the shipment in Accra have been included. There is no way to provide adequately for the necessary growth of a library that tries to keep up-to-date.

I hope that you are well and happily busy, and that your Christmas holidays were enjoyed. Things seem at last to be catching up with our cowboy. My gloomy predictions about the last election were happily proved false in the Senate. Perhaps there may be a chance that we can get out of the doldrums in 1988.

All the best.

Love,
Bonnie

February 9, 1987
Dear Bonnie,

Today your long awaited letter arrived. Your letter of Nov. 6 came Nov. 18 and I answered Nov. 26, but you must not have received it. Do you suppose someone appropriated it because it was so bulky for I filled it with clippings? Perhaps it looked like money. On December first I mailed a package of food weighing about 22 pounds via the Catholic Service Center. On the 18th of December I sent by air mail a Christmas package containing a tie, handkerchiefs, a date booklet and a filler of medical supplies. After a long wait for an answer to my letter, I sent another one on Jan. 21st with a birthday card enclosed. Perhaps this letter has also failed to reach you. I did miss your letters so I began rereading those you sent in the past. I have kept them all.

In the letter I mailed January 21, I told you that Anne called me about Harvey; I did not see it in the papers. I am sorry, Bonnie, that you have lost a good friend. I talk to Anne on the telephone and have invited her to lunch when we are no longer snowbound. I will try to help her for it is a shattering experience. She greatly appreciated your letter of condolence; she read it to me over the telephone, and it was very beautiful. You are very sensitive and possess great depth of feeling.

I am including the *N.Y. Times* article by Arthur Schlesinger. It is one that Anne shared with me and wanted sent to you. I have made copies of it for Anne. It is excellent. I do believe that Reagan's "chickens have come home to roost." Most assuredly he is an arrogant liar. It baffles me to realize that people are not more perceptive.

I am very happy that the *Christian Science Monitor* continues on its journey. If there is any trouble about it, do let me know.

My busy days continue with four Polish students and a fifth returning after a new baby. The Social Concerns Committee of CRCC meets regularly. I am troubled by the problems single mothers and their offspring have to endure. There must be some way we can help them. I have a report to give Thursday. There have been a number of interesting meetings of the Jewish Concerns Committee and the various sub groups.

Do keep well and enjoy your beautiful surroundings.

As ever,
Edna

February 28, 1987
Ghana, West Africa
Dear Edna,

Such is the perversity of the mails that both your letters, of January 17 (mailed 21) and February 9 reached me together yesterday. I am tremendously relieved, for I was getting seriously worried. I think now all our correspondence is accounted for. Your letter of November 26 was lost, probably because of its bulk, as you suggest. But it may not have been purloined by a light-fingered postal clerk. I think it more likely that the government opened it because it is strictly illegal to send in currency without having cleared it in advance. I suggest that, much as I enjoy the clippings, you restrict yourself to one small one, because your letters are more valuable to me than the clippings. I did, however, much enjoy Schlesinger's article that you and Ann sent me. The comment is just right.

Neither of the packages has yet arrived. That does not surprise me, as they got caught in the Christmas rush. I doubt that the food package will get here before spring. You remember that the one you sent last winter was received after I had left in April, put aside for me all summer, and consequently not opened until October. The other package should arrive sooner. I shall be on the lookout for it. I much appreciate your generosity. But I wonder if the trouble, the expense, and the uncertainty of shipping direct to me is justified. It really would be better, when you want to send things, to do so through West Park. People come out to visit us from time to time, and each brings some things. Fr. Superior is with us now and some at least of your December gifts could have come with him. Also from time to time we ship parcels—library books, etc.—though the Franciscans, who send out a huge iron container regularly. Your packages could go in that. The best plan would be for you to get in touch with The Rev. Boniface Adam, OHC, Holy Cross Monastery, West Park, NY 12493. Telephone, if you call during the business day Monday-Friday, (914) 384-6660 (at other times you are likely to get an answering machine) or (914) 384-6698. He can tell you what the prospects for sending things to us are in the immediate future.

I do indeed appreciate the _**Monitor**_, which comes regularly though the intervals are erratic. I must admit I am following Reagan's discomfiture with unholy glee. But as he is essentially a matinee idol, I doubt that he will really lose his popularity. That the Democrats have recaptured the Senate, by a large margin and <u>before</u> the Iran fiasco, is hopeful, but so far they have seemed to be so timid and disorganized that it is not really encouraging. God bless America!

Hob's death has been a severe blow to me. As you know he and I went not only to official reunions together, but also to Old Guard get-togethers when I was at home. Also, like you and two or three others, he was a faithful correspondent. That means much when one is living away from home. I still, however, have no idea how and why he died. Stewart another classmate, referred to Hob's sudden death in a one line note at the top of his Christmas form letter. Your mention of it in your last two letters is the only other word I have had. If you could give me a brief account of the cause and circumstances, I should appreciate it.

I am glad you are in touch with Ann. She must have been devastated. Hob was always worrying that she would go first, and so was I. A widower is always so much more alone and helpless than a widow. I am glad Hob was spared that. I trust Ann has by now been able to pick up the threads of their life again. I am glad she got my letter. She is not much of a one to write, so I do not expect to hear from her. Again I should be grateful if you could keep me informed as to how she is doing if you are able to keep in touch with her.

I share your frustration at not been able to talk things out. Correspondence at best can touch only on the main points, and then only superficially. But everything has its price, and I cannot but feel my work here is worth the sacrifices it entails. Classes at the seminary are going better than ever this year. I seem to be presenting my material in a more simplified and organized way, and the students are getting used to me. Their response and apparent enjoyment is encouraging. Two of the papers one class handed in last term were as good as a summary of our discussions as I could have written myself, and six others ranged from satisfactory to very good.

On March 6 we consecrate our chapel. It is dedicated to the African Martyrs. I enclose its collect. As I want to send this with the Superior, to be mailed in the USA, I cannot wait to describe the service. Because all the bishops were away until early March, we have had to postpone it until the last day of his visit. He goes, in fact, right from the service to the plane.

I hope your efforts to get the state to provide free nursery schools are successful. As you say, they are essential. Those of us who had the advantage of growing up in homes where reading, art, manners, and culture were taken for granted had a tremendous head start in life. From childhood I fully expected to go to college (although neither of my parents had) and I always enjoyed school more than vacation. Children brought up in squalid, illiterate homes, often through no fault of their parents, have little chance of escaping their environment, and little encouragement to do so, unless the state steps in and supplies some of their deficiencies. And the ages 3 to 5 are the crucial period.

So keep up the good work. I am sorry I took longer than you to get around to writing a second letter, but I kept thinking yours might have been delayed by the Christmas confusion. But now at last all is well. Thank you also for the birthday card.

Love,
Bonnie

A GENERAL LETTER
March 1987
Ghana, West Africa

Greetings from Quaquesalem!

That is the name we have given to the area where our new monastery is. We have at last been able to complete it in time for the Superior's visitation. Before he leaves, the chapel will have been consecrated. We had to postpone the service until the last day of his visit because all the Ghanaian bishops were away at a Synod until then.

Since I want to send this with the Superior so that it can be duplicated and distributed, and he rushes off to his plane as soon as the service is ended, I cannot wait to describe it to you.

The chapel is dedicated to the African Martyrs. The collect which has been written for the occasion is:

O God of never failing love, you have sanctified the soil of Africa with the blood of many martyrs and made them the seed of your Church: Grant that we, encouraged by their example and upheld by their prayers, may devote our lives to your praise and service; through our Savior Jesus Christ who gave his life for us and now lives and reigns with you and the Holy Spirit, one God, in glory everlasting. Amen.

You may want to use it occasionally in remembering us. The chapel is central to our life and ministry here.

The work in Kumasi seems to be off to a good start, although the negotiations about the property that is to be deeded to us are still in process. The additional room in our monastery here in Cape Coast has not yet been occupied, as we had hoped, by new postulants. Those in Ghana have not yet decided to come. One we hope to receive from Cameroon we have been holding off until we can make sure of his resident visa. The government has become more fussy about issuing them. But our five novices continue to do well and we hope one will take his annual vow before long.

Seminary goes well, especially as far as my classes are concerned. I seem to be communicating better every year, so both the students and I are enjoying the courses more. I am also kept busy these days incorporating the books I collected last summer into the library. Its new room is a great improvement over the crowded area where it was at first. But with the books that are now being shelved, the new room is already filled up. A living library never has the space it needs for expansion.

The Bible and Common Prayer Book Society of the Episcopal Church gave us 50 copies of the 1979 Prayer Book last summer. I have thereby been able to give each seminarian a copy and they are enthusiastically received. This Province has yet to make its revision of the Prayer Book and I am eager that the American book shall be taken into account.

I hope you and yours have a good Lent and Eastertide.

As ever,
Bonnie

ANOTHER GENERAL LETTER

[No date given, assume March 1987]
Ghana, West Africa

Greetings from Quaquesalem!

That is the name we have given to the area where our monastery is now located. We have been living in it since last April, but it has taken us until the beginning of this month to get it completed. Now all the rooms are adequately furnished and in use.

This month our chapel was consecrated. It is dedicated to the African Martyrs, of which there is a goodly company, ranging from those of the first three Christian centuries in Egypt and North Africa, through the recent martyrs in Uganda, to those who are suffering for Christian principles in South Africa today.

The chapel is truly beautiful. It is large, light, and airy, with simple furnishings and good space for the celebration of our liturgies. The altar is especially striking, as it has a central bar relief panel on which is painted a dove of peace flying over the keyboard of a piano. The latter is a symbol that Aggrey, a native Ghanaian, used to indicate the interdependence of the black and white races. The panel was designed by one of our African members and executed by a local craftsman.

Since the monastery is well out in the country, with nothing around it but fields, we are at last enjoying real quiet. It is a delightful contrast to living in the middle of a girls' school. We also have nice gardens, both flower and vegetable. We raise pigs, rabbits, chickens, and ducks. A constant breeze keeps the house cool, because every room has cross-ventilation that catches the prevailing winds. Sometimes it is almost like living in a wind tunnel.

The walk from here to the seminary takes me about an hour. The younger brethren can make it in forty-five minutes, but I have learned to take it easier. Most of it is on paths through the fields or along a country road, which I find very pleasant. I try to make it at least twice a week to keep up my exercise. My health remains good and weight stays just where I like it.

I am enjoying my teaching this year more than ever. I seem to be communicating better as I learn to simplify and organize my material and the students get used to my ways. The monastery is also thriving, with some good recruits in training. We have recently been able to open a second work of the Order of Kumasi.

Perhaps this letter is almost too cheerful, but I think we should share our joys as well as our sorrows. I cannot refrain, however, from mentioning one of the latter which we all share. Hob's death was a special blow to me. You all recall that he and I traveled to recent reunions together and he was one of my most faithful correspondents. Happy as one may be in a foreign field, letters from home are always appreciated.

I hope all goes well with you.

As ever,
Bonnie

March 20-24, 1987
Dear Bonnie,

It was good to receive your most interesting letters, including the Greetings from Quaquesalem, for Easter. Your collect is beautiful. I am happy that you are living amidst such peace and beauty. And you have given so much to others. Teaching is indeed a fulfilling experience; it is one heaven sent opportunity.

I promise you that I will not send you any more packages directly. I did not realize that you had to pay a duty on them in Africa. Somehow the obvious often fails to dawn on me. If you will let me know what the packages cost you, I will send a check. Do I send it to you, or to West Park?

I continue to keep in touch with Ann. She has already written you two letters and is surprised that you have not received them. She said that the one you sent her had been opened and then re-sealed. She told me that Harvey had his heart attack December seventh and was taken to the hospital that day. During his ten day stay, he responded beautifully to treatment. On his last day at the hospital, he was given a stress test on a treadmill just before the hour they intended to release him. However, during the test, he collapsed and died. The officials tried unsuccessfully to revive him. Ann was not at the hospital at the time; she was awaiting him at home, for the relatives were ready to bring him back. Think of the shock that hospital call brought to Ann, who was waiting anxiously to receive him. She was quite disturbed with the callous way the doctors handled the situation. Since that time she has learned of about six other similar mistakes. Not until Harvey was hospitalized did he inform Ann that several months previous to his attack he had suffered pains in his chest. He ought to have told Ann so that she could have made him see a doctor. During those months he had worked very hard outside raking mountains of leaves for disposal. Neighbors and friends have been most thoughtful. Within a week, I expect to have her here for lunch—weather permitting. Now it is most spring-like, but one never knows what the morrow will bring in N.E. Ann seems to be bearing up as well as can be expected. Everyone has to find his own way out.

I have been most concerned about the system of values so prevalent in to-day's society of the young, especially in our state colleges. I am appalled! *The Christian Science Monitor* of January 30th included a pull-out section of some twelve pages on "Moral Education." I bought up all I could find in both Hartford and Boston. Since I attend all the meetings of the Board of Trustees for the four CT. State Universities, I passed them out to the head of the system and all the members of the Board. Then I sent a copy to each of the presidents of the four universities. For one president, I carefully underlined significant portions, for he is one for whom I have no respect, and I felt he needed a bit of assistance. I received two acknowledgments—from the two best presidents; one was a fine letter of appreciation and understanding from the president under whom I taught many years. When I retired, I had been chairman of the Advisory Council to the Board of Trustees since its inception. Previously, I had served as salary chairman, treasurer, secretary, and president of the Faculty Association of the four colleges. At the same time, I had worked in an official capacity for the Connecticut Education Association, the National Education Association and the Connecticut State Employees Association. Now, however, we are living in a new era. I still believe that we have to live with hope, faith and courage. I feel that I must do whatever I can to help. This situation is so unfair to the students. If our older citizens do not strive to set good examples, we have no right to expect higher standards for the young.

As a member of the Denominational Concerns Committee at my church, I promised to report on one of the five resolutions to be discussed for consideration as one of the three final resolutions to be submitted for voting on the Final Agenda of our 1987 UUG General Assembly. It is the resolution I deem most important. I have enclosed a copy for I believe you will agree with its import. I worry about the future of our democracy. We owe a real debt to all the newcomers to our country to preserve our principles so that they can find a true refuge here and can help us improve conditions.

On April 5th I promised to lead a discussion on "The Future of Our Children" at our church forum. This will be related to the report I shall submit at the Spring Retreat our CRCC Social Concerns Committee (the one you visited) will hold on April 8th at Our Lady of Calvary Retreat Center in Farmington. It is a very beautiful place conducive to productive thinking. We meet from five to nine. I'm going to take our Vice Chairman, whom I like—she is fair, unassuming, and intelligent.

I have attended many meetings of the Christian/Jewish Task Force and take a very fine woman who lives in West Hartford. She belongs to the Congregational Church, the same denomination my grandmother, Harriet Bangs Lane, followed. I do believe I have descended from all kinds of Protestants. We usually meet at the Greater Hartford Jewish Community Center in West Hartford. We are planning spring conferences including an Inter-faith Cedar Celebration at the University of Hartford.

I am still enjoying my Polish students who are very faithful and appreciative.

I will write you again in another week after I have had Ann here for lunch.

Do keep well and happy.

Edna

April 17, 1987
Ghana, West Africa
Dear Edna,

Yesterday was Williams' day for me. Besides your good letter, I received one from Anne and the fall <u>Alumni Review</u>. I particularly appreciated your account of Hob's death. Since I never received Ann's first letter, I had not known the details. It really must have been a shock to have received the news when she was awaiting his return. Ann may be right in thinking that the doctor and hospital had been somewhat negligent, but as I have written Ann, I am sure it was an honest mistake and one aided and abetted by Hob who, if I knew him, was raring to get out. She was looking forward eagerly to having lunch with you and I trust it has taken place by now.

There is no problem about the duty on your packages. It is only recently that the government here has begun to enforce its regulations to the letter, and beyond the letter. One of our USA citizen members, whom the Order wanted to station here, who came over and was behaving properly, was refused a residence visa and told to get out of the country at once. There was not the slightest justification. At the same time customs started charging exorbitant fees. The Catholic Service decided that some packages, including apparently your food package, were not worth the duty and refused them. Fortunately they did not refuse your Christmas gifts, for I should have hated to miss them. The duty was paid by the Catholic Service, and as there were other packages in the lot, I have no idea what was paid by us for yours. So let it go. I was concerned only to keep you from sending other packages that would not reach me.

Please note our new address at the top of the preceding page. We now have a box at the Adisadel branch, which is nearer our monastery. It also is a lockbox of which we have the key. At the main office the boxes are rusted shut, so the mail has to be kept in bins and handed out at the counter. Your letter and Ann's were not the only ones we failed to receive. I have written the change of address to the Monitor, but it has not yet started to come to the new one. We shall keep the old "box" until the end of the year in case mail is still sent to it.

I read that article on morals in the *Monitor* with great interest. We do need to raise standards in that area, especially in our educational institutions. It is good that Dolores has you to uphold and champion her. Please give her my best. I do think, however, that we must be careful to distinguish between universal moral obligations and customs of our traditional culture. I fear we have not only failed to give full integrity as persons to members of minority groups, but have also been too insistent that they adopt our culture and thereby deprived ourselves of many contributions they could have made to our American way of life, which as American citizens is theirs as well. Living in Africa, where the local culture has been so badly damaged by colonialism and missionary condemnation (to the great detriment of Christianity) I am particularly sensitive to the situation.

Your resolution is excellent and I hope you succeed in getting the General Assembly to pass it. I wish other Churches would be as specific. Keep up the good work. Take care and continue to enjoy life.

Love,
Bonnie

May 16, 1987
Dear Bonnie,

It was so good to receive your letter. This past month I have been snowed under with my various activities that descended all at once. My sister-in-law, Florence, the one you met, thinks that I spend too much time on all my causes. At least, they keep me out of mischief—unless one of them brings down the wrath of the Mafia round my head.

Ann has been here for dinner—rather than lunch because I was overwhelmed by my income tax—which I had postponed until the last minute. She looks good and seems to be taking everything in her stride. She is strong and has good friends as well as thoughtful neighbors. We call each other on the telephone. We agree on politics, and she is quite perceptive.

The *Christian Science Monitor* has received your new address, and I have renewed your subscription. I find it most worthwhile.

I still maintain that the weakest link in education is administration. Too few people are willing to stand for justice when the cost is high. Materialism surely reigns in our country today, and truth is seldom revered, let alone recognized. Even though I know the task is monumental, I am not giving up.

I attended a reception at Central Connecticut State University to honor returning president F. Don James and his wife. He was my president and a very fine man—the best of the four Connecticut University presidents. His wife who is Swiss born is a perfect presidential wife—honest, gracious, supportive, and most perceptive. The occasion revealed elegant simplicity. I met many of my old friends.

The CRCC Christian-Jewish Task Force, of which I am a member, sponsored a dialogue session on Christian Jewish relations at one of our Christian churches. Our executive director, the Rev. Roger Floyd ran the meeting quite effectively. I don't believe I shall ever understand why someone is threatened by someone else who holds a different religious point of view. It has never bothered me—I do not believe that God is responsible for the evil in this world. For me He represents all that is good and beautiful. Please feel free to set me straight. Your religious background is more pervasive than mine.

In our Social Concerns Committee of CRCC I have been asked to form a subcommittee to look into the problem of the education of the very young (three to five year olds). I have asked one Hispanic and one Black to help because it is their people who seem to be short-changed. The Reverand you met and liked when you visited our committee is eager to serve. It will probably take 20 years to convince the government that this is their obligation to mankind, but we must begin.

The Rev. Roger Floyd, our CRCC director, looks at me and says, "You are always thinking, aren't you? You even think in terms of what ought to be?" Is that the way I strike you? I suppose we never see ourselves as others do.

As ever,
Edna

May 23, 1987
Dear Bonnie,

In reviewing the literature involving you I learned that you received an honorary doctorate from the General Theological Seminary. This is a long deserved reward for your superb intelligence, manifold accomplishments, and innumerable contributions to the welfare of mankind. How like you in your modesty to refrain from telling me yourself. I know that you graduated third in your class at Williams, and everyone expected you to become a college professor. And you have to open the eyes of your students to those values which reign supreme.

I am happy for you—for your being.

As ever,
Edna

June 4, 1987
Ghana, West Africa
Dear Edna,

Your letter of May 16 and the parcel you sent last December finally arrived on the same day!! I am most grateful for both. The contents of the package have come through well, and they will be welcome, especially as the Prior and Novice Master leave for Chapter at the end of this month and I shall be in charge of this house until August. The cookies, nuts and fruit will sweeten our life greatly.

The news in your letter is also appreciated. I am glad to keep in touch with Ann. She writes me regularly and it means much to me to be hearing from the both of you. It is not always enough to endure evil patiently. Sometimes we are called to "take arms against a sea of troubles and by opposing end them." I have your friend in my prayers.

I also rejoice that you are battling for the education of the very young. That is the key to rescuing the under privileged children from the handicap that makes further public education for them a farce. They enter school incapable of understanding what goes on + are passed from class to class in that same condition. No wonder they revolt or give up.

I especially appreciate your offer to finance a trip for me to England this summer. That is tremendously generous of you. But I am planning and hoping to spend the summer here. My health remains good and August-September is the best weather in Ghana. I have several jobs I want to accomplish before seminary reopens. Its library needs a shelf check. I am rewriting my class notes for the Proclamation course in the light of an excellent contribution by the students who took it this past year. I may have an entirely new course to teach next year for which I shall have to do the research and organization. Finally, I should like to write a book, again based on the content of the Proclamation course. So you see I shall, like you, have enough to keep me busy—and out of England.

The Monitor has been coming to our new address for the last few weeks. I am most grateful to you for renewing the subscription. I read each copy cover to cover.

You were so right about Hart. I remember you objected to him as a candidate in 1984. I felt then, on the basis of his platform and his electability, that he was preferable to Mondale. Now the problem is which of the 7 dwarfs, as the Monitor calls them, can get the Democratic nomination—and will he have a chance? Perhaps the best policy would be for the convention to draft Cuomo. Oh well, keep hoping and happy and don't work too hard.

Love,
Bonnie

June 18, 1987
Ghana, West Africa
Dear Edna,

Your letter of May 23 has arrived. It was written most fittingly on the 50th anniversary of my ordination to the priesthood. We had a very happy celebration here, with the bishop of the diocese present as well as representatives from the neighboring Religious Communities (Roman Catholic), seminaries, and friends. Little did I think when I was ordained that I should spend that anniversary in Africa. God has been very good to me, and given me a rich and varied ministry.

My doctorate was conferred by General so long ago (1976) that I rarely think of it—only when I notice the gown hanging in my closet, which I brought over to wear at seminary commencements. I should have been wearing it today, but we had to close the seminary early this year. Cape Coast had no running water since May 10. We got so little rain in the rainy season that the city reservoir is too low for the water to reach the outflow pipes. We still have not had enough rain to improve the situation and none seems to be in sight. We have dug a couple of wells on our place that are yielding enough water for washing and we truck in our drinking water. In Africa we have most of the modern conveniences, but they tend to break down, so one has to learn to cope. It adds to the fun.

As I told you in my last letter of June 4, I am planning to spend the summer here, so I cannot accept your most generous offer of money for travel. I do deeply appreciate it, however. We are having an important meeting of the Order this summer at which the Prior and Novice Mast of the house had to be present. I elected to stay and keep the store. It is just as well. My proclamation course with the seniors at the seminary went so well this year and I learned so much from them that I am rewriting my notes. In addition, the Rector is transferring my Church History to a new man whose field that is, so I am taking on two new courses—one on Prayer for the first year men and one on the Life and Letters of Paul. Since I have never taught either of them I have much research and organization to do. I am already at it and enjoying it greatly.

We are still enjoying the goodies you sent in the box last December. They have ept remarkably well and the cookies were only slightly broken. I hope you are having a happy summer and that all your interests and enterprises are prospering.

Love,
Bonnie

This will be mailed in USA, so may reach you before mine of June 4, mailed from here.

July 8, 1987
Dear Bonnie,

It was good to receive your two letters; they are ever heartwarming. Forgive me for congratulating you ten years later. The Alumni Review of Williams—1987 Winter mentioned the occasion in 1986. Upon reviewing my mail of long ago, I found that I had remembered the honors then, but I thought you had just received another academic recognition. Nevertheless, you deserve all the tokens.

I have duly checked on some of your friends. Anne is all right and busy. I am trying to persuade her to write some stories and then submit them to magazines, etc. She read one to me over the telephone. I thought it was beautiful and sensitive. I called Elizabeth in New Hampshire. She seemed good although her voice was not normal, but I could easily understand her over the phone because of some device attached at her end. She wanted to be remembered to you. She thoroughly enjoyed your visit last year.

Just imagine—six months for that package to arrive! I am surprised that it was edible. If you will let me know what it cost you to receive it, I will send you a check. Do you prefer a cashier's check to a personal check? Which is safer? I don't want you to be short of money.

You certainly are going to be busy this summer, but I wish the condition of the water there would improve. I hope your students realize how fortunate they are to have you. You surely possess a superb outlook.

Thank you for your prayers for D. I am sure they helped and she appreciated them. At her arbitration, she was on the stand over five hours. I am sure that she held her own, maintaining her integrity and perspicacity. She had endured this situation more than ten years. She must not stay there beyond September; her health cannot withstand a longer stint.

The last two Mondays in June I chaired a committee from my church to sponsor Honor Court at the Salvation Army in Hartford. We try to help the alcoholics stay out of jail by depending upon Alcoholics Anonymous. We served them the very best food we could find. They are pathetic, but trying to overcome. One can only think, "There but for the grace of God walk I." I always bring flowers and an attractive table cloth. When I taught I always felt that an attractive classroom made it easier for students to be good.

At the last meeting of the Social Concerns Committee of CRCC, as part of my responsibility for the Devotions, I quoted from your book and finished the simple poem by Leigh Hunt—"Abu Ben Abba."

How the people in this country can admire and applaud President Reagan is beyond my comprehension! Our citizens have grown more avaricious and more stupid with the years. Heaven help us if Robert Bork is elevated to the Supreme Court. There is something about his face and manner that I do not trust. Reagan has sponsored more unworthy individuals than one can imagine.

Usually around sundown I take my daily walk even though it takes me twice as long to walk a mile. It is worth it. My doctor gave me a clean bill of health this June after my annual physical. I do not take any medication and he approves my vitamins, and diet.

This spring nature has been most bountiful. The trees, shrubs, and flowers have been glorious. I could have served you a beautiful breakfast on my cool, decorative back porch. On sale, I bought a pretty white table with white yellow cushioned chairs. I finally found a capable gardener—the father of my little high school friend Nancy—of Portuguese origin. My flowers are lovely and cheerful.

I shall miss seeing you this year!

Keep well and happy,
Edna

September 2-7, 1987
Dear Bonnie,

Is something wrong? I have not heard from you since the 26th of June. Did you not receive my letter of July 8th? Or did your answer go astray? Each day I look for a letter, but none comes. I do hope you are well. To be sure, you had a very busy summer! After fifty years of devotions, you have earned rest and more free time. It is indeed a most generous gift you have made to mankind—I respect and admire you for it. I am delighted that you had a celebration of your ordination. Is there something you want that I can send you in honor of your 50th anniversary? I can ask your friends at West Park to carry it. And when I send your Christmas gifts by the same route, what do you truly want? In the choice of food, I am never sure of your desires, and I truly want to give you what you would most enjoy.

Saturday Anne came to dinner. Since it was Harvey's birthday, she said that it helped to get away. We ate on the back porch where she could enjoy the flowers, shrubs and above all, the western sky. Food always tastes better outdoors—that must be the Danish in me. Anne is bearing up very well. Her neighbors have been most considerate and helpful.

We have endured a hot, humid, but rainless summer. The latter part of August has proved to be more bearable, however. This summer I did not participate in any jaunts but pursued my various duties—tutoring, meetings, etc. This fall I may try some foliage trips. Mrs. G, who helps me with my housework, wants to travel with me. She is a fine, sensitive woman who lost her husband a year ago.

Our NARAL (National Abortion Rights Action League) of which I am a member in Hartford is anxious to protest the nomination of Robert Bork. I attended a meeting at headquarters to prepare to participate in gathering around the area to alert the women to the many dangers Bork represents. I have promised to speak at two meetings so far. I have collected many news clippings about the man. To be sure, he is brilliant, but he is extreme and bent on the wrong path. I fear that he would lead the other members of the Supreme Court astray. Reagan's regime seems interminable. Not only is he dishonest, but he is vain as well.

We have a new minister in our church—of a Finnish background and only thirty years of age, but he shows the wisdom of a sixty year old. He has a delightful wife and an adorable baby daughter. We are fortunate to have him.

Two of my pupils have applied for American citizenship; they are excellent candidates and are parents of two promising boys. Sometime papa brings his younger son—age four—along when he has his lesson. Fortunately, I keep blocks and crayons available. I always enjoy children. I meet delightful ones—of all ages in the grocery store and on my daily walks.

Your courses sound both fascinating and challenging. You are living proof that the brain grows keener with use.

As ever,
Edna

October 20, 1987
Ghana, West Africa
Dear Edna,

According to my records, which I think are accurate, I last wrote you on June 18th. That is much too long for you not to have answered. So I fear another of your letters has somehow gone astray. I am taking the opportunity of a visit by Br. William Sibley, the Prior of our house in Toronto, to send this letter with him, when he returns on Friday, to be mailed in Canada.

I hope you are well and have had a good summer. I enjoyed mine here and was able to get in good work in preparation for two new courses I am teaching this year. The weather, however, this year was unusual for my experience here so far. In July we had a hot, humid spell with no rain. Then in August the rains started and continued almost daily until last Saturday, when we had a heavy thunderstorm. Since then it has been clear, the longest spell (three days) in months. The inconvenience to me has been the muddy roads which has made walking, my only exercise, extremely difficult.

Seminary has been going for nearly a months and I am enjoying my classes more than ever. The new courses seem to be working out well and the old ones better than ever. As you well know, teaching is great fun, and the men this year seem to be more responsive than ever.

I have been hoping against hope that your letter would turn up. They are making some repairs at the main Post Office and that seems to have delayed the delivery of second class mail. I am still receiving back numbers of the Monitor. But it does not seem to have affected first class mail unless your letter has got lost en route. In case it has, it is past the time when I shoal be letting you know of the problem.

I trust you are happily busy and hope that your many enterprises are prospering as well as can be expected. You are a champion not, I trust, of lost causes, but of causes that are difficult to accomplish. But if anyone can do it, you will.

Love,
Bonnie

November 5, 1987
Dear Bonnie,

It was such a joy to receive your long awaited letter today. June 26th was the last time I heard from you. On July 9th I answered, but I have heard nothing since. Thinking my letter may have gone astray,

I wrote again on September 9th. When the middle of October came to be and still no letter appeared, I began to worry that you might be ill so I called the Holy Cross Monastery. As far as they knew you were well. When I asked for the Rev. Boniface Adams, they gave me the number in New York City. When I tried that location, I had to leave my number because no person answered. Later the Rev. David Hoopes called me. He assured me that you were well but very busy. When I enquired about the possibility of my sending a Christmas package to you through their good auspices, he said it would be possible if I sent it to New York City by December first. He gave me another telephone number to call. I will try that mode of delivery. When November rolled around and no word came from you, I decided that you no longer cared to write to me—so I did not want to bother you.

Thus, your November letter was a welcome surprise. Your *Christian Science Monitor* should reach you every week. I always send my letters first class air mail. I do not understand why my letters go amiss so often.

I have had a busy but uneventful summer. I passed all my health tests with good marks. I would rather have good health than all the money in the world. I am grateful to my ancestors. I have enjoyed tutoring my four Polish pupils. Two of them passed their citizenship tests with flying colors. They took their older son age seven along. When the examiner asked the boy to name the colors of the American flag he did, but at the same time he openly pointed to the flag waving outside the window. They have two fine, intelligent sons.

I still serve on the Social Concerns Committee of the CRCC as well as the Christian Jewish Task Force. I also helped the National Abortion Rights League to defeat the nomination of Robert Bork to the Supreme Court. Now I must assist in defeating Ginsberg. If we don't get rid of Reagan soon, we shall lose our country. He's a nitwit + a liar. I cannot stand that man!

D. has been transferred and she is very happy and productive. The superior prior president has been succeeded by another who is a scholar and a man of integrity. Thank you for your prayers. Another month at her former college would have broken her. I cannot bear to see fine human beings abused. I shall attend the monthly meeting of the Board of Trustees again to-morrow; I have been regularly for two years. It is comforting to know that you are out there somewhere. I missed you.

As Ever,
Edna

December 5, 1987
Dear Father Hoopes,

It is most considerate of you to offer to accept responsibility for finding someone who will be able to deliver my package to Bonnie Spencer in Ghana. I mailed the parcel first class December third from Newington Post Office and insured it for seventy-five dollars. I am enclosing a list of the contents so that the courier will be able to declare the contents if he is asked. I am also including a check for fifty dollars that I hope will ease the path for both you and the man who will be carrying this bundle.

I will call you one day this coming week to make sure that you have received the gift and to answer any questions that you may have.

Thank you once again for your kind thoughtfulness. I am sorry to add to your problems. May you have a joyful Christmas.

In appreciation,
Edna May Sole

January 7, 1988
Cape Coast, Ghana
Dear Edna,

Your letter is a great joy and relief to me. Like you in the summer and fall, I was imagining all kinds of awful things happening. I feel I must apologize for not having written sooner to tell you I had not heard from you, but with my researches for my two new courses and then the opening of the seminary I kept putting it off in the hope a letter from you would come. I am baffled as to why your letters do not come through. They are correctly addressed. Letters from others, as far as I know, have arrived safely. Note that even this registered letter, post marked November 7, only reached Adisadel yesterday—two full months!!! My only suggestion is that the thickness + shape of your stationary may be a factor. If you were to use lighter paper and an air mail envelope, or an air mail letter form, it might come through better. As you remarked about an earlier letter that I did not receive, you suspected that the government may have thought it contained money and opened it. I also think that likely. I have received letters in ordinary envelopes, especially Christmas cards, but there must be some reason why yours do not come through.

First let me tell you that I expect to go to the USA for the summer, probably arriving in mid-June but going almost at once out to California. But from early July until mid-September I expect to be centered at West Park, so I shall be able to visit you. This can be arranged definitely when I get home.

I hope this reaches you before Timothy telephones you. I wrote to ask him to do so last week. If he calls before you get this you may think that even your registered letter did not reach me, unless you arranged for a return notice—and even that should not get to you much before this letter.

Everything goes well with me. I was able to get my two courses worked out over the summer and they seem to be going well. My old courses keep up all right, especially the Proclamation course for the seniors. Last year's class was so responsive that I reworked much of the material in the light of what I learned from them, and this year's class is even more responsive + enthusiastic. I have already had one good paper from them and expect a second when classes start again on January 18.

I am glad D has been transferred. It is a shame when the administration stifles a good teacher. Unfortunately, state run institutions sometimes get involved in corrupt politics. Please give her my best wishes.

I knew when Reagan was elected that would be the end of the Supreme Court for at least a generation. Unfortunately Carter did not have a chance to appoint anyone, so soon all that Justices will be appointees of Nixon or Reagan. I am glad that at least Bork was stopped. I have not had the <u>Monitor</u> since mid-December. (The reason for that is that the Post Office here takes a holiday from December 23-January 3 and second class mail gets held up. It will probably not be delivered until next week, if by then they catch up with the first class mail.) So I do not know whether Ginsberg made it. I presume he did because the Senate cannot go on rejecting Reagan's appointments forever, and he will never nominate anyone except an ultra-conservative. I pray there will be a change of party next November, but I am not hopeful, because the Democrats do not seem to have a feasible candidate. Even if they find one, he will have a hard time defeating any Republican unless there is a major economic collapse before the summer. Republicans mean prosperity and they will stay in office as long as it lasts.

I cannot tell you how happy I am to be in touch once more. I hope the New Year is bringing you much prosperity and joy. Keep up all your good works.

Love,
Bonnie

January 29, 1988
Dear Bonnie,

Your beautiful letter of January 7th arrived and was most welcome. It is truly amazing that my registered letter of November 7th took two months to reach you. Where did the post keep it? Your suggestions concerning the form of my mail are most relevant. Perhaps you have now received my aerogramme I sent two weeks ago before your letter arrived. In the future I will follow your instructions concerning the envelopes.

It is wonderful that you are coming home this summer. I shall be delighted to have you visit me. It has been two years since I have seen you. Stay as long as you wish—any time; just let me know when.

I am sorry that the delivery of your *Monitor* is so capricious. After Bork failed to get senatorial approval, Meese induced Reagan to nominate Douglas Ginsburg, a member of U.S. Court of Appeals in Washington, D.C. since Nov. 1986, but he proved himself unworthy in many ways. Drug use in his student days as well as during his years as a professor at Harvard, the appearance of conflict of interest when he was a senior Justice Department official as well as other factors made him a dubious candidate. He was <u>not</u> an outstanding professor of law at Harvard.

The latest nominee is Anthony Kennedy of California (Stanford and Harvard). The Senatorial Committee has approved him unanimously.

I made myself listen to Reagan in his State of the Union address. I still fail to see why people fall all over themselves in admiration of such a Dodo.

As ever,
Edna

January 16, 1988
Dear Bonnie,

It is two months since I have heard from you. I answered your last letter dated October 20th, the day I received it. It must be that you have not received that one letter. In that letter I explained to you that I had not heard from you since June 26th. I answered on July 9th, but I had heard nothing from you. I wrote again on September 8th. When no letter appeared by the middle of October, I began to worry that you might be ill so I called the Holy Cross Monastery but they assured me you were well <u>but busy</u>. When I asked for the Rev. Boniface Adams, they gave me a number in New York. When I called, I had to leave my number. Later the Rev. David Hoopes called me and assured me that you were well but very busy. He agreed to be responsible for the delivery of my Christmas package to you. Thus, I mailed it to him Dec. 5th along with a check for fifty dollars to ease its passage.

When I called him later, he told me that no one was due to travel to Ghana until July so he mailed the package directly to you. I have a late birthday gift for you and plan to try a direct mailing to you—but heaven only knows. This failure of the mails is most distressing. Does this fate afflict only my mail? When are you coming out of Ghana? I miss you. Will write next week.

As ever,
Edna

P.S. Keep well and happy. Perhaps no one will steal this—no stamps and no enclosures.

February 9, 1988
Cape Coast, Ghana
Dear Edna,

When your letter of January 16 reached me today, I thought at first that it was an answer to mine of January 7, in which, as I trust you now know, I asked you to use Air Mail envelopes or letter forms. But of course my letter had not time to reach you and you decided on your own to use the form. It goes to show that great minds run in the same channel.

Also today I at last received you Christmas package. My bright idea of sending it to West Park only delayed and complicated the problem further. What went wrong, as far as my scheme was concerned, was that the person from here who attended the administrator's conference in January this year stayed on in America instead of coming right back. So there was no one traveling from West Park here after Christmas. But the package has arrived and is greatly appreciated. The tie, socks, handkerchiefs, linens, etc., are all lovely. And the goodies will be much enjoyed not only by me but also by the Brethren. Refreshments like that make our community get-togethers more pleasant and sociable.

I hope our correspondence will now get through all right. The failure of your letters to reach me must have been because they were suspiciously bulky. The government is very concerned about money entering and leaving the country. Having opened your letters and found them just personal matters, they covered their embarrassment by throwing them away. So the answer is the use of air mail equipment which is what they expect. So far as I can tell, yours were the only letters that did not come through; at least I have not heard from anyone complaining that I have not answered one from them. My only regret is that I did not realize sooner that the failure to hear from you was because your letters were going astray. Instead, I was busily worrying that you were sick.

The first semester at the seminary is now ended and I am pleased with the papers and examinations I have received, with as always a few exceptions.

I am looking forward to being home for the summer, and especially to seeing you. I shall get in touch by phone after I get there so that we can make our plans. I am sorry the winter had been bringing you so much cold and snow when you wrote and I hope things have become better since. I have just received a letter from Tuscon telling me that they had snow on Christmas Day, the first time in recorded history. Climate in USA seems to be behaving peculiarly. But at least in New England it keeps changing.

May you and all your works be blessed and prosper.

Love,
Bonnie

February 28, 1988
Cape Coast, Ghana
Dear Edna,

Your second letter on an airmail form, written January 29, reached me shortly after I had written you, on February 9, in answer to your first air mail form and thanking you for the Christmas package which had reached me. I hope you have received that letter. Because of it I have delayed answering your second. I now can report that last

Tuesday we had a party for Fr. Rodel-Miller, CHC, who has just joined us to teach at the seminary. We were able to include some of your goodies and they were much appreciated by all.

Thank you for the information about the Supreme Court appointment. I am glad the most conservative candidates were rejected. I presume that if Kennedy was unanimously approved by the Senate committee, he has now been confirmed, and that he is at least more open to decent ideas than most of Reagan's appointees. Let us hope this will be the last one he can appoint. The Court has already become so conservative that human rights do not have much chance with it. And it is bound to get worse if there is not a change of administration next fall.

It is hard to follow the course of nomination of presidential candidates with only intermittent news. But in my usual pessimistic view, I expect a Republican will win the election. Of their candidates Robertson (or whatever his name is) is horrible. I am not impressed by the others. Perhaps Dole is the best. The problem of the Democrats is that they do not have a feasible candidate. Unless there is a major recession before the election, I do not think they have a chance. A government that has brought prosperity is never defeated.

Things go on here much as usual. Seminary has begun its second term. I was pleased at the results in my courses of the first term grades. The subject in which I am most interested and which I feel makes the chief contribution is Proclamation, with the seniors. They have written two good papers already and seem to be enthusiastically engaged on the third.

I look forward to my furlough home and to seeing you. It is too early for me to arrange the schedule of events during it, but I shall get to work on it as soon as I get home. I shall give my visit to you priority, though it may not come in the early part because of my trip to California and possibly to Toronto.

One decision we have pretty well settled on here is that I shall go home permanently after Chapter meets here in June 1989. Although I hate the thought of ceasing teaching, I think it better, if I can hold out till then, to quit while I am still ahead rather than peter out. I shall find plenty of interesting + I hope fruitful things to do in the USA.

All best wishes for you and your activities, especially in politics + social service. I am eager to talk them over with you.

Love,
Bonnie

March 6, 1988
Dear Bonnie,

It was so good to receive your letter of February 9th and I am grateful that your Christmas package was finally delivered. Perhaps by now my letter of January 30th has reached you. I was delighted to learn of your long awaited trip to your native land. I wrote you that I would be happy to have you visit me and stay as long as you wish. Just let me know when. It will be two years since I have seen you.

February was not my lucky month. I think I came down with the new flu; at least a bad bout with sinusitis and bronchitis, but the x-ray revealed my lungs in good order. I felt as though I were inhabiting another planet, but now I have recovered. My sister-in-law scolds me for not giving in sooner. I have never been good at giving up. Fortunately I am a hardy soul.

As ever,
Edna

March 26, 1988
Dear Bonnie,

It is always a delight to hear from you—including your last letter written February 28th. I hope you will still receive The Christian Science Monitor; if not, please tell me.

According to the latest reports—George Bush is way ahead with the Republicans and Dole is expected to withdraw. To me, Bush is such a weakling and nothing but a carbon copy of Reagan.

Our president is boldly calling Ollie North a hero and declares that neither he nor John Poindexter is guilty of all the charges filed in the Iran-contra affair. He believes these men broke no laws and committed no crimes. I think Ronald Reagan should be impeached. He is a liar and an ignoramus. Albert Hakim and Richard Secord were also indicted by a federal grand jury March 16. The four have pleaded not guilty to all charges.—The standards in this country have certainly reached a new low.

On the Democratic side—Dukakis appears to be in the lead with Jesse Jackson and Albert Gore following. My last <u>Bostonia</u> published by Boston University maintains that "the Duke's entire record in the area of public higher education is nothing to write home about." In fact, the article goes on to claim, "The state college system under Dukakis continues to be ripe with scandal, inefficiencies, and educational mediocrity."

I read three newspapers a day as well as the <u>U.S. News & World Report</u>. Our CT. Public Television is the best station—especially for its depth in political news. Gore's wife is exactly right when she criticizes the morals of many T.V. programs.

I rejoice with you in all that you have given to your students at the Seminary. They are far richer through you—only the riches of the spirit and the mind endure.

It will be wonderful to see you again—it has been so long. There are many things I want to discuss with you. Do tell me what you want to do. I am glad you are coming home.

As ever,
Edna

April 8, 1988
Cape Coast, Ghana
Dear Edna,

Your welcome letter of March 6 has been gratefully received. I trust you have long since received mine of February 28. I am sorry to learn of your illness in February. Mine came in the latter half of March. I had my first attack of malaria in the over five years I have been here. A new strain has developed immunity to the usual prophylactics. Mine was a light attack but it came at the end of the term before the spring vacation which was followed by Holy Week and Easter. Like you, I refused services. I got through but the strain left me weak. This doctor gave me a thorough examination and says I am physically fit. But malaria has its depressive affects, and as you can see from my handwriting, my coordination is not all is should be. But I feel myself again. I have no classes until May, so shall get a good rest. Nothing to worry about.

The <u>Monitor</u> has been coming with unusual regularity and promptness, which has been appreciated both because it has given me interesting reading matter and because it has kept me abreast of the primaries. The latest reports the one in Illinois. To me it is clear that Bush is certain to be the next president. No other Republican has a chance of being nominated. No Democrat or combination of candidates can defeat him. My feeling is that Gore and Jackson would have the best chance, but Gore does not seem to have captured the public imagination. Jackson and Dukakis might have a chance, but not the other way round. The Duke is too liberal for this election. Jackson seems to be emerging as a genuine national figure, not just a black who makes an impression.

So Bush it will be. Like you I do not trust him. I do not think he is a man of real moral principles. But he has two points in his favor. He has a modicum of intelligence—something entirely lacking in Reagan, and he has not, so far as I know, been "born again." That religious camouflage for reactionary conservatism is the greatest danger in American politics.

There is one further consideration. The economic situation in USA and the world is very precarious. I am sure there will be a crash of some kind in the next four years. If the Democrats were in power it would be blamed on them, and the Republicans would get in power for the next 30 years. So let the Republicans have the Presidency in 1988 and take the consequences of their lack of human concern. Perhaps by 1992 the USA will be ready for a Democrat.

I hope you can read some of this. It does not mean feebleness of mind or body, but temporary difficulty in coordination. We both must use the brakes occasionally. See you soon.

Love,
Bonnie

May 8, 1988
Dear Bonnie,

Your letter of April 8th was greatly appreciated. I am concerned about your malaria attack and hope you will carefully follow the doctor's directions and not overdo. I am sure that you have a strong constitution, but you must be careful. I had no trouble whatever reading your handwriting. Your letters are always most interesting and eagerly awaited.

I share your political concerns and deductions, but perhaps the future will provide a ray of hope. The Iran scandal and the Noriega one in Panama may prove too great a hurdle for Bush. Surely this V.P. lacks courage and honesty. The voters are indeed blind if they cannot ascertain that. I also suspect he will resort to the low road as he goes forth.

I am currently reading <u>The Closing of the American Mind</u> by Allan Bloom. 'How Higher Education Has Failed Democracy and Impoverished the Souls of Today's Students'. He is scathing indeed and rightly so. He quotes many of our leading philosophers—from Plato on and analyses our current relationships. He doesn't seem to miss any of our many problems. How did we ever permit society to reach such a state? And some forms of religion to-day worry me— especially those T.V. evangelists. It seems that to-day our people are so engrossed in materialistic matters that they completely ignore the spiritual side. They cannot possibly find happiness and fulfillment along that route.

Since April 19th I have been on jury duty at the Superior Court in Hartford. I am currently sitting on a case in the Criminal Court. One case they opened to me they refused to let me sit because I knew one of the attorneys. I didn't remember him although his face and name were familiar, but he remembered me. My commitment is supposed to last for one month. The jurors seem to be quite decent and civilized. I did have an interesting discussion with one lady who said that she thought white lies were permissible. I told her that my mother informed me when I was a little girl that there were no white lies—a lie is a lie. Another juror—a man—is an admirer of Ronald Reagan— even to the jelly beans. Of course, I am not reticent about my views. We are not allowed to discuss the case or even read about it let alone view it on T.V.

As ever,
Edna

May 1, 1988
Cape Coast, Ghana
Dear Edna,

Your letter of March 26 has been left unanswered for so long a time, because when it arrived I was recovering from a bout of malaria—the first I have had. We were in the last weeks before spring vacation, and I kept up with my classes, which probably increased the period of weakness after the illness itself was over. I am fully recovered now, and looking forward eagerly to classes that start next Monday.

The <u>Monitor</u> is coming with regularity and less delay than usual. I almost always receive it, but sometimes two or three issues arrive together. I have been able to follow the primaries well, though the news in the <u>Monitor</u> is about two weeks late when it reaches me. Any of the three leaders in the Democratic Party would be all right with me, as long as the party is not split by his nomination. I still do not think any of them has a chance of election, unless the stock crash of a week or so ago has repercussions that result in a real slump in the economy. The <u>Monitor</u> that would deal with the crash has not arrived yet. Someone heard of the crash on the radio and all it said was that it was the biggest ever. If there is a real recession, I think Dukakis would be the best of the Democrats to deal with it. I understand that he had done well in rescuing Massachusetts from the economic doldrums. I regret that his record in education is so poor, but state school + college systems usually maintain an independence from the state which makes it hard for a governor to handle them. The entrenched authorities can always claim that the government is violating academic freedom if he tries to reform the system. As president I think any of the three leading Democrats would reduce the military budget and give the money saved to education or other social services.

But I fear that Bush will win the election with another landslide unless we have a full economic crash. A <u>Monitor</u> has just arrived. It speaks of the trade unbalance and says Wall Street was jittery, but the big drop that the radio mentioned (the largest ever, they said) must have occurred too late for that edition, if it happened at all.

I hope all continues well for you. I shall get in touch with you as soon as I can when I reach West Park. Meanwhile, don't work too hard.

Love,
Bonnie

May 22, 1988
Dear Bonnie,

Your good letter of May first arrived on May twentieth. It was most reassuring to learn that you have fully recovered from your bout of malaria. Please be sure that you do not over do.

Today the <u>Hartford Courant</u> announced a possible federal surplus. It seems that Social Security is starting to accumulate a large reserve that if left untouched, will soar into the trillions of dollars in the next 50 years. "At the moment, these annual surpluses—about $40 billion this year and expected to rise to $77 billion in 1992—are merely off-setting a part of the budget deficit." Many fear that Congress will consider using the surplus for other government programs. Personally I believe that the future is most uncertain. Neither the members of Congress nor the voters possess the necessary wisdom.

Apparently Gov. Dukakis is facing a budget problem in Mass. The Mass. residents and corporations are paying $252 million less in state taxes this year than expected. He maintains that the revenue shortfall is merely temporary. [*The following has a line through it-not sure if that means it's crossed out:* Chief executives of Conn. companies according to a recent survey took home an average yearly pay of $1.83 million. It just goes to prove that human beings in our society are not reimbursed according to their real contributions.]

I agree with your assessments of the political candidates, but I doubt that the South will ever vote for Jackson. Racism still lurks beneath the surface in this country. I do not know when we shall ever reach the level where the character of the individual is rated first. This is why we have so much misery in our midst. In spite of everything, I still fight for what I believe.

I finally finished my jury duty and we reached a decision—after much debate. It was an interesting as well as enlightening experience. In our group we had one black man who really knew what the work out there was like. I think the others were surprised that the two of us agreed so often.

As ever,
Edna

June 18, 1988
West Park, New York
Dear Edna,

Here I am again at last. I had intended to telephone, but it is so difficult for me to hear over one that a letter is better. The trip home was a nightmare. No fault of the airline, indeed the service they provided in Amsterdam was an electric car and an attendant who took me right to my seat on the plane. But the shock of not being able to cope for myself produced an emotional depression, which has now passed. The aftermath, however is a fear of travel. I use a cane and that leaves only one arm for carrying luggage, holding on to banisters, etc. I leave for California on the 21st + return on the 29th. It is an easy trip as far as getting on and off the planes, etc., goes, so it will be a good test. When I get back we can see what we can do about getting together.

I received your letter of May 8, but did not answer it because you would not have received the reply by mail before this. I agree as usual with all you say about the degeneracy of the country. My problem with the coming election is that I feel that the situation is like the Hoover-Smith election (Bush rather reminds me of Hoover). But after 8 years of prosperity (for the rich vs. the poor) under a stupid president—Coolidge, vid., Reagan, there was bound to be a crash. Thank God Hoover won and the crash was rightly blamed on the Republicans. I really hope to see Bush get elected and take the consequences of his predecessor's stupidity.

We can talk this all over when we see each other. I have been too busy recuperating from the trip and settling in for the summer to catch up on the news. So we shall wait until I am back from California. Meanwhile keep busy and happy.

Love,
Bonnie

June 26, 1988
Dear Bonnie,

Your letter of June 18th was most welcome, but I distressed about your difficult trip home. I trust the Dutch to provide the necessary accommodations. I always enjoyed the airports in Amsterdam and Copenhagen the most. I well understand your problems with your baggage. But please don't fear travel; you will soon be able to cope— with some adjustments. I wish I had been there to help.

On the 22nd of May I mailed you a letter to Ghana but you probably did not receive it. I telephoned you at West Park on the

21st of June and left a message to call me and reverse the charges. I thought you were at a meeting until I received you letter of June 18th in the afternoon of the 22nd.

I do want you to visit Connecticut—stay a week or more. My house is all on one floor with no stairs to climb; I can make accommodations very easy for you. If it is possible for you to reach Connecticut, I can pick you up wherever you say; otherwise I can drive to West Park to pick you up and bring you to CT. I think I can find someone to accompany me. D is leaving for India on the 30th, but perhaps Mary would be willing.

I do want to see you and talk with you; we need a long visit.

As ever,
Edna

July 22, 1988
West Park, New York
Dear Edna,

We seem to be out of communication again. I wrote you when I returned from Africa, on June 18, and I have never had an answer. As I said in my letter, I was going out to Santa Barbara for a meeting and then returning to West Park. I discussed possibilities of our getting together and expected comments on them when I got back. But I do not think any came. I express a bit of doubt in the last sentence because shortly after I returned I collapsed into unconsciousness for 4 or 5 days, and was somewhat woozy when I came to again. It is possible I received a letter from you in that period and answered it, but I have no record of it.

The illness was very strange. Fr. Wilson thought he saw signs of a heart attack and I was taken to the Benedictine Hospital in Kingston in an ambulance. I remember being examined—heart perfectly OK—on various things and then I passed out. I woke up 4 or 5 mornings later thinking it was the next morning. I think the basic problem was an aftermath of the malaria I had in Africa; at least that was one of the things they tested. When I came to I was feeling perfectly well—no pain, fever, etc., but very weak. It took several days therapy to get so I could walk with a cane. I still need a cane to steady me, but all is well now. They gave me all the tests and they came out all right. I got out of the hospital last Tuesday.

I am going to spend the rest of this month and the first ten days of August quietly recuperating here. Then I go to Toronto for the rest of the month while the members of this household are in New Hampshire on vacation. That is no trip. I just am put on the train at Poughkeepsie and met on arrival at Toronto. This was planned before my illness, as I am eager to see the members of the Order stationed there.

But it has been decided that I am not to go back to Africa. So there will be time for us to get together in the fall. After the Toronto trip I shall see how I feel about traveling on trains, subways, etc. It is a little difficult with a cane, especially getting up and down stairs. But it may be possible for me [to] visit you. I shall certainly make the effort. In any case, something will be arranged so that we can get together.

I think the most sensible thing is to let the <u>Monitor</u> subscription to Africa run out. The men there glanced at my copy, but none read it consistently.

Let me emphasize again, I am now perfectly well and happily settled into the house here, which is where I want to be. My legs are getting stronger every day; probably I shall soon be walking around the house without my cane. But I shall continue to need it when I am outside.

I hope you have been well and busy, and will continue so during the next month. I shall see you as soon as it can be arranged.

Love,
Bonnie

July 31, 1988
Dear Bonnie,

Your beautiful, welcome letter of July 22 arrived Tuesday, July 26, and I telephoned you Wednesday.

I received your letter of June 18 on Tuesday, June 22 (afternoon), when you informed me that you were leaving for California on the 21st. Not knowing that on that date you were leaving for California, I telephoned you at West Park, but was unable to reach you, so I left word for you to call me and reverse the charges.

On June 26th, I answered you letter of June 18th. On June 30th you called me, and I was relieved to hear from you. I had been deeply distressed about your very difficult trip home from Ghana.

When you informed me by telephone on the 30th of June that it would be too hard for you to visit me then, I did try to find someone to accompany me to West Park. Since all my friends were busy, I was unable to find a companion and I did hesitate to make the journey to and from all by myself in this day and age of evil.

I am deeply concerned for your welfare and agree with you that it would not be prudent for you to venture forth until you feel better. Please do let me know what your doctor thought Friday. Do take care after that bout of malaria in Africa. Your rest in Toronto should restore your health and raise your spirits; I am happy for you.

I should love to have you visit me in the fall if it is feasible. Otherwise, I will try to make it when and wherever you say. I can take you anywhere. Above all, take care of yourself. I am extremely grateful that you are not returning to Africa. You are needed here! The reliance on a cane is a minor matter. If all else fails, I am sure that I can pick you up at West Park in the fall. I truly want you to do whatever it is that you wish to do. Whenever you wish to telephone me, you are free to reverse the charges. I have never been guilty of saying things I do not mean. Thank you for being so frank with me.

I have acquired three new Polish pupils—mother, father, and son—a whole family. They have much in common, but they are at different stages. They arrive here together once a week, and I am experimenting just as I did when I was teaching for a living. In some areas I teach them together and in other facets separately. It is quite challenging. The son is a teenager who is repeating grade 10 in high school. When his parents first told me about him, I suggested that he come along too for it is a dreadful waste for him to spend the summer without improving his English. On the first night, I took time to admonish him concerning his association with his American acquaintances. We have many (too many) American teenagers who are hardly models. He appears to be an intelligent, upstanding youth, and his parents are admirable. I will not stand by and see unworthy American youths discredit promising foreigners.

I will follow your advice and let the <u>Christian Science Monitor</u> subscription to Ghana run out. Would you like me to send you a local subscription to the Monitor at West Park? May I again ask what can I do for you?

I continue to use my cane outside and take my dark walk around eight p.m., after the sun goes down. We have had a long spate of hot, humid weather including the most unhealthful air I have ever known. I try to keep my house as comfortable as possible. The trees around are most helpful and one floor is convenient. My car is still standing up, and I have passed my tests with the doctors; I just have to watch my cholesterol. My surgeon refuses to approve a driving license for the handicapped for me. I suspect he still thinks my bones are good.

I am still working on committee for the Capitol Region Conference of Churches. I am serving on two that involve Christians and Jews. The other night I engaged in a rather heated argument with one of our evangelical ministers. He accused us of attempting to placate the Jews. I told him that was an insult. I don't attempt to placate anybody. I feel that we come together to better understand each other, to respect the beliefs of others, and to work together for a better world. In all the 49 1/2 years I taught (I began at seventeen), I never had any trouble over religion; I have friends of all faiths.

As ever,
Edna

August 6, 1988
West Park, New York
Dear Edna,

It is just as well that you could not find someone to drive with you last month, at least the first half of it, for you would have found me in the hospital. On the Sunday after I telephoned you (July 3) some of the Brethren thought I was having a heart attack and sent for an ambulance. I must already have been only half conscious, for I submitted without protest. Ordinarily I would have raised the roof at such nonsense. I remember the ride to Kingston and the beginning of the examination in the emergency ward. Then I passed out. I woke up in the morning, thinking it was Monday, the next day, and I discovered it was Friday. The four intervening days have been totally wiped from my memory. I am told I was unconscious, with periods of delirium, and a few intervals of consciousness. I know nothing about it, and when I remark that to those who cared for me, they reply "Just as well."

When I came to, I was very weak and it took five days of therapy to get me to where I could walk with a cane. Since I got home I have been recovering my strength, and now have it back. I never was in any pain during my illness and my heart is perfectly sound. I tried to get the doctor to tell me what caused it, but he avoided my question. Aftermath of the malaria was the basis, I think, because they medicated me for that. But what else was involved, if anything, remains a mystery.

But, thank God, it is over and I am well again. On Thursday next (Aug. 11) I go to Toronto for the rest of the month. It is an easy trip. Someone puts me on the train at Poughkeepsie and I am met at Toronto. Just sit on the train all day. When I get back I shall telephone you about our getting together. I am becoming more convinced that my vocation is to stay at home in this house and say my prayers. I shall take part in the work of this house but probably only go out on necessary errands, doctor's appointments and the like, all in the vicinity. I shall have several in September, checking up on things. I could not attend to things in Africa. But there will be some free days and perhaps you could come over on one of them, <u>provided</u> you get someone to drive with you. You must <u>not</u> make the trip alone. If you cannot get here, we can substitute telephone calls and letters.

I would indeed be grateful for a subscription to the <u>Monitor</u>, addressed to me personally at this house. (No need for it to start until September.) The house gets the **New York Times** daily, but it is placed in the guests' common room, and when we have a houseful it is almost impossible to see it. If you send me the <u>Monitor</u>, I shall be able to keep up with the news, and after I have read it, put it in the Professed Common Room, where the members of the Order can get at it.

Please don't worry about me. I am as fit as a fiddle. I think this strange illness had an important part in God's preparation of me for the new form I believe my vocation will be taking. We can discuss this more later. Meanwhile have a good summer and don't work too hard.

Love,
Bonnie

P.S. All my tests with the doctors at the hospital came out all right.

September 6, 1988
West Park, New York
Dear Edna,

Just a note to say that I am looking forward to seeing you on Saturday, 24 September. It will be best for us to go out for lunch because there is a big retreat going on here, so our meals will be in silence. Also because of the size of the group, it would not be possible to put you up for the night. But again, you indicated that you would prefer a motel or hotel, if you decide to stay over. I am eager to see you.

Love,
Bonnie

September 16, 1988
Dear Bonnie,

Thank you for your note of September 6th. We are planning to drive to West Park the morning of the 24th. I shall take you and D to lunch. Do you have a suggestion for the place—the best possible? Unless unforeseen factors intervene, we expect to return to

Connecticut late in the afternoon. D suggests that it is not that far. Do you remember that it was D, a former student teacher of mine, who drove me to West Park to bid you farewell when you were preparing to leave for your term in Africa? That was a rather sad occasion for me. She was the one who was treated so unjustly—and you prayed for her. Finally, she was transferred, where she is happy and productive. Your prayers helped. She was an excellent student who possessed high ethical standards.

We are hoping for beautiful weather to enhance your magnificent scenery; the moon will be full. If you wished, we could take you take you back for a visit; then I could get someone to return you to West Park. Connecticut also has some beauty spots.

My minister, who has a wife and baby daughter, is only 30 yrs. old, but has the wisdom of a man of 60. He is sponsoring a Book Discussion Group that meets every Thursday morning. Our first session is this Thursday and we are reading Habits of the Heart by Robert N. Bellah. It is quite timely.

I continue to meet with my Polish students for two hour sessions every week—two pupils on Thursday and three pupils on Friday. I am still working with the Capitol Region Conference of Churches including the Social Concerns Committee, the Early Childhood Committee, the Christian, Jewish Dialogue. We have been trying to gain support for the passage of the ABC Bill—The Act for Better Child Care Services (S. 1885) (H.R. 3660). It will cost our country $2.5 billion in the first year, but our children are worth it. The bill is now cleared for a vote on the floor of the House as well as the Senate some time in Sept. Both houses will stay in session until the first week in October. If it doesn't pass by then, we shall have to begin all over again. In CT. both our Senators and all of our Congressmen except Rowland are for it. The bill was introduced in the Senate (S. 1885) by Senator Christopher Dodd of CT. and in the House (H.R. 3660) by Rep. Dale Hilder (D. Mich.).

I do not like George Bush—I do not trust him. His silver spoon must have been plated, but then, I never did set much store by those silver spoons. When I was knee high to a grasshopper, I learned to esteem neither money nor social status. His choice of Quayle proves him to be a poor judge of character. If the voters in this country selected Bush, we shall have reached a new low—and after eight years with a dodo.

I am deeply concerned about the condition of our schools. I must begin to attend the monthly meetings of my town's Board of Education. I continue to attend those of the Universities' Board of Trustees. Some people are glad to have me there.

I shall be very happy to see you on the 24th; it has been a long, long time. I hope all goes well with you. Is there anything that I can bring you?

As Ever,
Edna

September 25, 1988
West Park, New York
Dear Edna,

It was so good to see you and D yesterday and I much enjoyed the luncheon. I also greatly appreciate the handkerchiefs. And we did have fine weather.

I think we covered most of the items in your letter. I did forget to ask if the Child Care Bill has passed? As I have seen nothing about it in the papers, I presume it is still in progress.

I am glad to see in today's paper that the election is still a toss-up. So Dukakis still has a chance. It may depend on the debates. The 37% undecided are probably people who will be swayed by them, not what the candidates say, but how they come over on TV. I distrust these TV elections for the choice has little to do with the real issues. However, whoever is elected, he has promised to do something about education. If the military spending can be cut back, especially star wars and if our interference in the internal affairs of other countries can be checked, there may be some money for education and other worth-while projects. Dukakis should do a better job than Bush in this area.

352

Please give my best to D when you get a chance. I rejoice that she is now happily situated. I pray all your interests develop satisfactorily. Keep up the good work.

Love,
Bonnie

October 5 and 6, 1988
Dear Bonnie,

Thank you for your letter of the 25th. It was most welcome. It meant a great deal to me to be able to see you at long last. You looked wonderful—as fit as a fiddle. Somehow I seemed unable to reach you; it was probably my own fault.

As usual I agree with all your political assessments. In the Bush Dukakis debate, I felt that the Governor was far superior. He seems more caring and genuine in his concerns for people. Why can not the average voter sense this? I have never been able to understand why so many are bewitched by charisma.

I do believe that little children are often more sensitive to the inner being than sophisticated adults. Every college should require the completion of a thorough course in philosophy taught by the most enlightened professors.

Across the street live two little boys—seven and ten years old—Matthew and Timothy. The younger one always hails me with gusto. The other day he informed me that he would like to see what my house looked like inside. Thus, I gave him a personal tour and a large piece of cake to take home. He liked my home but preferred the back porch—probably the color scheme—plus Mother Nature appealed. He had delightful manners. Children are so natural—they have always charmed me.

A friend of mine, whom I met at our meeting of Christians and Jews, thoroughly enjoyed your book <u>God Who Dares to Be Man</u>, which I lent her. In fact, she has ordered one to keep for herself. We enjoy talking about many subjects; she is like a kindred spirit. She has a fine husband who was formerly a school administrator in West Hartford. I pick her up to attend these meetings for the CRCC. In fact, if you have any more copies, I will buy another to pass around. I am enclosing a check for fifteen dollars. If it is not enough, let me know.

The ABC Bill (Child Care) is still hanging in the Senate. If it is not passed this week, it will probably be lost for this year. They have attached two other bills—one on child pornography and one on parental leave. Following the advice of the Connecticut Association for Human Services, I called Senator Lowell Weicker in Washington, D.C. to support the bill and vote for cloture. I called about 30 people to contact him also.

The last Christian Science Monitor included an excellent article by Norman Cousins on page 14.

I gave your message to D; she enjoyed you—so did I.

As Ever,
Edna

October 13, 1988
West Park, New York
Dear Edna,

Thank you for your letter. It was indeed good to see you. But your remark that you seemed unable to reach me endorses my feeling that somehow we communicate better by letter. I suspect we tend to expect too much of a vis-a-vis contact. They are necessary from time to time, but I think our correspondence is more important.

The Monitor comes regularly and is much appreciated. Also the first issue of the magazine arrived. I particularly enjoyed the article on Christianity in U.S.S.R. I did not know before of the "Communist Christians." Their existence is important. My only fear is that the Russian Orthodox is so imprisoned in its tradition that it will be unable to make any contact with them. I enjoyed Cousins' article. In the international political field, the inability of USA to dialogue with Communism is what prevents our government from appreciating genuinely popular movements, not only in Central America, but in Africa and Asia as well. Our concept of democracy is the capitalist status quo in this country and its economic exploitation of the Third World. It looks now as if we shall reelect that concept in Bush by a huge electoral voter majority. Our only hope for change is an eventual economic collapse, which I still think will be best if it comes when a Republican president is in office.

Thank you for your check, which covers the copy of <u>God Who Dares</u>, that has been sent to you. Perhaps it is better if the ABC bill goes over to the next term so that the cowboy with not veto it. Keep up your good work.

Love,
Bonnie

October 28, 1988
Dear Bonnie,

It was a pleasure to hear from you. The books arrived—two of them—so I am enclosing another check for the second one. My friend bought the second one for $12.95 and was delighted, for the one she ordered through the library had not arrived. She said that if it did come, she would donate it to her church library. She attends the Congregational Church in West Hartford. She was impressed by your book. The books were beautifully packaged—better than any other parcel I have ever received.

Somehow I think that the news media are unfair to Dukakis, and Bush surely travels the low road—just as I anticipated.

This week I went over to Weicker's headquarters to help in his election. He is campaigning for another term as U.S. senator. He is from Connecticut, a Republican, but he has shown integrity, courage, intelligence, and commitment. He has often differed with Reagan. While I am registered Democrat, I always try to vote for the best candidate irrespective of party affiliation. I told the Democrats that they ought to run Lieberman who is opposing Weicker for Governor.

I believe Weicker has proved to be an able senator and should be returned. Our present Governor O'Neill appoints too many cronies who are not the best to our boards and commissions. I still feel that our educational system is most inept in its provisions for the teaching of government. An understanding cannot be obtained through books along. First hand contact is essential.

I agree completely with your views regarding U.S. performance in the international political field. Bush is both blind and deaf when he regards himself as an authority in this area. A little education is never enough.

We just have to begin all over again with the ABC bill. At the different meetings I attend I try to emphasize the importance of the education of the three, four and five year olds. I am always pounding away at the theory that proper education is the only way to establish tolerance and understanding among people of various economic levels, races, religions, and nationalities. However, I do believe too many do not know what education means.

I agree that our correspondence is important (You write good letters), but I also believe that it is helpful if we have more vis-a-vis contacts. You are a sensitive person and very intelligent, but I see you so seldom. You are always welcome to visit me—unless you find it boring. I can pick you up somewhere if necessary.

Your letters have meant a great deal to me. Keep happy and well.

As Ever,
Edna

November 5, 1988
West Park, New York
Dear Edna,

Thank you for your check. Holy Cross Publications felt sufficiently recompensed by your first check, so I am giving your donation to the Order staff which appreciates it greatly. I am glad that your friend found the book helpful.

The <u>Monitor,</u> both the newspaper and the magazine, continues to arrive regularly. I am most grateful for them. I note that the <u>Monitor</u> is still hopeful for Dukakis, suggesting that the polls could be wrong. By the time you get this the matter should be settled. I still think Bush will have a large majority in the Electoral College, but I am voting for Dukakis.

I agree with your assessment of Weicker. The only possible objection is if the Republicans win the Senate and thus get the committee chairmanships. But Weicker's reelection will not change that situation. Our only safeguard against Bush-Quayle is a Democratic Congress. The Supreme Court is already lost and will become totally conservative Republican before Bush's term is over.

I am sorry ABC failed this time, but even if it had been passed, probably the cowboy would have pocket-vetoed it. I hope things will go better next time, especially if the Democrats keep Congress.

I did not mean to imply in my last letter that I considered vis-a-vis contacts unnecessary. I hope you will be able to visit me here from time to time, but I shall be most uncomfortable if you undertake the drive alone. As I explained while you were here, my present lifestyle rules out trips away from the monastery, so I cannot accept your invitation to stay with you. I shall, however, act on your suggestions that I telephone you from time to time. If for any reason you are particularly anxious for me to call, just telephone here and, if I cannot be reached, I shall call you back. Meanwhile all the best.

Love,
Bonnie

November 21, 1988
Dear Bonnie,

Your letter was most welcome, and your telephone call was a delightful surprise. I called you Sunday night, but you were not there—you were away. Call me anytime. I did not write the weekend I promised because events proved to be most unexpected. Very early one evening when I drove to the market, I stupidly drove upon the sidewalk on a dark corner. I feared that I would never be able to get that car off the walk. After scraping the car amid many loud rumblings, I finally succeeded. To my dismay, my two right hand tires were hopeless, and the rims looked peculiar. Another strange grocery customer kindly tried to help me in my dilemma. Thus, I managed to call the AAA to come for my disabled car. After the lapse of nearly an hour, the truck with its attendant arrived to take charge of the situation. Fortunately, he was resourceful and possessed a good sense of humor. He had to pick me up as though I were a bag of flour to put me high up in that big truck. After depositing me at my home, he proceeded to tow the wounded car to his garage for repairs.

In a couple of days, my brother Charles who lives in Wethersfield, the town over the hill, took me out of town to the garage to get my car. He knows about automobiles, but I never did have any mechanical sense. My old friend—the Oldsmobile, looked much better with all wheels in good order. Then on Friday, I took the critter to a garage in New Britain where they cater to this particular brand. Now my white Olds is in fine shape and I feel better. I am truly grateful that no one was hurt in my mishap. When one goes forth in the day, she never knows what awaits her.

This Thanksgiving as I told you I am entertaining most of the members of my family; my brother Clifford and his second wife (his first wife died years ago), his daughter Suzanne, my niece, who represents the only family member of her generation, as well as her daughter with her husband and the three year old little girl who is lively and precocious. Everyone loves Stephanie. We are having roast leg of lamb instead of turkey with all the fixings. As I said, before you would have been most welcome.

The election proceeded as you predicted. At least we have a Democratic Congress. Somehow our voters must become better informed.

As Ever,
Edna

Thanksgiving Day, 1988
West Park, New York
Dear Edna,

Just a note to thank you for your letter and to express hope that your plans for this day are working out well. I know it means much to you and your family to be together at this time. I appreciate your telling me something about them.

Sorry to learn of your car accident, but as no great damage was done and all has come out well, that also is a cause for thanksgiving.

I was in New York Sunday for an anniversary celebration of our Priory in Harlem. I fear it is usually difficult to get me on the phone here. I keep silence in the mornings, so I am not called to the phone at that time. In the afternoons I am often out for a walk, or working somewhere not easily accessible to whomever answers the phone. If you need to get in touch, the best plan is to leave a message for me to call back. Otherwise I shall make use of the privilege you have given me to call you from time to time.

We are in the midst of our family celebration of Thanksgiving with all the Brethren home and a few guests. It will be dominated by food, as is characteristic of this holiday everywhere.

I am beginning to get seriously to work on a couple of books I want to write. They are the fruit of my teaching in Ghana.

All the best.

Love,
Bonnie

December 6, 1988
Dear Bonnie,

Thank you for your Thanksgiving message—it was a delightful thought.

The picture D took of you is excellent. She is flourishing and as busy as a bee. Your two new books will make a real contribution; your gift of expression is both unique and crystal clear. I am anxious to read them.

My Thanksgiving celebration was successful except that my niece Suzanne was unable to make it because two days before she broke her leg skiing in Vermont where she escapes for relaxation. However, she is mending on schedule. My little grandniece was a joy to behold. The good Lord did not give me any children of my own so I have always derived great pleasure from other people's offspring . . .

I continue to enjoy my Polish pupils and my work with the Capitol Region Conference of Churches. I find my experience with the Jewish and Christian people stimulating and challenging. They are good people. I am enclosing a page given us by our Director to guide us in our discussion of approaches we can take to enhance positive Christian-Jewish relations. This brief outline of Kohlberg's stages of moral development he feels is pertinent to our understanding of why people act as they do. I understand the progression, but I question the age level for each stage. I am sure it did not take me that long to reach the level and I don't think it takes everyone so long. In our educational system, we must facilitate the progress. Do you have time to react to this sheet?

I am still a doubting Thomas concerning the progress of the political picture.

Will you please tell me what you would like for Christmas?? Be sure to send me the size and color. I will send you a present, but please help me in the selection. Please call me.

Edna

December 8, 1988
West Park, New York
Dear Edna,

Thank you for your letter. I am replying at once to answer the questions you raise.

I think the analysis of morality is fundamentally sound. The points on religious morality correctly analyze the reasons for the similarity of religious and secular principles. The difference in my opinion lies not in ideas of right and wrong but in the motivation and power to follow them. And the freeing or restricting depends on whether the moral drive is based on love or duty. So much noisy morality is grounded in duty—not duties one fulfills but duties they impose on others.

As to the ages, they are just average approximations. Individuals differ in terms of the value-shaping forces, especially in the family, but also in the culture and mores by which one is surrounded. I am sure long before ten years old I thought cheating, lying or stealing were bad because they were wrong.

As for the Christmas present, you sent me a wind breaker jacket some years ago. I left it in Africa because I expected to need it when I went back. Then I forgot to include it in the things I asked them to send after me. By the time I discovered that, I knew someone else had and appreciated it highly. I did not have the heart to ask him to give it up. So if you would like to send me another for Christmas, it will be greatly appreciated by me. I do not know the size, but you guessed right last time. (My waist is 36") The red one last time was fine, but I leave the color to you.

I shall try to telephone you before Christmas. I pray all continues well with you.

Love,
Bonnie

December 19, 1988
Dear Bonnie,

Thank you for answering my questions so promptly and beautifully. I agree with you that the moral drive should be based on love, but so many do not know what love is. That too shows that the importance of love is not generally recognized and consequently not understood. Little children sense it when they find it. Education has many lessons to learn. As we guide the young to adulthood, we too often fail to reveal the power and quality of love. Somehow too many come to prize the material side of life—much to their sorrow. Surely the moral tone of our country has a long way to go. But we must persevere. Without hope and faith we are lost.

Last Monday, the twelfth, I sent your Christmas present, the red jacket from Abercrombie & Fitch. If you do not like it, you may exchange it. Is there anything else you want for the New Year?

Saturday I took my niece Patty, her little one, Stephanie, and my brother Clifford to see The Nutcracker. Stephanie will be only four in January, but she thrives on theatrical productions. I expect to spend Christmas at Patty's house. Children always make Christmas more meaningful—especially when they are little.

As usual, I am late in all my Christmas preparations.

I do hope you telephone me before Christmas. I do not have any luck calling from this end.

Your Christmas card was beautiful.

As Ever,
Edna

December 26, 1988
West Park, New York
Dear Edna,

Your letter reached me just before Christmas. I hope you had a happy day with your niece and her children. Our Christmas is without children, but it has its values also. The Midnight Eucharist is always a glorious event. There is quite a congregation that comes from all around here, most of whom we never see at any other time. After the service we have a celebration. Then on Christmas we take things easy, with Communion at 9 followed by brunch. The dinner—just ourselves and residents—is at 4:30. Before it there is an exchange of gifts, each member of the Order buying one for another whose name he drew out of the pot. So we have a good family time.

I must admit I am favorably impressed with the persons Bush has selected for his cabinet, and by the way he seems to be mending fences with Congress and others. However, there have been no clear indications of policy, so this all may be show.

I shall telephone you next month. Meanwhile, I hope 1989 brings you much joy.

Love,
Bonnie

January 3, 1989
Dear Bonnie,

Thank you for your good letter. I wish I could have shared your Midnight Eucharist, and I am happy that you had family sharing on Christmas Day.

On that day, I enjoyed Christmas at Patty's house—especially with little Stephanie, who continues to amaze me with her depth of perception and understanding despite her age of nearly four. She is fascinated by her books—these are the presents I have the most fun purchasing. So many of the world's little children never have this experience. Our country still fails to realize the importance of these early years. A little education is never enough anywhere, especially in a democracy. And we still do not teach people how to be loving parents.

I agree with your Bush observations—including your skepticism. I grow increasingly wary of our educational system. We need more teachers who truly care, and we must start earlier. You can do nothing for children unless you love them.

To me, Shamir is bad news; he surely impedes progress in solving the crisis in the Middle East. Bowles article in the ***Christian Science Monitor*** of December 30th analyzes the situation very clearly.

On New Year's Eve I never venture forth on any roads to compete with the many drunks who venture abroad. With my T.V. I thoroughly enjoyed the program from Lincoln Center—"The New York

Philharmonic New Year's Eve Gala" featuring tenor Placido Domingo. So many of the T.V. programs are tawdry and cheap. My favorite channel is Public Television.

On New Year's Day I went to D's house for tea. I always enjoy her parents as well. I have told them that the State should have subsidized them to bear ten children in addition to the two daughters they raised so successfully. D is happy and busy.

Sometime Mary, my best friend, and I will visit you—Don't worry—it won't be soon. Mary's people came here from Switzerland and they are very fine people. Her sister and her husband sent me Kingdoms in Conflict by Charles Colson. I have yet to read it, but you probably already know it. Can you share your points of view? Mary is a widow; her husband was a pediatrician. She reads widely and helps humanity whenever she can.

Forgive me for being late with your birthday card.

Telephone me whenever you feel like it and reverse the charges. I am always happy to hear from you.

As Ever
Edna

January 10, 1989
West Park, New York
Dear Edna,

Your good letter and birthday card duly arrived and are much appreciated. I am answering the letter, so that I can do justice to the various points you raise. I shall telephone you later in the month. It is good to have voice-to-voice contact, but, even with my hearing-aids, I find it difficult to converse seriously on the phone.

I rejoice that you had so happy a Christmas at Patty's. I am sure the contribution of your presence and gifts added much to their pleasure as well. The proper education of children must begin in their earliest years. The problem is that those born into poverty have not resources in the home to encourage learning. If the day care program is made available to them, and is properly conducted with competent teachers, it could serve as a head-start course. That is essential to prepare children for school. It is especially necessary for those to whom English is a second language. When children enter the first grade unable to understand what is going on, they never look on school as a place of learning. But a competent day-care-head-start program would be very expensive. It might cost as much as one of these latest (useless) planes the Air Force is building. Obviously the government will not cancel one of them merely to educate the poor.

Bush is apparently not the pure fake that his predecessor has been. He may even show some intelligence. But with the Republican Party pressuring him to tend mostly to the interests of the wealthy capitalists, including the skilled laborers, there is little chance that he can do anything for the really poor, even had be the desire to do so.

I am delighted that we are not (pretending?) to negotiate with the PLO. The only contribution we could make to near-east situation would be to back the Arabs to the point that Israel has to grant them full rights and sovereignty outside its present <u>official</u> borders. Of course, the USA can never do this. Any elected official would not be reelected if he tried, the Jewish vote being what it is. So I see no real hope in the situation, unless the Arabs themselves can pull it off without our help. The willingness to talk with the PLO may indicate some chance of our letting the Arabs accomplish what they can without our active opposition.

I do hope you and Mary can drive over sometime. I remember her well from our first visit in London together. It will be good to see her again, and of course to see you.

I keep busy writing my book, which leaves little time for reading in other fields. I do not know Carlson's <u>Kingdoms in Conflict</u>. I shall be interested in your comments on it.

I hope 1989 is being good to you and will continue so. There has been considerable activity during the past 30 days, including several trips to New York (by car down and back—I refuse to go by public transport or to spend the night). I hope now I shall be able to stay at home uninterruptedly for a while.

All the best.

Love,
Bonnie

P.S. I enjoyed and agree with the <u>Hartford Courant</u> article. Thank you.

January 19, 1989
Dear Bonnie,

Your beautiful letter was greatly enjoyed; I always look forward to a message from you. I ever agree with your philosophy—it is a great comfort.

Last Sunday at church we heard from Dr. Elliott Williams, from the Connecticut State Department of Education. He explained most clearly our need to pursue vigorously the goal of racial/ethnic equity and desegregation in Connecticut's public schools. After the service, we met for a discussion period in our chapel. I never can keep still at a time like that. I had to emphasize our need in this democracy to provide public education for all our children from the age of three. We should have a mix of all our little ones in the best possible environment. Why don't more people realize how we now waste two most important years in a child's life? Next Sunday we vote on the resolution. I told them that we all need to get out to have an impact on our government: Boards of Education, Town Councils, State Legislatures. If religion refuses to improve the world, what will? I feel sure that we will endorse the Resolution.

Reagan maintains his customary pose to the very end. Our people are indeed stupid not to see through him. At least Bush is more intelligent, but what you mention about the pressure of the wealthy capitalists is all too true. The people could produce a change—the machinery is there—but they do not care enough. Our educational system does fail.

Monday night two of my Polish pupils (husband and wife) took me to the Bushnell to see some famous Polish dancers. It was a beautiful program—songs and dances—most colorful. The performers showed such joy in what they were doing. People all over the world have so much in common. I have enjoyed my pupils greatly—they are so responsive.

Each day I plan to walk 45" to 60". The air is most invigorating. Do call—when you want to. I know the book you are writing will be a fine contribution; you have a way with words.

As Ever,
Edna

January 31, 1989
West Park, New York
Dear Edna,

Your letter and the enclosures arrived on Monday after the phone call. I decided to let a short interval pass before I answered. But have been working hard on my book, to have things ready for the editor when she turns up again, and more time has gone by that I intended.

I hope the meeting on desegregation went well and that the motion was passed. It is most important that we stop thinking the race problem in America has been solved. So, all the pressure that can be put on society and the government should be exerted. At best, it will be a long, long time before equality is reached, and there will be no progress so long as we remain complacent.

It looks as if child care has some chance. If it is provided, the important thing will be to see that those in charge of the children are competent to being their education. A child who grows up in a home where the parents are near illiterates, still has little chance of learning even today with all the TV programs, computers, et al. Reading is still an essential.

I am proud of myself. In the last three weeks I have mastered a word processor to the point where I have been able to type the first three chapters of my book onto a disk and print them out. I was leery of it at first, as I am of all machinery. But its great advantage is that you can correct typing mistakes with no trouble, and edit the copy without having to type the whole thing over. I find it very useful.

I had not known that Bush had cast the deciding vote for chemical warfare in the senate. To think Reagan had the temerity to attack Lybia for doing what he was having the USA do! He was a total fraud. I shall not live to see his final rating by the historians, but my guess is that he will be placed among the poorest 10 presidents.

I hope all continues well with you.

Love,
Bonnie

February 13, 1989
Dear Bonnie,

Your last letter was most happily received. I am anxious to read your new book—when it is ready. I will send you the purchase price. I gave my extra copy of your last edition to my church library, and they were most appreciative. And I shall send for another copy of your new book to give to our library. I am also proud of you with your mastery of the word processor, but would know that you could do it for you have a superb mind. I share your aversion to machinery.

Our church meeting on desegregation went very well indeed. The resolution was passed with only one nay vote. I continue to be most interested in the federal and state support of enlightened child care and follow its course diligently. I agree with all your ideas. I am hoping my church can find effective means to speed its progress.

Saturday night I was invited by some Unitarian church members to a Valentine Party—Potluck. Instead of playing games, we talked, discussing with deep interest the current problems of our American society—marriage, perplexities of youth, drugs, crime, government—including personal philosophies. There were no dull moments. I missed you at the party. We needed you. We agree that we needed to strive for maturity—a deeper understanding and a willingness to put forth a helping hand. I made some brownies to bring. If you wish, I can bake and send you some for your friends. I made my own recipe. I am not a highly experienced cook, but my recipes tend to be original. In fact, if there is anything you need or want, I can send it to you. I am a fairly good shopper.

Perhaps sometime in March we can visit you—Mary, D and I. I will take you all out to dinner—you select the spot. Is there any day that is best for you? When we have a feasible date, I will get in touch with you for your approval.

As ever,
Edna

February 26, 1989
West Park, New York
Dear Edna,

This should have been written much sooner, but I have been so occupied with finishing my book on Paul, that I did not even check the dates in March. Now that I have, I find (alas!) that there are difficulties. Monday, March 6 would be all right, but I have left this letter so long unwritten that by the time you get it, it may be too late for you to come on that date.

The next two Mondays are impossible as far as I am concerned—indeed so is the whole week of which they are beginning. March 12-17 we have Elderhostel, which will keep me busy, and March 19-25 is Holy Week, in which I shall not want to go anywhere. Monday 27 March might be possible, though it is the day after Easter. That however might make it easier for D and Mary to be free to come.

On the other hand, if it seems preferable to defer the visit until April, all the Mondays except the first (April 3) are open. (April 3-7 is another Elderhostel.) One advantage of waiting until April is that the weather may be better. This has been such a crazy winter that blizzards in March would not surprise me.

As I mentioned above, Paul According to Paul is now finished in first draft. The editor who is helping with it, however, has not yet seen it. If with some further changes she thinks it is worth publishing, I am hoping she will help find someone to put it out. I can write books without too much trouble, but to find a publisher is very difficult.

Monday

Last night we had another dusting of snow, which seems to be all we are capable of this winter. The sun is now out, so the snow will be gone at noon. I still keep well. An open winter like this is always bad for the health—the germs do not get killed off. But so far I have been lucky.

The Democrats will never capture the presidency again until they espouse liberalism, whether they call it that or something else. For it is not the word that is important but the concept and the application of it. I find myself more and more relieved that Bush was elected. He may not be much, but in the campaign Dukakis showed himself to be a fool, and a pigheaded one at that. I am glad we have been spared him. I hardly dare hope Tower will be kept from being Secretary of Defense—but it would be a good thing if he were. I look forward to seeing you whenever it can be arranged.

Love,
Bonnie

March 4, 1989
Dear Bonnie,

It was good to receive your letter Tuesday. Your suggestion concerning the selection of April for visitation is indeed wise. What is your preference—Monday, April 24, Tuesday, April 11, Tuesday, April 18 or some other date?

Just Mary and I expect to visit you. D is snowed under with work and commitments, but she is happy and productive.

We need a new governor in this state—one who does not rely on old political tricks. I continue to attend the meetings of the Board of Trustees for the four State Universities, but I am not impressed by the members of the Board. If it is convenient for you, we shall arrive around 12 noon and take you out to dinner. You select the place.

I would expect you to be able to write books without too much trouble and am eager to read your new one. What do you have to do to get a publisher? I am enclosing a check for another copy of <u>God Who Dares To Be Man</u>. Inadvertently in my last letter I mentioned that I had given my extra copy to my church library. I really gave it to the library of the Capitol Region Conference of Churches in Hartford. With this copy I will keep my word and give it to my own church library. Occasionally I mix my churches. Yesterday a young man from Jehovah's Witnesses dropped by to carry out his mission, but I find it difficult to follow their line of reasoning. I was polite but questioning. I believe that everyone needs some kind of religion and I respect the individual's choice.

I am troubled to-day by the meaning of ethics to the average American. We are not willing to put forth the thought and energy to solve the problems of this democracy. I do not trust John Tower, and neither do I trust George Bush; he is just a front.

I was happy that you telephoned. I like your voice. Call whenever you wish and reverse the charges.

I hope to see you eventually.

Edna

March 11, 1989
West Park, New York
Dear Edna,

This letter was delayed because I was waiting for the Senate's decision on Tower. Thank heaven we are spared him as Secretary of Defense. I suppose the final appointee will not be much better, but at least he could not be worse. I was not as upset by Tower's alleged drinking and promiscuity as I was by his association with the armament manufacturers and with Reagan's policy of huge expenditures on exotic weapons. We could finance our needs in education, housing, and welfare—including free Medicare for everyone—if we cut the defense budget back to where it should be. Thank you for the check for the book. It has been mailed, and should have reached you by now.

Having suggested postponing your visit to April, I hate to pick the latest date in that month you propose. But Monday is best for me, since it is our day off, so April 24th is my preference. However, I should be telephoning you after Easter, and we can discuss the matter further then if you wish. I am considering the Beekman Arms in Rhinebeck for dinner. It is one of the oldest inns in the country, so is worth seeing, and it serves good meals. I shall telephone before you arrive to make sure it is open that day. If you get here around 12 noon, that will be fine.

I have finished my book on Paul, and the editor has it. I hope for her comments and corrections next week. Then I think I can get it into shape. The problem then will be to find a publisher. The editor, who is helping us, seems more uncertain about religious books than I expected. But I am sure her company will come up with something in the end.

I do not trust Bush either, though I do think he has qualities better than Reagan's. For instance, he seems able to change his opinion— witness his recent statement that he is open to considering some form of gun-control. Reagan could not change his opinion because he never had one. His policy was benign drift, with a confident smile, that overwhelmed the American public via TV. Bush lacks that "charm" also, which is another point to his credit.

I do hope you do not think the postponing of your visit reflects any reluctance to have you come. It is just that March is such a busy month, with retreats, Elderhostel, and Holy Week, which is a very special time for us at the monastery. After Easter Week, things begin to quiet down. I pray that you have a blessed Easter.

Love,
Bonnie

March 24, 1989
Dear Bonnie,

I agree with you about the supreme importance of Tower's questionable associations with arms manufacturers, but I have never respected alcoholics and womanizers; they come a dime a dozen, and I question their judgment. Congress saved the day. Many of us communicate with our congressmen and later complimented them. Our Senator Dodd shocked me; I never admired his father when he was our senator. I had always thought Christopher must have inherited his good points from his mother. The subsequent choice for Secretary of defense seems to be wise. I just recently received a letter from Senator Dodd explaining his position. I chastised him. Later I will send you a copy of his letter.

The books arrived on time and I have duly given it to my minister, for our library. He was most appreciative. Some of us meet with him to discuss books every other week. Presently we our discussing *The Closing of the American Mind* by Allan Bloom. I think Bloom is on the right track in writing about "How Higher Education Has Failed Democracy and Impoverished the Souls of Today's Students." I am anxious to read your new book on Paul. I will order three right now. Just let me know the price. Surely our value system has taken a nose dive. Philosophy has become an unknown quantity. People seem most interested in the joy of the moment and lack depth of thought and feeling.

Edna

April 1, 1989
West Park, New York
Dear Edna,

Senator Dodd surprised me at first, but one of the brethren here who keeps up with such things told me that when his father was in trouble of some kind the only person who stood up for him was

Tower. I am not sure that personal feelings like that should determine a senator's vote, but I got the impression that Dodd waited to be sure his vote was not needed to defeat Tower and then felt he was free to return the debt. I think what I had against Tower most of all was that he made such a fool of himself trying to get approved.

Bloom's book sounds interesting, but I am so busy with my own books at the present that I should not have time to read it. Today I got the comments from the editors—very sound and helpful, but they will require a good deal of rewriting. I am glad to do it, but it will take time. Then I have also started the other book. I have a first draft of what I hope may be the first chapter. But I have considerable reading to do before I can write the rest of the book. I cannot tell when or if the book on Paul will be published as I do not have a publisher yet. I shall bear in mind your desire for three copies.

I hope the Interfaith Seder goes well and all your other projects. I shall try to call you again before the 24th.

All the best.

Love,
Bonnie

April 15, 1989
Dear Bonnie,

It was a good hour's walk—rain and all—a good time for meditation.

I wrote to both senators—Dodd and Lieberman about John Tower and received very good answers from them. I think what you wrote about Dodd was true.

Your work on your books is most admirable, and I do not want to interfere with your progress in any way. I am most interested in your book about Paul.

The Interfaith Seder was interesting, but this one experience has enlightened me sufficiently. My various activities do not allow much grass to grow under my feet. At present, my income tax is a nuisance, but I am grateful to my attorney's helper.

Monday the seventeenth in Hartford at the South Congregational Church we have the Spring Assembly of the Capital Region of Churches. The various churches are working together as they should.

Edna

April 30, 1989
West Park, New York
Dear Edna,

Thank you for the grand luncheon. It was so good to see you and Mary again. The atmosphere of Beekman Arms was pleasant; even if the food was not all it might have been. But the important thing was we were together and I greatly appreciated it.

Thank you also for the splendid gift—you have such good taste in ties.

I am glad you wrote Dodd and Lieberman. It is so important to let our delegates to Congress know what we think. I am bad about this. But Monihan and our Representative McHugh are usually on the side of the angels, and D'Amato is beyond redemption.

You are right, of course, in attributing the moral breakdown of our society to inadequate education. But as long as graduates from our most prestigious schools and colleges are busily enriching themselves at public expense, it is hard to blame young people whose poverty deprived them of education and who are unable to find employment, for expressing their frustration in criminal ways. And I am beginning to be convinced that all the violence portrayed on TV and in the movies, encourages crimes like that mob of youngsters in Central Park. But even if we improve the educational opportunities to the full, we shall have to wait for another generation of school children before they can have a beneficial effect. Meanwhile, I believe organizations to take young people out of the slums and put them to work on construction projects such as FDR set up would greatly help. Of course, the Republicans will provide no such help.

All goes well here. Do not work too hard at all your interests—but keep them up!

Love,
Bonnie

May 10, 1989
Dear Bonnie,

It was good to receive you last letter. Our visit to see you at West Park was most rewarding. The scenery, the weather, the Beekman Arms, especially the dining area, have all left happy memories, but most of all it was as always a joy to be with you. I would have enjoyed pausing at your monastery a bit, but I did not want to impose on Mary who had the long drive home facing her. We made the trip before darkness descended.

I agree with your views concerning education, as well as the cheap and violent TV programs. You arc right about the FDR programs, but Reagan ushered in a questionable era. Since FDR and Truman, we have not done so well. Greed and dishonesty have taken over. Our people continue to pursue goals that will not bring them true happiness. I have never revered money and social status.

I am trying to interest the minister of my church, the father of a wee daughter and the Capitol Region Conference of Churches (I belong to the Social Concerns Committee) in providing a program to improve parenting. Being an effective parent is the most important role an individual can play in society. I always felt that as a teacher I was obligated to teach my students whatever had been neglected in the family. You would be surprised what I had to teach (I was never bored teaching—it was a joy.) We are still working on the ABC Bill before Congress.

We really do need to work hard to improve our political system. The Public TV Channels are the best. Why doesn't TV portray some of our beautiful English literature?

Next week at my church, the Christian Jewish Task Force (of which I am a member) of the CRCC is sponsoring with the Jewish Federation a public forum "The Rise of Organized Hate Groups in America." We are planning a reception afterward.

Friday my cousin Althea from Florida and a friend of hers are visiting me for a few days. My tulips and daffodils are cheerfully nodding their heads. My crab apple and dogwood trees are beautifully decorative. My daily walks are rewarding and the neighborhood children are friendly and cheerful.

Edna

May 20, 1989
West Park, New York
Dear Edna,

It was a delightful luncheon party and we had the weather with us. Between then and now we have had some dismal days—much needed rain but not pleasant for an outing. For the last few days it has cleared up and spring is in its riotous bloom. I also wish we could have had some time at the Monastery also, but we got through lunch so late and did a bit of sightseeing on the way back. Perhaps we can work things better next time.

I thought the editorial in the Monitor the other day, contrasting Carter and Reagan, was exceptionally well taken. As President, Carter was not great, but he is a good man of real integrity—too good I fear for the White House.

The goings-on in China over Gorbachev is fascinating. I hope some real steps toward liberty result from it. But I fear those who are clamoring for democracy do not realize what they will get if they succeed. We could tell them something about how corruption, inefficiency, an overwhelming bureaucracy, and exploitation with indifference of the poor flourish in USA. Perhaps socialist democracy can avoid some of this—I hope so. I am afraid our problems are indigenous to capitalistic democracy.

Poor Ireland. The way the British have been treating that country since the Middle Ages is one of the scandals of history. South Africa's oppression is small potatoes in comparison.

Keep well and happy.

Love,
Bonnie

June 1-12, 1989
Dear Bonnie,

Your last letter was most welcome. It seems such a long time ago that I saw you. If it is convenient for you, perhaps Mary and I can visit you again sometime this month since you feel unable to come to Connecticut.

On the thirtieth of June my brother Charles and his wife Florence are celebrating their fiftieth wedding anniversary. It has proved to be a very happy union. He was in World War II from the beginning to the end since he was a member of the CT. National Guard, and this unit was one of the first state organizations to be called. He could have gained the right to remain home, but he felt it was his duty to serve. Florence continued to work at Travelers and remained a loyal spouse. You remember them—for I took you to their house when you were here.

The recent holidays did not find me on the road for I think too many careless drivers are abroad. I still drive my 1981 Oldsmobile with pleasure, but I don't travel afar by myself, although I do go forth at night to my meetings. I continue to find ice rather treacherous where I encounter it. My neighbors are wonderful—children and all.

My newest Polish pupil, a young woman of 25 who has been in this country about three years is doing very well and is quite delightful. Since she lives with her aunt in Hartford, I feel she is afforded some protection. I always try to prepare my students for their citizenship tests because I want them to become citizens. They will be far safer then.

The month of June is my month for general health tests, and so far I am doing very well. I suspect you pray for all your friends—thank you.

As usual, I agree with your political perceptions. Carter was a good man of real integrity, but too many lacked the understanding to see it. Somehow I doubt that most Americans appreciated the value of a democracy—even ours could be much finer if we all exerted ourselves a little more. I tremble to think of the future awaiting the people of China. Such cruelty with utter disregard for humanity is beyond my comprehension. The last issue of <u>Time</u> had an excellent article entitled "Our Violent Kids." It is the best description and explanation I have seen. American youngsters lack admirable models, and if we do not change our ways, we are going under. It is truly frightening! My definition of a Christian is one who follows the teachings of Jesus; we have never had a better teacher. Our children lack spirituality as do their elders—not all but too many of them. I always felt that the spirit abroad in the classroom was on the utmost importance. I tried hard to make everything as beautiful and serene as possible.

Edna

June 19, 1989
West Park, New York
Dear Edna,

Your letter was most welcome. I remember meeting your brother and his wife. Please give them my best wishes. I hope their anniversary celebration is a great success.

Speaking of that, I have a golden anniversary (Life Profession) coming up myself. On next 6 January there will be a celebration of it here. The guesthouse is being reserved for any who would like to come and spend the weekend. The service will be at 11 a.m. on the 6th. I realize that the weather in January may make it impossible, but if you and Mary or whoever, are able to come, it will be a joy to me.

I am glad to learn that you have another Polish pupil. You are doing a great service to them. The situation in Poland is remarkable. I do hope they can work things out together without a disaster as in China.

I hope your health tests continue to go well. I must have a series of them next month. I am feeling fine, but it is always well to check.

I look forward to seeing you and Mary on July 10th. Meanwhile may God bless and keep you.

Love,
Bonnie

July 2, 1989
Dear Bonnie,

It is always so heartwarming to hear from you.

My brother's anniversary celebration was a great success. A little over one hundred friends came to the American Legion Hall in Wethersfield where it was held. The best part was the happiness both Florence and Charles revealed. There is nothing like a good marriage.

If the weather permits, I will surely come to your golden anniversary on the sixth of January. I hope Mary can make it. It probably would be wise for us to plan to come Friday, the fifth and stay over—in order to make the Saturday 11 a.m. service—if that is possible.

The world is still unstable, and it is not surprising. The situation in China is shocking. I am glad Yale pulled their students out. Man surely does not understand how to use power prudently—not even in the U.S. The Reagan regime was a disaster and we are not recovering wisely. While Bush is more intelligent than his predecessor, he leaves much to be desired. Our people do not <u>think</u>; in fact, that is where our schools fail. History is too often poorly taught for we do not learn from the mistakes of the past. However, I do still have hope that Dodd's ABC Bill will be successful in the House now.

Reagan surely ruined the Supreme Court with his appointments. The abortion picture looks gloomy indeed. I still maintain that the crime is to have a baby you do not intend to love and care for. No child can thrive without genuine love, but too many have no understanding of the meaning of love. Life does not begin with conception. I certainly would not have wanted to be born to parents who did not want me. These creatures who maintain that we need more babies that can be adopted are not thinking clearly. Many of these unwanted babies have poor genes and too many would-be parents lack the background and understanding essential to the rearing process. I am prepared to wage some heavy political battles.

Mary and I are looking forward to being with you on the tenth of July. We expect to arrive around noon on that Monday. I am taking you both out to lunch; you decide the destination. We had such a good time on our last trip.

Take good care of yourself.

Edna

July 4, 1989
West Park, New York
Dear Edna,

Thank you for your generous gift. It is a real help to us and much appreciated.

I look forward to seeing you and Mary next Monday. I shall be expecting you to arrive at about 12 noon. The weather is so changeable these days; we can only hope it is in one of its favorable moods.

Love,
Bonnie

We have prayed for the children—their care and education.

July 25, 1989
Dear Bonnie,

We thoroughly enjoyed our visit with you. It was good to see you and be with you. You always lift my spirits. I gave Mary your message. I have known Mary for many years and she is my best friend. She is sensitive, considerate and as honest as the day is long. She came to the college from Pennsylvania to teach years ago and later married a pediatrician. She is now a widow. It was a happy marriage.

Stella, a native of Poland is also a widow—who had a wonderful husband. She keeps me with my house one day every other week and is most considerate and dependable. She has two grown children, a son and a daughter who has two little boys. It's a fine family. She helps my brother Charles with his house one day every week. Stella and her husband put both their children through college. I hope she can find time to give Mary a little help with her house.

I am very fortunate with my little house for it is most comfortable and easy to keep. I have no cellar stairs to fall down, and it is reasonably cool. I am so glad we planted all those trees around the house. When we bought the place, there was not one thing growing. Now my flower gardens are quite pretty and I enjoy breakfast on the back porch shielded by the trees and my hemlock hedge. I have considerate neighbors all around. I try to take my hours walk between seven and nine at night when the sun does not burn. Nature is always rewarding.

I agree with your estimate of Reagan. He was popular because most of our citizens do not know how to think. Their standards are low and cheap.

I am happy for you that you are going to have the opportunity to visit in Toronto where you want to be. Perhaps it will be cooler there. How are you going to get there? I do not think our planes are very safe to-day. I am enclosing a check for you to spend on yourself. Have a good time!

Edna

July 16, 1989
Dear Edna,

Thank you for your visit and please thank Mary again for the luncheon. It was good to be with you again. The restaurant was not all I should have liked—though I certainly enjoyed my meal—but the decor could have been better. The problem is that so few restaurants around here are open for lunch on Mondays. I am still angry at Mariner's Harbor for telling me they would be there when they weren't.

I notice today that the *NY Times* has an article on the front page pointing out how much the poorest 1/5 of our population have suffered in lower standards of living thanks to Reagan. His continued popularity baffles me, but eventually history will be written and he will be judged more correctly. In my opinion, though he was not our worst president, he was close to it.

Bush continues to cut a good figure. I do think he is really trying to face up to our problems and find a solution, though I do not always agree with his findings. I am beginning to think he may be endurable for the next 7 1/2 years. Of course, if we have a depression he probably will not get a second term. He reminds me more and more of Herbert Hoover.

As I think I told you, I shall be on retreat August 1-10, after which I go to Toronto, returning on the 30th. I hope you have a good summer. All the best.

Love,
Bonnie

August 6, 1989
Dear Edna,

Your letter should not remain unanswered any longer. I had planned to write from Toronto, but I have decided that would be much too late. I do not leave for there until 14 August. I return here on the

30th. If for any reason you want my address there, it is Holy Cross Priory, 204 High Park Avenue, Toronto, Ont. M6P256. (416) 767-9081.

There is not much to say. The retreat is going well, I think. It is always hard to judge. The weather was excellent the first few days, but this weekend has been hot and miserably humid. However, I do not mind it as much as I did before I lived in Africa. The weather was never this bad there, but continuous hot weather has got me acclimated to it.

I have not been able to spend the check yet, since I do not go out while in retreat. But I have an appointment to go with someone else on a shopping trip on Friday 11 August. I cannot tell you how grateful I am to you for making it possible.

One keeps hoping something can be done to get the hostages released. But at the moment the hard-liners seem to be coming back into power.

I hope you keep well and are enjoying yourself.

Love,
Bonnie

August 17, 1989
Dear Bonnie,

It was a joy to receive your good letter last week. I do hope that your Toronto will bring you a refreshing change.

To date, I have made no plans for a vacation. Perhaps the coming fall will produce some interesting ideas.

My last Polish student passed her American citizenship test; and I am very happy for her. I believe she will prove to be a welcome addition to our country. I have enjoyed my associations will all my Polish pupils.

As Ever,
Edna

August 17, 1989
Holy Cross Priory, Toronto, Canada
Dear Edna,

Just a note to tell you that I have now spent your generous gift on clothes I needed. They include a pair of dress slacks, some T-shirts and socks, and a splendid pair of Birkenstock sandals. I am most grateful to you for enabling me to get them. They will last me a long time.

I had meant to telephone you after the Long Retreat, but I was so busy with getting ready to leave for Canada that it slipped my mind. I am happy to be up here for the rest of this month. Some of my favorite members of the Order are stationed here, including Fr. Turkington, just ahead of me in Profession among those still alive. He and I worked together at St. Andrew's School for six years. So we are both glad to see each other.

I hope you will be able to get over to the monastery sometime in the fall. Meanwhile have a happy summer.

Love,
Bonnie

P.S. Please excuse the blots on the reverse side. Apparently the printer's machine was not as clean as it should have been. I did not notice them in time to get a better sheet.

August 31, 1989
Dear Bonnie,

It was a joy to talk with you and receive your letter from Canada. Now it is good to welcome you back to the U.S., but I am happy that you had the change in Canada and also had the opportunity to communicate with old friends. Your recent purchases sounded fine, and if you need any other articles, first let me know—I am sure I can find them for you.

What was the Canadian reaction to our world problems?

The satisfaction so many human beings find in promoting rampant cruelty is completely beyond my comprehension. The depths to which they descend is frightening. I wish parenthood were not so easy to achieve. Too many fail in their role and far too many have poor genes to bestow in the first place. If people only used their minds there would be no racism. One of our college professors—a white Southerner—maintained that in 300 years we should all become kind of coffee colored. It will come in time. We do not follow the teachings of Christianity. You did; you gave your all. We are far too lenient with our drug lords the world over. We must give far more money to help Columbia to fight its battle. The future of China looks bleak, but I continue to have some hope for Gorbachev. Last night on our Conn. Public Television station, which is our best channel, I witnessed a review of his whole life and was duly impressed. The MacNeil-Lehrer news hour is the best news program on the air—in my opinion. It has depth. The U.S. must continue to do what it can to improve the world situation.

My last Polish student passed her American citizenship test, and I am very happy for her. I believe she will prove to be a welcome addition to our country. I have thoroughly enjoyed my association with all my Polish pupils.

As I take my early nightly walks around my neighborhood, I enjoy the children of all ages as well as the adults.

I would enjoy visiting you at your monastery this fall if I can arrange it. Tell me the time that would prove most convenient.

I am glad you are back in this country. Call me whenever you feel so inclined.

As ever,
Edna

September 13, 1989
Dear Edna,

It looks as if Monday either 9 October or 16 October would be best for me. Will either of those days be satisfactory for you?

I must admit that I took my time in Toronto as a holiday from world problems. The local paper, when I could find it, had little world news and I did not see the Monitor. I cannot see that taking off the two weeks has had any difference in my attitudes, or for that matter in the world's problems, most of which seem unsolvable. I am glad I have no direct responsibility in those areas.

I spent my time in Toronto mostly in secular reading, chiefly some excellent novels. The word processor has not yet been fixed and that seems to be a psychological block to writing the book I am engaged in, although, since I write it first in longhand, there is no reason why I cannot get on with it. This week, however, I am engaged in teaching a course in an Elderhostel and that is taking all my energies. I am finding it fun and I think the participants are enjoying it.

I hope we can work out a date in October. Meanwhile, enjoy yourself.

Love,
Bonnie

October 27, 1989
Dear Bonnie,

Perhaps I shall arrive before you receive this note. Mary and I plan to land at your monastery at noon on Monday, October 30th. I shall take you both for dinner. You choose the spot. It will be so good to see you for I have missed you. This summer and fall I have not taken any trips so far. I have spent my time teaching my Polish pupils, who are progressing beautifully. I have also continued to function on my various committees. I must be one of those people who are naturally driven by causes. I try to help individuals who are in trouble—and there are plenty of those. D is happy and flourishing superbly in her new positions. They are fortunate to have her. The prior head of her department who has happily retired left behind him a real mess. The new woman who replaced him is intelligent, honest and perceptive. She appreciated D, who works very hard and has fine values.

I have been grateful that you had the opportunity to enjoy Toronto and I am glad you are reading some novels; they are good for you. And your students are most fortunate to have you for their teacher. A fine person is indeed a comfort in this worldly place.

As ever,
Edna

November 11, 1989
Dear Edna,

Sorry to be so slow in answering your letter I received before your visit, but I have been learning to operate the new word processor, and then I had to be away for a two day conference. Thank you for sending me D's address. I shall enclose your invitation with this letter, and mail one to Mary and D at the same time. It will be grand if all of you can come, but I have my fingers crossed as to the weather. Last weekend I was in Brooklyn conducting a day of devotion. They sent a car for me and arranged for me to be driven back or I should not have gone. Even then I found it tiring. I guess my traveling days are over.

It was so good to see you and Mary. The Casa Mia did seem nice—I am glad you liked it. We shall try it again sometime.

I must say I am pleased at the way the elections came out. The Democrats still seem to be in control on the local level, and that probably counts for more than the national does. I am sorry the two major black candidates won by so small a margin, but at least they won. For my money they were much the better of the two candidates in each race, and it is for that reason, and not their color that I welcome their victories.

Don't work too hard.

Love,
Bonnie

Christmas, December 24, 1989
Dear Bonnie,

The pressures really build at this time of year. I am glad you are being careful. Remember—you are truly needed in this troubled world.

As usual, I agree with your political observations and conclusions. If some of our American leaders had not encouraged Noriega in the beginning, we would not be faced with such horrible results. One analytical gaze at Noriega's countenance ought to have served as a warning. Too many believe that a desired end is justifiably reached by any means.

In Connecticut, we are not adequately serving the needs of our children. Our state departments are neglecting the welfare of our young. There is no excuse for this in one of the wealthiest states in the union. No wonder our jails are overcrowded. I am still trying to get some of our ministers to sponsor gatherings of men and women to discuss the needs of good parents. Guiding the young from the very beginning is our most important task. In neglecting our children we are wasting our money. And I still believe in planned parenthood and abortion. The sin is to have a child you do not plan to love and care for.

Yesterday, I had a pre-Christmas dinner with my brother Charles and his wife Florence. (you visited them in Wethersfield when you were here)

Tomorrow I shall spend Christmas with my other brother—Clifford and his daughter Suzanne as well as his granddaughter Patricia who has a wee one called Stephanie. Christmas needs children.

I have mailed my Response Card to attend your Fiftieth Anniversary Celebration. I would not miss that! I do hope the weather is kind! I plan to come with Mary and D. We are expecting to stay for the luncheon. They did not feel they could spend the night.

You have bestowed a beautiful gift on humanity. It means a great deal to me that you are out there somewhere.

As ever,
Edna

December 29, 1989
Dear Edna,

   Your letter and check arrived. It is much appreciated. I am putting the money aside, so that after the anniversary I can buy some clothes I need.

   I am just recovering from a bout of the flu. It has left me very weak. I am taking things very easily—we have two days off to recover from the Christmas celebrations. I hope to be back on schedule by Sunday for my birthday, but even after that I shall attempt little work until the anniversary celebration is over.

   I look forward eagerly to seeing you, Mary and D on that occasion. I am glad you were able to spend Christmas with your brothers. Christmas is essentially a family festival. That is why we insist that we spend it with our monastic family here.

   Love,
   Bonnie

January 8, 1990
Dear Edna,

   You have been so generous to me that I have a hard time keeping up with the thanks I owe you. I assure you that your gifts are much appreciated and will be put to good use.

   I was so sorry you were late for the service, but it was good to see you. Thank you also for the book which I have already started and am enjoying immensely.

   Despite the aftermath of the flu I deeply appreciated the honor of the occasion and seeing so many friends from such different aspects of my life—past and present. The difficulty of such affairs, however, is that there is not time for a real visit with anyone. But we communicate best by correspondence when we have time to think through and express our judgments on current affairs. In that area, we seem to have got through the Panama crisis rather clumsily but without too much damage, though I cannot be hopeful that Quayle's visit will do much to reassure the Latin Americans. However, the Lord seems to be taking care of us, which is what counts most.

It was good to see you even briefly and I am grateful for your presence as well as your gifts.

Love,
Bonnie

January 9, 1990
Dear Bonnie,

It was indeed painful to have missed the service for the celebration of your fiftieth anniversary. It still hurts. I am sure that it was beautiful and rewarding. Your monastery gives forth a peace and beauty all its own. I deeply admire all that you have given to the world though these many years. If there is any way I can help I want to do so.

Mary is an excellent driver but somehow she missed the turn off the highway we traveled so long and thus we had to retrace our route many, many miles. That made us late. I did not know the route and so I was not much help—She drove as fast as she reasonably could but to no avail. Mary was quite distraught. She has been a true friend these many years. Your luncheon was fine and held in a most beautiful room, but I wish we had made the service. I hope you will find it in your heart to forgive me.

With much remorse,
Edna

January 15, 1990
Dear Edna,

I was disappointed for your sake that you did not get to the anniversary in time for the service, but it certainly was not your fault. And Mary's missing the turn was an understandable mischance. So there is nothing to forgive, only something to regret. But it meant much to me to see you and I am glad you enjoyed the luncheon.

Your gifts have been so many and so beautiful that I am running out of ways to thank you. But the book you gave me is simply splendid. I had read the review of it in the <u>Monitor</u> and had made a vague intention to be on the lookout for it. I read it at once and enjoyed every word. Rarely has a book so entranced and moved me. I am passing it around, but keeping careful track of its whereabouts so that I can be sure to give it to Timothy when he returns from his second trip to South Africa. The diocese of Johannesburg there is a companion diocese to New York, so our relationship is close and Timothy is one of the persons who keep up the contacts. I am sure he will be fascinated by the book. In my opinion it is the best novel written in English in the century. I am most grateful to you for the chance to read it.

Many happy returns of your birthday. Sorry I could not wish them to you before the event.

I seem to have thrown off the aftermath of the flu at least. I am back at work on my book—finished the 9th chapter yesterday, just in time to give it to my editor who turned up unexpectedly.

Love,
Bonnie

April 8, 1990
Dear Edna,

Thank you for your nice long letter. I am looking forward eagerly to being with you the 23rd-25th. I am glad that Mary will be able to drive us to West Park on the 25th. I am sorry I have an appointment that afternoon but we shall have time for a nice drive and lunch on the way. I shall telephone you from Dr. Brewer's when I find out what arrangements are best for her.

I am well, though I spilt some boiling water on one foot and am having to go around with it barefoot while the new skin grows. Nothing serious or painful—just annoying. I have finished my book on biblical spirituality. I hope to get a copy off to an English (rather Scottish!) theologian who has promised to write a forward. Also I shall send the revised material to my editor friend so that she can make her revisions. I hope she will have more success in finding a publisher than she has for my book on Paul. But we both knew the Paul book would be hard to sell. There are so many books about him.

I learned about Harvey's family's feelings about Anne from her one time I visited her after Harvey died. I think it was prejudice against a foreigner. But they did put on a very fine memorial service for her. I did not go back to the parish house to see them, as I knew none of them, but one of them, seeing my name in the book of those present, wrote me afterwards. As you say, Anne was a very fine woman and made a real place for herself in her adopted country.

Thank you for the **World Monitor Magazine**. You are most kind. I read it and the paper through whenever they come. I find them the best source of news—though we do get the **N.Y. Times**. I put them out for others to use and several are beginning to read them also.

I look eagerly forward to seeing you on Monday the 23rd.

Love,
Bonnie

April 26, 1990
Dear Edna,

Thank you very much for the delightful visit. I greatly appreciated the opportunity to be with you. Please thank Mary again for the dinner at her home, and for driving us over. It was too bad we had rain on the way here, but I trust the weather was more pleasant on your way home.

I am trying to get caught up with my correspondence. It is surprising how it piles up if one is away for a week.

I hope you have a blessed Eastertide.

Love,
Bonnie

June 3, 1990
Dear Bonnie,

It seems ages since I have seen you. Do come for a visit any time that is convenient for you and stay as long as you like. I have plenty of room and all kinds of food. It will be so good to talk with you; there are manifold topics. Connecticut has many interesting sights as well as all kinds of people. June would be a delightful month if it is suitable for you—but choose your own time. If there are any special sights or particular activities you would enjoy, just tell me.

My activities with the Capitol Region Conference of Churches continue. I think it so important that people of all religions work together. We have very find leadership in the organization. I have never had any battles over religion. I was brought up to respect differences of opinion. I think I told you that my father was a Baptist, my mother a Methodist, my grandfather Lane Episcopalian and my grandfather Saunders an agnostic. I have friends of all persuasions.

Somehow I am hopeful that peace will prevail in the world. The exchange of college students with other countries is a very good idea. I have had the good fortune to teach all kinds of pupils so that I know it can work. We need a deep and genuine respect for each other; and a sense of humor will save many a delicate situation.

I am fortunate to have fine neighbors and I thoroughly enjoy the children. Some of them help with outside chores for which I pay them. I would indeed be a sad world without them

Edna

[includes pledges for Bonnell Spencer: 10-88, 3-89, 7-89]

June 25, 1990
Dear Edna,

June has been a busy month for me. On the first Sunday I preached in Kingston at the Baptism of my third cousin three times removed! Then I went to Williamstown for the Old Guard Reunion. David and his wife called for me at the monastery, drove me up, and returned me after it. They have to drive close by on their way from Pennsylvania to Williamstown. The reunion was very pleasant. Although it was not a year for an official reunion, there were 8 of us from 1931 present, with six wives. It made a nice companionable group.

We are now in the midst of our annual Chapter of the Order. That is occupying all our time each day. Almost the whole Order is present (or has been, some who have jobs have had to leave for them) and it has been good to see many who are stationed far away.

Between all these special events I have been working on my book-changing the Bible quotation to the New Revised Standard Version, which is a real improvement over the former translation. All through July I must concentrate on the book, incorporating the editorial suggestions that my editor gets to me. If I possibly can I should like to be able to start sending the book to prospective publishers by the end of July.

August we are in retreat here the first ten days. The last half of the month I may go to the South to visit some friends there. When I get back I want really to settle in to my life here, keeping the morning free for silence and prayer. That will make it difficult for me to get away for visits.

In many ways the best arrangement is for you to come here on Mondays—which is our day off. We really have more of a visit together that way than when I stay with you, and so much of the time has to be spent preparing meals. Would <u>Monday, July 16th</u>, be possible for you and <u>Mary</u> or <u>D</u>?

I hope you are enjoying the summer. So far we have had lovely weather for the most part.

Love,
Bonnie

September 23, 1990
Dear Bonnie,

It was so good to see you and be with you on our visit in July. You always lift my spirits. Since you do not feel it is feasible to come to

Connecticut, perhaps Mary B and I can drop in on you sometime in October before the snow flies. We can still take you out to dinner—wherever you wish.

I am so happy that you were able to go to Williamstown for the Old Guard Reunion. I am sure David and his wife were delighted to take you.

I trust your new book has reached the publishers and is well on its way. It will prove a worthy addition with all your gifts. I also hope that you were able to visit your friends in the South during August. You needed a change of scenery—you earned it.

So far, I have taken no trips this summer, but perhaps I can find a destination this fall. Warm, humid weather and I are not compatible, but the cold does not bother me. I have been busy with my pupils, and my Capitol Region Conference of Churches activities.

I attended the Honor Court for the alcoholics. That is a good experience for someone who has never had even a wee taste of the beverage. We do not start early enough to prevent the young from becoming addicts. I remember how strict my father was when I was only knee high to a grasshopper. He had never tried the stuff either. There was never any alcoholic beverage in our house. I don't even like the odor. George used to take a little, but never much. He used to accuse me of keeping it under the kitchen sink next to the cleaning fluids. I never objected as long as those who sampled it knew when to stop. I was always grateful for George's good sense of humor. Life without that quality would be impossible. I have weathered many a difficult moment with a timely bit of humor.

I go for a brisk walk every day; at night I carry a flashlight. My doctor checked me carefully and I passed. I thank God and my ancestors for my health.

I worry about our government. What do you think about David Souter? We must not overrule Roe v Wade. So many people become parents who should not even have one child. I know because I have taught their children! The drug problem is shocking.

What do you think about the situation in the Middle East? Certainly Americans should react more intelligently. We have rarely taught government wisely.

We need to teach people how to become parents.

As ever,
Edna

September 30, 1990
Dear Edna,

Delighted to get your letter. It had been so long since I heard from you that I was beginning to get worried. In fact, I was just about to write you to find out if anything was wrong.

I do hope that you can come over—would <u>15 October</u> be agreeable to you and Mary? That is a Monday which is best for me. If it is not suitable, let me know as soon as you can, and I shall try to find another date.

Nothing has been accomplished in regard to my books over the summer. Fortress Press turned down my book on Paul, after giving it much favorable consideration. But they already have too many books on Paul. I think Liturgical Press is considering it at the moment, but nothing much happens in the summer. Renni, who helps with the editing, has been on vacation and has sent me no more pages of <u>Marriage</u> with her comments. I am hoping to hear from her any day now.

I find that much needed work is being done for alcoholics these days. Several members of the Order are recovered alcoholics and are much engaged in counseling. Also fine work is being done with families of alcoholics, especially those who suffered from alcoholics in their childhood. All this is an important ministry.

Souter is sure to be confirmed and I think he is the best we can hope for with the Republicans in the White House. He may overthrow Roe v Wade, but it will eventually be restored again. A national government unconcerned about the rights of the oppressed cannot last forever in this country, though things may get worse before they get better—especially if we have a depression.

Our hands are tied in the Middle East because we have to back the Israelis in their seizing of Arab territory, so it is hypocritical for us to object to Iraq doing so. The only solution is to settle both problems at once, by both sides withdrawing, but of course, the USA will go to war before permitting that. We are politically dominated by the Jews.

I do hope to see you soon. All the best.

Love,
Bonnie

I am distressed about D and have her in my prayers.

November 18, 1990
Dear Bonnie,

It was so good to hear your voice the other day. I have owed you a letter for a long time—too long, but I think of you every day. Call me whenever you wish; I hesitate to call you lest I choose the wrong moment. My daily activities are not so important as yours.

Edna

Note on Dec. 26, 1990 she moved to Guilford, Ct.

February 1, 1991
West Park, New York
[To Mary B]

Dear Mary,

Thank you for your letter. When because of your absence from your home your answer was delayed, I tried to get you on the phone, but Directory Assistance informed me that no such person was listed. I then found D's number and called her. She gave me Edna's address and phone number and I called her. She seemed a bit confused at first as to who I was, but she eventually caught on and we had a good chat. She neither enthused or bemoaned over being in the retirement home, so I hope she is becoming reconciled. I was emphatic about its advantages for her.

The niece has done exactly the right thing. She had to see that Edna had the necessary care. Not only could her brother and his wife not cope with her, but it was dangerous for her to be alone. As you have pointed out her memory span is very brief. I found that true when I last visited her. The morning you were coming to bring me home she asked me three separate times how many days longer I would be able to stay with her.

I shall try to reach her by telephone over the weekend, and keep in touch that way for as long as she continues to recognize who I am. It may not be long before she is unable to do so. Incidentally, she has not yet written me as she intended when you reminded her that she has my address. It is too bad, but I think we shall have to recognize that from here on out communication with her will be difficult, if not impossible. But I shall do my best.

I hope 1991 is treating you well. All best wishes.

Love,
Bonnie

P.S. I suspect the reason why I could not get your phone number was that I had your name spelt wrongly in my address book. That is now corrected. If there are any major changes in Edna's situation or condition I should be grateful if you would inform me of them.

October 24, 1991
West Park, New York
[To Mary]

Dear Mary,

So sorry to learn of your illness. I shall have you in my prayers. It is good that the operation was successful and the radiation treatment is working and will soon become unnecessary. You are very wise not to attempt too much while under treatment.

I telephoned Edna and got her on a good day. She was mentally alert and seemed reconciled with the home. As usual, I had a hard time convincing her that I cannot visit her in Guilford. The necessity of changing trains en route and the difficulty of staying in a strange place overnight are my reasons, but she finds it hard to accept them. I must admit a further and a more important reason is that she is so irregular about meal times. It upsets my internal schedule. I shall keep writing her, as well as telephoning. I think she enjoys the letters best of all.

May God bless you and give you health.

Love,
Bonnie

March 21, 1996
West Park, New York
[To Mary B]

Dear Mrs. B,

Your card and note for Bonnie Spencer arrived this morning, and I thought you would want to know that he died on February 22. His death was quite sudden, which was a blessing—he would have hated any lingering illness—and it has been quite a shock to us.

I know he will be in your prayers, and do pray for us, as well.

Sincerely,

Assistant Superior

Edna May Saunders Sole died on March 14, 1996 at the age of 92. She suffered from Alzheimer's disease in the last several years of her life.

His and Her obituaries follow.

Appendix

Class Notes for the 25th Reunion, Williams College, Willliamstown, MA

BONNELL SPENCER, O. H. C.

Home Address: Mount Calvary, Order of the Holy Cross, Santa Barbara, California

Single

Bonnie apologizes for his picture being formal, saying that "people are always snapping pictures of the 'quaint monks' but rarely send copies." We've all known of Bonnie's dedicated life, but a straight recital of it, in his own words, is the best we can think of: "After two years at Oxford on the Moody Scholarship, went to General Theological Seminary, New York, to prepare for the ministry in the Episcopal Church. Was ordained deacon in 1936 and priest in 1937 by Bp. Manning. Right after being made a deacon, went to the Order of the Holy Cross, West Park, N.Y., to try my vocation to the monastic life. Was made a Novice in 1937, junior professed in 1938, and took my life vows in 1940. In 1938 began preaching Missions and sermon courses in parishes, which has been my chief occupation ever since. Also was one of the founders of a prayer guild for young people called The Servants of Christ the King, of which I was Director until I went to Tennessee. During the war years, had a huge correspondence with the members in the Armed Forces. In 1940-1 was stationed at Kent School, rather as a supernumerary. Returned to West Park, 1941-6, and was for a while Novice Master and Editor of The Holy Cross Magazine. In 1946 was sent to our house in Tennessee, St. Andrew's School, near Sewanee. That year I was chiefly preaching in the South, but in 1947 was made Prior. As such, I had supervision of the House and School. Continued my preaching work as well, however, until 1953, when I had to take over as Headmaster of the School, in addition to Prior. Quite a combination! (St. Andrew's is a boarding school for about 120 boys. One of our alumni is Jay Wilson, Williams '56.) Found school work most stimulating, but was glad to be relieved last summer and transferred to Mount Calvary in Santa Barbara, a Retreat House for men, of which again I am Prior. A very peaceful contrast to St. Andrew's. Besides supervising the House, I am getting around the West preaching. In the course of the years I have published two books, They Saw the Lord, a series of meditations on the Resurrection Appearances, and Ye Are the Body, a layman's history of the Church. The latter was a textbook for a course on Church History I taught at St. Andrew's. There have also been innumerable magazine articles and pamphlets. This bare recital of facts sounds rather stuffy, I fear, but nothing very exciting has happened, or remarkable been accomplished. Just tried to do the jobs as they came along, and have met, worked with, and perhaps occasionally helped, lots of swell people—especially the boys at St. Andrew's. The greatest fun I have had, I guess, was directing the dramatics at the School. The boys turned out some remarkable performances of Shakespeare, Moliere, Galsworthy, etc. (Shades of the Little Theater and Cap and Bells!) But it has all been good right down the years, and still is. It doesn't add up to much, but I can only hope the rest of '31 has had as good a time as I have." Isn't it like the man! The self-renunciation of a life dedicated to serving God and man, and his self-renunciation in that life.

Class Notes for the 50th Reunion, Williams College, Willliamstown,

BONNELL SPENCER O.H.C.
Order of the Holy Cross
Holy Cross Monastery
West Park, New York 12493

As we all know, Bon Spencer is an Episcopal priest. He is the only member of our class who has the facilities for getting us through the Pearly Gates. He can't do it for us, he can only help. Also, he can't help all of us, only those who are qualified.

Bon is not aware of it, but he has had a remarkably fine career in the Order of the Holy Cross. He started with two years at Oxford and then went to the General Theological Seminary in New York. He is now one of its most distinguished alumni, having been awarded an honorary degree of Doctor of Divinity in 1976.

After graduation from the Seminary, Bon entered the Order of the Holy Cross, was ordained as a priest in 1937, and has spent the rest of his life serving the Church. At first the Order sent him on preaching missions throughout the U.S., visiting every state except Alaska. For a number of years, he served at St. Andrew's School in Tennessee where he was a teacher and eventually Prior. As Prior he not only administered the school but taught and continued his preaching missions. It was a terribly busy time and a relief to be transferred to the Order's monastery in Santa Barbara where he served as Prior. Later he served as Prior of a monastery in Texas.

A great experience for Bon was his appointment to the Church's Standing Liturgical Commission which undertook the huge task of revising The Book of Common Prayer. His special responsibility was the Committee on Christian Initiation, that is, Baptism and Confirmation, but as a member of the Commission he had the opportunity to comment on and make suggestions with respect to all phases of the book. If you read the new version, you will know that some of the wording is Bon's. It was for his work in this assignment that he was given his honorary degree by the General Theological Seminary.

Bon has published four religious books: *THEY SAW THE LORD*, meditations on the resurrection appearances, *YE ARE THE BODY*, a church history, *SACRIFICE OF THANKSGIVING*, on the Communion Service, and *CHRIST IN THE OLD TESTAMENT*, on the types of Christ. He has also written many pamphlets and magazine articles. He was also editor of the Breviary of the Order of the Holy Cross.

All this adds up to a wonderfully gratifying life of great accomplishment. An advantage of monastic life is that it is like being a member of a large family into which younger, fresh minds are always entering, keeping the older ones mentally vigorous and alert and giving them more time for prayer, study and counseling of other members of the family and their guests. It is never necessary to retire.

Appendix

Sunday Freeman

Kingston, N.Y.
Sunday Feb. 25, 1996

Brother Howard Bonnell Spencer

West Park: Brother Howard Bonnell spencer, OHC, an Episcopal Benedictine Monk who ordained at Holy Cross Monastery, West Park, New York, died Thursday at Benedictine Memorial Hospital in Kingston. He was 86 and was born in New York City Dec. 31, 1909, son of the late Bonnell and Viola Bogart Spencer.

Known as "Brother Bonnie" he was educated at Trinity School in New York City and received a Bachelor's degree at Williams College in Williamstown, Mass in 1931. In 1933 he graduated from Exeter College in Oxford University, England with a graduate degree in Literature.

In 1933 he entered the General Theological Seminary in New York City and was ordained a deacon of the Order of the Holy Cross on June 7, 1936. On May 23, 1937 he was ordained a priest and life professed on Jan. 4, 1940.

He was Novice Master from 1943 45 and from 1963-65, was prior of St. Andrews Monastery in Swansea, Tenn. from 1947-55, Headmaster of St. Andrews School from 1953-55, served as prior of Mount Cavalry Retreat House in Santa Barbara, California from 1955-59 and was founder and brother in charge of Whitby House in Grapevine Texas from 1967-71 and assistant superior from 1971-72.

He previously served as the Director of the servants of Christ the King, a national youth organization; as president of the Associated Parishes Council, was a member of the standing Liturgical Commission and chaired the Christian Initiation Committee.

He also taught at St. Nicholas Theological College in Cape Coast Ghana, West Africa from 1983-88. A former editor of the Holy Cross Magazine he published numerous books including: "What Has God to Do with Marriage", 1939, "They Say the Lord". 1947, 1983, "Ye Are The Body", 1950, 1963, "The Church in Christianity", 1951, "The

Sin Against the Holy Ghost", 1955, "A Functional Liturgy", 1961, "Anatomy of Selfishness", 1962, "Sacrifice of Thanksgiving", 1965, "Christ in the Old Testament", 1966, "Dietrich Bonhoffer "Prophet for Our Times" 1966, "Sacrament of Reconciliation", 1967, "God Who Dares to be Man", 1980

He also edited "A Four Office Breviary", 1968 and "A Monastic Breviary", 1976. In 1976 he received a doctorate of divinity from General Theological Seminary.

His brother, Eugene Bogart Spencer, died previously.

A Solemn Requiem Eucharist will be celebrated at 11 a.m. March 5 at at Holy Cross Monastery, U.S. Rte 9 W, West Park. Entombment will be in the Columbarium at Holy Cross Monastery.

Funeral Arrangements are under the direction of Simpson-Gaus Funeral Home, 411 Albany Ave., Kingston

Highlights of the Life of Edna Mae Saunders Sole

By Suzanne Saunders Taylor

After living a full life Edna Mae Sole died at the age of 92 on March 14, 1996, just three weeks after her devoted friend Rev. Bonnell Spencer had died in West Park New York on Good Friday. She did not know of his death. Her life did not go unnoticed and a major article about her was published in the March 15, 1996 Hartford Connecticut Courant.

I thought it would be helpful to highlight a few of her accomplishments and endeavors during her long life. In 1921, at the age of 16, she began teaching in a one room school and eventually pursued a Bachelor's Degree in Education from what was known as the Teachers College in New Britain. She continued her education at Boston University, earning a Master of Fine Arts there. She also studied at Trinity College and Oxford University in England.

Her many activities included holding various offices in numerous organizations. Foremost among them were the Connecticut Education Association, the Connecticut State Employees Association, the American Association of University Professors, the McCusker Memorial Scholarship Foundation, the Faculty Association of Central Connecticut State University, League of Women Voters, National Abortion Rights League, and the Council of Churches. She was a member of the Democratic Party, Delta Kappa Gamma Epsilon and the Boston College Club.

While not an original suffragette she fought throughout her life to protect the rights of women and children. In her last years of teaching she devoted her energies to inner city youth and took them camping and taught them ballroom dancing . . . During retirement she continued in the literacy program and spent many years helping Polish immigrants learn English.

She was proud of her ancestry as on her mother's side she was a descendent of the Lane Family of North Guilford, Ct. and on her father's side a descendent of the Van Cotts who settled New Amsterdam, in what later became New York.

A life-long Unitarian she espoused tolerance and good deeds. Her influence on me was considerable as due to her encouragement I earned a PhD and now teach and do research in the area of pensions and health insurance.

Mr. and Mrs. George H. Sole attending a committee hearing
at the Connecticut State Legislature

Edna Mae Sole in the garden at West park Monastery

Edwards Brothers Malloy
Oxnard, CA USA
July 15, 2014